California GOLD

California State Grange

Grange
Recipes
Are
Naturally
Good
Eating

Acknowledgements

The California State Grange wishes to acknowledge the persons who have made the publishing of California Gold a success.

To Joy Beatie, Director of Women's Activities for the State Grange, and all the women of the Grange who are a vital part of our organization. No one can deny their contribution to the success of any Grange program.

To the Grange Brothers and Sisters for sharing your favorite recipes. Your recipes help us to enjoy that bountiful harvest we have here in California.

To each and every person who has contributed of their time and effort in the production of the cookbook, we thank you.

William R. Booth,
State Master

Photography: Ray Borton

This cookbook is a collection of our favorite recipes,
which are not necessarily original recipes.

Published by: Favorite Recipes® Press
P. O. Box 305142
Nashville, Tennessee 37230

Copyright© California State Grange
2101 Stockton Blvd.
Sacramento, California 95817

Library of Congress Number: 92-32005
ISBN: 0-87197-355-3

Printed in the United States of America
First Printing: 1992   12,500 copies

Table of Contents

The Grange in California   4

California Gold   6

Appetizers   7

Breads   16

Cakes   34

Candies & Cookies   60

Desserts (including pies)   88

Meats   112

Poultry (& Seafood)   135

Salads   155

Side Dishes   175

Soups & Stews   187

Vegetables   195

Substitution Chart   215

Equivalent Chart   216

Nutritional Guidelines   218

Index   219

Order Information   223

Legend: Recipe Symbols

Microwave   V.I.P. Very Important Person

Special Diet   Under 30 minutes

The Grange in California

The Grange is a nationwide family fraternity which believes that the value of family—working together, playing together, being together—is the same in rural and urban America. In promoting close family ties, the Grange has found that there is a strong relationship between family and a safe, nurturing community environment. Therefore, the Grange strongly promotes community service.

The Grange's roots are in agriculture, and it is our belief that from agriculture springs most of the bounty that all families enjoy. From the clothes we wear to the food we eat, agriculture touches just about every aspect of our lives.

The first recorded communication relative to the establishment of a Grange in California was penned in 1870 by Mr. A. A. Bayley of Pilot Hill to Oliver Hudson Kelley, Secretary of the National Grange. As a result, Mr. Bayley organized the Pilot Hill Grange on August 19, 1870, with 29 Charter members.

Mr. W. H. Baxter of Napa County was appointed a deputy of the National Grange in 1871, but did not experience success in forming Granges in California until 1873. An attempt to monopolize grain sacks by a wheat cartel angered California farmers and at a convention of the California Farmers Union on April 8, 1873, in San Francisco, the California State Grange was formed. The State Grange was officially chartered in Napa, California on July 15, 1873. At this first session, the Grange proposed legislation that would regulate railroad fares, freight and port charges and voted to establish a plan for statewide irrigation. Other specific objectives were to establish a cooperative system of trade and to organize farmers banks.

In 1873, the Grange began working toward the development of state water resources. The first major project undertaken by the Grange was the development of a dam at Kennett in Northern California, now known as Shasta Dam. Plans included the development of electric power sites and an irrigation system for the Sacramento and San Joaquin Valleys. It was in 1873 that the Bennett Valley Grange hall was built with donated labor, a building which is still in active use as a Grange meeting place. It is the oldest Grange hall in the nation.

The first Grange Bank opened August 1, 1874, at 415 California Street in San Francisco. Grange warehouses were soon opened in Modesto, Merced, Yuba City, Woodland, Colusa, Dixon and Antioch. The first Grange newspaper was printed in April of 1877.

The first Junior Grange, then known as Juvenile Granges, was formed in Dinuba in January, 1928. The following June, a Juvenile Grange was formed in Hornbrook.

The Home Economics Committee, which is known today as the Grange Women's Activities Committee (GWA), first displayed their work at the 1933 Annual Session in Placerville. Rules governing the activities of the Home Economics Clubs were adopted the following year in Salinas.

In 1935, the National Grange held its annual convention in Sacramento, which opened November 13th in the Assembly Chamber of the State Capitol. It was also in 1935 that the first Grange Credit Union was formed in Butte County.

The Grange Constitution and By-Laws prohibits contributions to partisan political coffers. A study called The Philbrick Report disclosed that one lobbyist in the 1937 session of the Legislature received in excess of $170,000 in fees, while the entire expense of the Legislature that session was $144,000. The Grange introduced a bill through Assemblyman Hugh Donnelly of Stanislaus County which would have required lobbyists to register, to disclose the source of their lobbying funds and disclose their salary and all expense account funds which they received. The bill was stonewalled and it took nearly 40 years of effort before the passage of the 1974 Proposition 9 formed the Fair Political Practices Commission.

Today, the State Grange Legislative staff is actively involved with a wide range of issues supported by the membership, including education, health care, conservation, agriculture, taxation, commerce, consumerism, environment and water development and distribution.

In addition to legislative activities, today's Grange sponsors community service programs; deaf activities programs; Junior Grange activities; scholarships; talent, art and photo contests; sewing, toy making and cooking contests; youth activities; young adults programs and member services such as credit unions, insurance services and travel services. In California, the Grange is over 34,000 members strong and growing.

California Gold

California's Gold, found in the mountain streams of the Sierra by hearty 49'ers or as seen in the plains of waving fields of wheat under the summer sun have both contributed to the history and mystique of California. The early settlers came to California in search of gold, but it was the golden fields of wheat that grew from the brown soil that was the real future of the state. It was agriculture that proved to be the foundation for the state's economic boom.

This Grange cookbook is a celebration of the bountiful harvest we enjoy as a result of the diversity of our agricultural abilities. The rich abundance of different fruits and vegetables contributes to the quality of our life. We must remember that less than 2% of our population is now responsible for the production of the food and fiber that makes our standard of living the highest in the world.

Over 250 different crops and livestock commodities are grown within our state, with no one single crop dominating the state's farm economy. California has been ranked the #1 agricultural producing state since 1947. In 1990 California generated cash farm receipts of over $18.3 billion and over $70 billion in related economic activities. Our 30 million acres of farmlands are less than 4% of the U.S. total but we produce more than 50% of the nation's fruits, vegetables and nuts.

Almost without exception, ingredients for the recipes in this cookbook are grown within our state. In fact, eleven crops are grown exclusively (99.9%) within California: almonds, artichokes, dates, figs, kiwifruit, olives, pistachios, pomegranates, prunes, raisins and walnuts.

The ritual of the Grange teaches us that:

Since God placed man on earth, agriculture has existed. There is no occupation that precedes it, no order or association that can rank with the tillers of the soil. Before literature existed, before governments were known, agriculture was the calling of man. And all the fruits of social progress since then grow from the brown soil...

History shows that where agriculture flourishes, man flourishes also. California as the cornucopia of agricultural production in the United States blesses us with a bountiful harvest.

This cookbook is dedicated to the California farmer who produces food and fiber for 129 people—97 in the United States and 32 abroad.

APPETIZERS

ARTICHOKE DIP ⌛

Yield:
8 servings
Utensil:
round dish

Approx Per Serving:
Cal 510
Prot 10 g
Carbo 5 g
Fiber 0 g
T Fat 50 g
88% Calories from Fat
Chol 49 mg
Sod 843 mg

2 8-ounce cans artichokes, drained, chopped
2 cups grated Parmesan cheese
2 cups mayonnaise
¼ teaspoon garlic powder
1 tablespoon grated Parmesan cheese

Combine artichokes, 2 cups Parmesan cheese, mayonnaise and garlic powder in bowl; mix well. Spoon into greased 9-inch round dish. Sprinkle with 1 tablespoon Parmesan cheese. Bake at 350 degrees for 30 minutes or until golden brown. Serve with taco chips or crackers.

Marcy Mackey, Morgan Hill #408

THE HAYSTACK

Yield:
15 servings
Utensil:
platter

Approx Per Serving:
Cal 137
Prot 6 g
Carbo 9 g
Fiber 5 g
T Fat 9 g
58% Calories from Fat
Chol 15 mg
Sod 427 mg

1 16-ounce can refried beans
1/2 envelope taco seasoning mix
Tabasco sauce to taste
1 ripe avocado, sliced
1 1/2 tablespoons lemon juice
1/2 cup sour cream
1 4-ounce can chopped green chilies, drained
1 4-ounce can chopped black olives
1/4 cup chopped green onions
3/4 cup shredded Monterey Jack cheese
3/4 cup shredded Cheddar cheese
1/2 cup chopped tomatoes
1 to 2 cups alfalfa sprouts

Combine refried beans, taco seasoning mix and Tabasco sauce in small bowl. Spread in 1/2-inch thick circle in center of large platter. Beat avocado, lemon juice and sour cream in mixer bowl until smooth. Spread over bean mixture. Layer with green chilies, olives, green onions, cheeses and tomatoes, shaping into pyramid. Cover with alfalfa sprouts. Serve with corn or taco chips.

Rowetta Miller, Fieldbrook #771

HOT CHEESE DIP

Yield:
32 servings
Utensil:
slow cooker

Approx Per Serving:
Cal 79
Prot 5 g
Carbo 1 g
Fiber <1 g
T Fat 7 g
74% Calories from Fat
Chol 19 mg
Sod 324 mg

1 pound hot sausage
16 ounces Mexican-style Velveeta cheese
1 10-ounce can Ro-Tel tomatoes

Brown sausage in skillet, stirring until crumbly; drain. Heat cheese and tomatoes in slow cooker until cheese is melted, stirring occasionally. Stir in sausage. Serve with assorted chips.

Dean C. Ritchie, Wildflower #663

Hummus

Yield:
16 servings
Utensil:
bowl

Approx Per
Serving:
Cal 109
Prot 4 g
Carbo 20 g
Fiber 1 g
T Fat 2 g
14% Calories
from Fat
Chol 0 mg
Sod 213 mg

1 16-ounce can chick-
   peas
Juice of 2 lemons
1 small clove of garlic,
   chopped
2 tablespoons (generous)
   tahini paste

Salt, pepper and paprika
   to taste
Chopped parsley
1 tablespoon olive oil
4 to 6 rounds pita bread,
   cut into triangles

Drain chick-peas, reserving juice. Combine lemon juice, garlic, tahini paste, salt, pepper and chick-peas in blender container. Process for 30 seconds. Stir in 1/4 cup of reserved chick-pea juice. Process until slightly thickened. Pour into decorative bowl, smoothing with spoon. Sprinkle with paprika and chopped parsley; drizzle with olive oil. Serve with pita bread triangles.

Judy T. Massabny
National Grange Information Director

Mexican Layered Dip

Yield:
15 servings
Utensil:
round dish

Approx Per
Serving:
Cal 218
Prot 6 g
Carbo 12 g
Fiber 6 g
T Fat 18 g
69% Calories
from Fat
Chol 32 mg
Sod 452 mg

2 large avocados
2 teaspoons lemon juice
Salt and pepper to taste
1 16-ounce can refried
   beans
1 cup sour cream
1/2 cup mayonnaise
1/2 envelope taco
   seasoning mix
1 cup chopped green
   onions

1 4-ounce can chopped
   green chilies, drained
2 cups chopped tomatoes
1 hard-boiled egg,
   chopped
1 4-ounce can chopped
   black olives
1/2 cup shredded sharp
   Cheddar cheese
1/2 cup shredded
   mozzarella cheese

Mash avocados with lemon juice, salt and pepper in small bowl. Layer refried beans, avocado mixture, sour cream, mayonnaise, taco seasoning mix, green onions, green chilies, tomatoes, egg, olives and cheeses in 9-inch round dish. Serve with chips.

Sharon Blasingame, Rainbow Valley #689

ARTICHOKE SQUARES

Yield:
15 servings
Utensil:
baking dish

Approx Per Serving:
Cal 126
Prot 7 g
Carbo 5 g
Fiber 2 g
T Fat 9 g
64% Calories from Fat
Chol 73 mg
Sod 305 mg

2 9-ounce jars marinated artichoke hearts
1 large onion, chopped
1 medium clove of garlic, chopped
4 eggs, beaten
1/4 cup bread crumbs
1 teaspoon oregano
1 teaspoon pepper
Tabasco sauce to taste
2 tablespoons chopped parsley
8 ounces sharp Cheddar cheese, shredded

Drain artichoke hearts, reserving marinade. Chop artichoke hearts. Sauté onion and garlic in reserved marinade in skillet; remove from heat. Add artichokes, eggs, bread crumbs, oregano, pepper, Tabasco sauce, parsley and cheese; mix well. Spoon into 9x9-inch baking dish. Bake at 350 degrees for 25 to 30 minutes or until set. Cut into squares. Serve hot or cooled.

Edna Jones, Dows Prairie #505

BUTTER DIPS

Yield:
12 servings
Utensil:
baking pan

Approx Per Serving:
Cal 176
Prot 3 g
Carbo 22 g
Fiber 1 g
T Fat 9 g
44% Calories from Fat
Chol 24 mg
Sod 559 mg

2 1/2 cups self-rising flour
1 tablespoon sugar
1 teaspoon baking powder
1 teaspoon salt
1 cup milk
1/2 cup melted butter

Sift flour, sugar, baking powder and salt into bowl. Stir in milk until moistened. Roll out dough to 3/4-inch thickness; cut into strips. Pour melted butter into 9x13-inch baking pan. Place strips in pan. Bake at 400 to 425 degrees for 20 minutes or until light brown. Serve as hors d'oeuvres or for breakfast with jelly.

Gerry Freeman, Sanger #478

CURRIED CHEESE YUMMIES

Yield:
40 servings
Utensil:
baking sheet

Approx Per
Serving:
Cal 46
Prot 1 g
Carbo 3 g
Fiber <1 g
T Fat 3 g
62% Calories
from Fat
Chol 3 mg
Sod 113 mg

1/2 cup shredded American cheese
1/2 cup chopped black olives
1/2 cup chopped chives
1/2 cup mayonnaise

1/2 teaspoon curry powder
1/4 teaspoon salt
5 English muffins, cut into halves

Combine cheese, olives, chives, mayonnaise, curry powder and salt in small bowl; mix well. Spread on English muffin halves. Cut into quarters. Place on baking sheet. Broil 5 inches from heat source until bubbly. Serve hot.

John V. Maple
National Grange Executive Committeeman

STUFFED CHEESE ROLLS

Yield:
36 servings
Utensil:
baking sheet

Approx Per
Serving:
Cal 182
Prot 7 g
Carbo 21 g
Fiber 1 g
T Fat 7 g
37% Calories
from Fat
Chol 48 mg
Sod 546 mg

16 ounces American cheese
1 4-ounce jar pimentos, drained
1 4-ounce can chopped olives, drained

6 hard-boiled eggs, chopped
1 8-ounce can tomato sauce
Salt to taste
36 hot dog buns

Force cheese and pimentos through food grinder. Combine with olives, eggs, tomato sauce and salt in bowl; mix well. Spread mixture on hot dog buns. Place on baking sheet. Heat in 350-degree oven until cheese is melted. Serve immediately.

Harriet Wilson, Van Duzen River #517

HAM AND CHEESE BALL

Yield:
12 servings
Utensil:
bowl

Approx Per
Serving:
Cal 259
Prot 6 g
Carbo 3 g
Fiber 1 g
T Fat 26 g
87% Calories
from Fat
Chol 52 mg
Sod 340 mg

16 ounces cream cheese, softened
1/4 cup finely chopped chives
1 6-ounce can deviled ham
1/2 cup chopped black or green olives
1 cup finely chopped pecans

Combine cream cheese, chives, ham and olives in bowl; mix well. Shape into large ball. Roll in finely chopped pecans. Place on serving plate. Chill for 2 to 4 hours to overnight before serving.

Betty Lemon, Happy Camp #395

HAM AND CHEESE PUFFS

Yield:
12 servings
Utensil:
baking sheet

Approx Per
Serving:
Cal 168
Prot 6 g
Carbo 8 g
Fiber <1 g
T Fat 12 g
65% Calories
from Fat
Chol 102 mg
Sod 241 mg

1 cup water
1/2 cup butter
1 cup flour
1/2 teaspoon dry mustard
4 eggs
1 4-ounce package sliced cooked ham, chopped
1/2 cup shredded Cheddar cheese

Heat water and butter in 2-quart saucepan until mixture boils and butter is melted; remove from heat. Add flour and mustard all at once, stirring with wooden spoon until mixture forms ball and pulls away from side of pan. Add eggs 1 at a time, beating well after each addition. Stir in ham and cheese. Drop batter with large spoon onto greased baking sheet, forming 12 mounds 2 inches apart. Bake at 375 degrees for 35 minutes or until golden brown.

Caroline Nelson, Centerville #797

Party Pizza Cups

Yield:
20 servings
Utensil:
muffin pans

Approx Per
Serving:
Cal 142
Prot 7 g
Carbo 11 g
Fiber 1 g
T Fat 7 g
48% Calories
from Fat
Chol 22 mg
Sod 406 mg

12 ounces lean ground beef
1/2 cup chopped onion
1   8-ounce can tomato sauce
1 teaspoon Italian seasoning
1/4 teaspoon salt
1/4 teaspoon pepper
2   10-count cans biscuits
1 cup shredded mozzarella cheese
1 cup shredded Monterey Jack cheese

Brown ground beef and onion in skillet, stirring until ground beef is crumbly; drain. Stir in tomato sauce, Italian seasoning, salt and pepper. Spray muffin cups with non-stick cooking spray. Press 1 biscuit into each muffin cup, covering side and bottom of cup. Place 1 tablespoon of mixture of mozzarella cheese and Monterey Jack cheese in each cup. Top with ground beef mixture; sprinkle with remaining cheese mixture. Bake at 400 degrees for 12 minutes or until golden brown. Cool on rack in pan. Remove to serving plate. May also top with chopped green onions, sliced olives, sliced mushrooms or sliced green bell pepper before baking.

Gilda Evans, North Fork #763

Spinach Balls

Yield:
60 servings
Utensil:
baking sheet

Approx Per
Serving:
Cal 36
Prot 2 g
Carbo 2 g
Fiber <1 g
T Fat 2 g
59% Calories
from Fat
Chol 15 mg
Sod 85 mg

2   8-ounce packages frozen chopped spinach
1 cup grated Parmesan cheese
4 eggs, beaten
2 cups seasoned stuffing mix
1/2 cup margarine, softened
Salt and pepper to taste

Cook spinach using package directions; drain. Combine with Parmesan cheese, eggs, seasoned stuffing mix, margarine, salt and pepper in bowl; mix well. Chill for 15 to 20 minutes. Shape into 1-inch balls. Place on baking sheet. Freeze until firm. Remove from freezer. Bake at 350 degrees for 10 minutes.

Doris Ritchie, Wildflower #663

SPINACH PINWHEELS

Yield:
40 servings
Utensil:
bowl

*Approx Per
Serving:*
Cal 106
Prot 2 g
Carbo 10 g
Fiber 1 g
T Fat 7 g
*56% Calories
from Fat*
Chol 6 mg
Sod 176 mg

1 cup sour cream
1 cup mayonnaise
1 envelope ranch salad
   dressing mix
6 chopped green onions
   with tops
1³/₄ ounces bacon bits

2 10-ounce packages
   frozen chopped
   spinach, thawed,
   drained
1 10-count package
   large flour tortillas

Combine sour cream, mayonnaise, salad dressing mix, green onions, bacon bits and spinach in bowl; mix well. Spread thinly on tortillas. Roll up; wrap in plastic wrap. Chill until firm. Slice each roll into ¹/₂-inch thick slices. Arrange on serving plate.

Joan Berini, Capay #461

SPINACH ROLL-UPS

Yield:
40 servings
Utensil:
bowl

*Approx Per
Serving:*
Cal 96
Prot 3 g
Carbo 7 g
Fiber 1 g
T Fat 7 g
*60% Calories
from Fat*
Chol 6 mg
Sod 181 mg

2 10-ounce packages
   frozen chopped
   spinach, thawed,
   drained
1 2-ounce envelope
   ranch salad dressing
   mix

1 cup mayonnaise
1 cup sour cream
5 to 6 chopped green
   onion tops
¹/₂ to 1 cup bacon bits
10 flour tortillas

Combine spinach, salad dressing mix, mayonnaise, sour cream, green onion tops and bacon bits in bowl; mix well. Chill, covered, in refrigerator for 3 hours to overnight. Spread on tortillas. Roll as for jelly roll; wrap in plastic wrap. Chill for 2 to 3 hours. Slice into thin rounds. Arrange on serving plate.

Marian Tipton, Buckeye #489

Zucchini Finger Food

Yield:
15 servings
Utensil:
baking pan

Approx Per
Serving:
Cal 145
Prot 4 g
Carbo 8 g
Fiber 1 g
T Fat 11 g
69% Calories
from Fat
Chol 61 mg
Sod 220 mg

4 eggs, beaten
Garlic powder to taste
1/2 teaspoon salt
1/2 teaspoon dried basil
1/2 teaspoon parsley
   flakes
1/2 cup shredded
   Cheddar cheese
1/2 cup oil
1 cup baking mix
1 medium onion, chopped
2 cups grated zucchini

Combine eggs, garlic powder, salt, basil, parsley, cheese, oil, baking mix, onion and zucchini in large bowl; mix well. Spoon into greased 9x9-inch baking pan. Bake at 350 degrees for 20 to 30 minutes or until browned. Cut into squares. Serve hot.

Gladys Montgomery, Orangevale #354

Fruit Punch

Yield:
22 servings
Utensil:
punch bowl

Approx Per
Serving:
Cal 81
Prot <1 g
Carbo 21 g
Fiber <1 g
T Fat <1 g
1% Calories
from Fat
Chol 0 mg
Sod 30 mg

2 46-ounce cans red
   fruit punch, chilled
1 1/2 cups orange
   juice
1/4 cup lemon juice
1 10-ounce package
   frozen sliced
   strawberries, thawed
2 12-ounce cans lemon-
   lime soda, chilled

Pour 1 can punch into ice cube trays; freeze. Combine remaining punch, orange juice, lemon juice and strawberries in bowl; mix well. Pour into punch bowl. Stir in soda. Add frozen punch cubes. Garnish with orange slices or raspberry sherbet.

Dolores A. Barrow, National Grange First Lady

BREADS

CHEESY GARLIC BISCUITS

Yield:
12 servings
Utensil:
baking sheet

**Approx Per
Serving:**
*Cal 172
Prot 4 g
Carbo 15 g
Fiber 0 g
T Fat 11 g
55% Calories
from Fat
Chol 22 mg
Sod 362 mg*

2 cups baking mix
1 cup shredded Cheddar
    cheese

¹/₂ teaspoon garlic powder
³/₄ cup milk
¹/₄ cup melted butter

Combine baking mix, cheese, garlic powder and milk in
bowl; mix to form dough. Drop by teaspoonfuls onto
ungreased baking sheet. Brush with butter. Bake at 450
degrees for 10 to 15 minutes or until brown. Brush again
with butter.

Ora Saalman, Sierra Nevada #454

SUGAR-FREE APPLESAUCE-RAISIN MUFFINS ☺ � ⌛

Yield:
12 servings
Utensil:
muffin pan

1 egg
2 tablespoons oil
1¹/₂ cups unsweetened
    applesauce
2 cups unbleached flour

³/₄ teaspoon baking
    powder
¹/₂ teaspoon nutmeg
¹/₂ teaspoon cinnamon
³/₄ cup raisins

**Approx Per
Serving:**
*Cal 138
Prot 3 g
Carbo 26 g
Fiber 1 g
T Fat 3 g
20% Calories
from Fat
Chol 18 mg
Sod 29 mg*

Combine egg, oil and applesauce in bowl; mix well. Add flour, baking powder, nutmeg and cinnamon; mix well. Stir in raisins. Spoon into oiled muffin cups. Bake at 375 degrees for 20 to 25 minutes or until muffins test done. Remove to wire rack to cool.

**Mary and Don Johnson
National Grange Assistant Steward**

BRAN MUFFINS

Yield:
18 servings
Utensil:
muffin pans

1¹/₂ cups sugar
¹/₂ cup oil
2 eggs, beaten
2 cups buttermilk
2¹/₂ cups flour, sifted
2¹/₂ teaspoons baking
    soda

¹/₂ teaspoon salt
2 cups All-Bran
1 cup boiling water
1 cup raisins
¹/₄ cup chopped dates
1 cup chopped pecans

**Approx Per
Serving:**
*Cal 303
Prot 6 g
Carbo 49 g
Fiber 5 g
T Fat 12 g
33% Calories
from Fat
Chol 25 mg
Sod 319 mg*

Combine sugar, oil, eggs and buttermilk in bowl; mix well. Sift in flour, baking soda and salt; mix well. Mix in cereal. Stir in boiling water, raisins, dates and pecans. Chill, covered, overnight. Stir batter; spoon into greased muffin cups. Bake at 400 degrees for 20 to 25 minutes or until golden brown.

Billie Lee, Nevada Star #16

SUPER PECAN-CARAMEL ROLLS

Yield:
24 servings
Utensil:
2 baking pans

Approx Per Serving:
Cal 342
Prot 5 g
Carbo 49 g
Fiber 1 g
T Fat 14 g
37% Calories from Fat
Chol 48 mg
Sod 242 mg

6½ to 7 cups flour
2 envelopes rapid-rise yeast
½ cup sugar
1½ teaspoons salt
1 cup milk
1 cup water
½ cup butter
2 eggs
¼ cup packed brown sugar

¼ cup sugar
1 tablespoon cinnamon
¼ cup butter, softened
⅔ cup packed brown sugar
⅔ cup butter
6 tablespoons light corn syrup
⅔ cup coarsely chopped pecans

Mix 3 cups flour, yeast, ½ cup sugar and salt in large bowl. Heat milk, water and ½ cup butter to 120 to 130 degrees in saucepan; butter may not melt. Add to flour mixture; mix well. Beat in eggs at low speed. Beat at medium speed for 3 minutes. Stir in enough remaining flour to make a soft dough. Knead on floured surface for 5 to 8 minutes or until smooth and elastic. Place in greased bowl, turning to coat surface. Let rise, covered, in warm place for 30 minutes or until doubled in bulk. Combine ¼ cup brown sugar, ¼ cup sugar and cinnamon in bowl. Divide dough into 2 portions. Roll each portion into 12x15-inch rectangle on lightly floured surface. Spread each rectangle with 2 tablespoons softened butter; sprinkle with cinnamon mixture. Roll up tightly from narrow side; press edges to seal. Cut each roll into 12 slices. Combine ⅔ cup brown sugar, ⅔ cup butter and corn syrup in saucepan. Heat until butter melts, stirring to blend well. Spread evenly in 2 greased 9x13-inch baking pans; sprinkle with pecans. Arrange rolls in prepared pans. Let rise, covered, for 15 minutes or until nearly doubled in bulk. Bake at 375 degrees for 20 to 25 minutes or until golden brown. Cover pans with foil. Invert pans onto wire rack; let stand for 1 minute. Remove pans.

Shirley Hayes, Little Lake #670

PRUNE AMBROSIA PINWHEELS (U.I.P.)

1 envelope dry yeast
1/4 cup warm water
1/4 cup orange juice
1/4 cup sugar
1 egg, beaten
1/2 teaspoon salt
2 1/4 cups flour
1/3 cup melted butter

1/2 cup packed brown
  sugar
1/4 cup melted butter
1 tablespoon grated
  orange rind
2/3 cup chopped prunes
1/2 cup flaked coconut
Orange Glaze

Dissolve yeast in warm water in bowl for 5 minutes. Add orange juice, sugar, egg and salt; mix until smooth. Add 1 cup flour; mix well. Stir in 1/3 cup butter. Add enough remaining flour to make a moderately stiff dough. Let rise, covered, for 1 to 1 1/2 hours or until doubled in bulk. Combine brown sugar and 1/4 cup melted butter in bowl. Stir in orange rind, prunes and coconut. Roll dough into 9x12-inch rectangle on lightly floured surface. Spread with prune filling. Roll up from long side to enclose filling. Cut into 1-inch slices. Arrange 3 inches apart on greased baking sheet. Let rise, covered with waxed paper, until doubled in bulk. Bake at 350 degrees for 15 minutes or until golden brown. Drizzle Orange Glaze over rolls.

Orange Glaze

1/2 cup confectioners'
  sugar
2 teaspoons orange juice

1 teaspoon grated
  orange rind

Combine confectioners' sugar, orange juice and orange rind in bowl; mix well.

Mary Victorine, Region 1 GWA Director

SOURDOUGH ROLLS

Yield:
24 servings
Utensil:
2 baking pans

Approx Per
Serving:
Cal 125
Prot 3 g
Carbo 24 g
Fiber 1 g
T Fat 1 g
9% Calories
from Fat
Chol 3 mg
Sod 187 mg

4 to 5 cups flour
1 tablespoon dry yeast
2 teaspoons salt
2 tablespoons butter

1 cup hot water
3 tablespoons sugar
1½ cups Sourdough
   Starter

Mix 1½ cups flour, yeast and salt in bowl. Combine butter and hot water in mixer bowl. Add sugar, beating constantly. Beat in Sourdough Starter. Add yeast mixture; mix well. Mix in enough remaining flour to make a firm dough. Knead on floured surface until smooth and elastic. Place in greased bowl, turning to coat surface. Let rise until doubled in bulk. Shape into rolls. Place in 2 greased baking pans sprinkled with cornmeal. Let rise until doubled in bulk. Bake at 500 degrees for 20 minutes or until golden brown.

Flora Pearson, Millville #443

SOURDOUGH STARTER

Yield:
6 cups
Utensil:
gallon jar

Approx Per
Cup:
Cal 231
Prot 7 g
Carbo 48 g
Fiber 2 g
T Fat 1 g
3% Calories
from Fat
Chol 0 mg
Sod 2 mg

3 cups flour
1 tablespoon yeast

2½ cups warm water

Combine flour, yeast and warm water in 1-gallon jar; mix well. Let stand, covered, in warm place. Use starter any time after 24 hours.

Flora Pearson, Millville #443

APRICOT AND PRUNE COFFEE CAKE

Yield:
12 servings
Utensil:
tube pan

Approx Per Serving:
Cal 522
Prot 7 g
Carbo 82 g
Fiber 4 g
T Fat 20 g
33% Calories from Fat
Chol 116 mg
Sod 247 mg

1/2 cup packed light brown sugar
2 tablespoons butter
2 tablespoons flour
1 teaspoon cinnamon
3 cups flour
1 1/2 teaspoons baking powder
3/4 teaspoon baking soda
3/4 cup butter, softened

1 1/2 cups sugar
4 eggs
1 1/2 teaspoons vanilla extract
1 cup sour cream
3/4 cup chopped dried apricots
3/4 cup chopped prunes
2 tablespoons confectioners' sugar

Mix first 4 ingredients with fork in bowl until crumbly. Sift 3 cups flour, baking powder and baking soda together. Cream 3/4 cup butter at medium speed in mixer bowl until fluffy. Add sugar, beating until light. Beat in eggs 1 at a time; beat for 3 minutes. Add vanilla. Beat in flour mixture alternately with sour cream. Beat for 1 minute longer. Fold in fruit. Layer batter and brown sugar mixture 1/3 at a time in greased and floured tube pan. Bake at 350 degrees for 55 minutes. Cool on wire rack for 20 minutes. Remove to serving plate. Sift confectioners' sugar over top.

Evelyn McWalters, Berry Creek #694

COFFEE CAKE

Yield:
12 servings
Utensil:
baking pan

Approx Per Serving:
Cal 433
Prot 5 g
Carbo 57 g
Fiber 1 g
T Fat 21 g
43% Calories from Fat
Chol 21 mg
Sod 144 mg

2 1/2 cups flour
3/4 cup sugar
1 cup packed brown sugar
1 teaspoon cinnamon
1/8 teaspoon salt
3/4 cup oil

1 egg
1 cup sour milk
1 teaspoon baking powder
1 teaspoon baking soda
1 cup chopped walnuts

Sift flour, sugar, brown sugar, cinnamon and salt into large bowl. Add oil; mix well. Reserve 1/2 cup mixture for topping. Add egg, sour milk, baking powder and baking soda to remaining crumb mixture; mix well. Spoon into oiled 9x13-inch baking pan. Sprinkle with reserved topping and walnuts. Bake at 325 degrees for 30 minutes or just until coffee cake tests done. Cool in pan for 10 minutes. Remove to wire rack to cool.

Barbara G. Gourley, Welcome #791

GERMAN BEER COFFEE CAKE

Yield:
16 servings
Utensil:
bundt pan

Approx Per
Serving:
Cal 446
Prot 5 g
Carbo 70 g
Fiber 3 g
T Fat 17 g
34% Calories
from Fat
Chol 58 mg
Sod 227 mg

3 cups flour
2 teaspoons baking soda
1 teaspoon cinnamon
1/2 teaspoon allspice
1/2 teaspoon cloves
2 cups chopped dates
1 cup chopped walnuts
1 cup butter, softened
2 cups packed dark
  brown sugar
2 eggs
2 cups beer

Mix flour, baking soda, cinnamon, allspice and cloves in large bowl. Combine a small amount of the flour mixture with dates and walnuts in small bowl, tossing to coat well. Cream butter and brown sugar in large mixer bowl until light. Beat in eggs 1 at a time. Add flour mixture alternately with beer, mixing well after each addition. Stir in date and nut mixture. Spoon into greased and floured 12-cup bundt pan. Bake at 350 degrees for 1¼ hours or until coffee cake tests done. Cool in pan on wire rack for 10 minutes. Remove to rack to cool completely. Let stand, wrapped in foil, for 24 hours before serving. Garnish with confectioners' sugar. This recipe had been a family secret for more than 100 years.

June Pertl, Happy Camp #395

CRISPY COOKIE COFFEE CAKES

Yield:
36 servings
Utensil:
baking sheet

Approx Per
Serving:
Cal 145
Prot 2 g
Carbo 22 g
Fiber 1 g
T Fat 6 g
35% Calories
from Fat
Chol 13 mg
Sod 126 mg

1 envelope or cake yeast
1/4 cup lukewarm water
2 eggs, beaten
1 cup milk, scalded,
  cooled to lukewarm
4 cups flour, sifted
1/4 cup sugar
1 teaspoon salt
1 teaspoon grated lemon
  rind
1 cup margarine
1 cup sugar
1 tablespoon cinnamon
1 cup raisins

Dissolve yeast in lukewarm water in bowl. Add eggs and milk; mix well. Mix flour, 1/4 cup sugar, salt and lemon rind in large bowl. Cut in margarine until crumbly. Add yeast mixture; mix lightly. Chill, tightly covered, overnight. Divide into 2 portions. Roll each portion into 12x18-inch rectangle on floured surface. Sprinkle rectangles with mixture of 1 cup sugar, cinnamon and raisins. Roll up tightly from long side to enclose filling. Cut each roll into 1-inch slices; place on greased baking sheet. Flatten with hand. Bake at 400 degrees for 12 minutes. May glaze if desired.

Grace Bussell, Region 9 GWA Director

Rhubarb-Strawberry Coffee Cake

Yield:
16 servings
Utensil:
baking pan

Approx Per Serving:
Cal 419
Prot 5 g
Carbo 67 g
Fiber 2 g
T Fat 15 g
33% Calories from Fat
Chol 27 mg
Sod 401 mg

4 cups 1-inch rhubarb pieces
1 16-ounce package frozen sliced sweetened strawberries
2 tablespoons lemon juice
1 cup sugar
1/3 cup cornstarch
3 cups flour
1 cup sugar
1 teaspoon each baking powder and baking soda
1 teaspoon salt
1 cup margarine
1 cup buttermilk
2 eggs
1 teaspoon vanilla extract
3/4 cup sugar
1/2 cup flour
1/4 cup margarine

Combine rhubarb and strawberries in saucepan. Cook for 5 minutes. Stir in lemon juice and mixture of 1 cup sugar and cornstarch. Cook for 4 minutes or until thickened, stirring constantly. Cool. Mix next 5 ingredients in bowl. Cut in 1 cup margarine until crumbly. Add mixture of buttermilk, eggs and vanilla; mix until moistened. Spread half the batter in greased 10x14-inch baking pan. Spread fruit mixture over batter; top with remaining batter. Sprinkle mixture of remaining ingredients over coffee cake. Bake at 350 degrees for 40 to 45 minutes or until golden brown.

Marguerite Connor, Happy Camp #395

Streusel-Filled Coffee Cake

Yield:
9 servings
Utensil:
baking pan

Approx Per Serving:
Cal 326
Prot 4 g
Carbo 49 g
Fiber 1 g
T Fat 13 g
35% Calories from Fat
Chol 46 mg
Sod 278 mg

3/4 cup sugar
1/4 cup butter
1 egg
1/2 cup milk
1 1/2 cups sifted flour
2 teaspoons baking powder
1/2 teaspoon salt
1/2 cup packed brown sugar
2 tablespoons flour
2 teaspoons cinnamon
2 tablespoons butter, softened
1/2 cup chopped walnuts

Combine sugar, 1/4 cup butter and egg in mixer bowl; mix well. Beat in milk. Sift in 1 1/2 cups flour, baking powder and salt; mix well. Mix brown sugar, 2 tablespoons flour, cinnamon, 2 tablespoons butter and walnuts in bowl. Layer coffee cake batter and walnut mixture 1/2 at a time in lightly greased 8x8-inch baking pan. Bake at 375 degrees for 30 to 35 minutes or until golden brown. May add 1/2 cup raisins to batter if desired.

JoAnn V. Welch-Russell, North Fork #763

Wesson Oil Coffee Cake

Yield:
15 servings
Utensil:
baking pan

1 cup packed brown
  sugar
3/4 cup sugar
2 cups flour
3/4 teaspoon salt
1 teaspoon nutmeg

2/3 cup Wesson oil
1 cup buttermilk
1 egg
1 teaspoon baking soda
1/2 cup chopped walnuts
1 teaspoon cinnamon

Approx Per
Serving:
Cal 290
Prot 3 g
Carbo 42 g
Fiber 1 g
T Fat 13 g
39% Calories
from Fat
Chol 15 mg
Sod 192 mg

Mix brown sugar, sugar, flour, salt, nutmeg and oil in bowl. Reserve 3/4 cup of the mixture. Combine buttermilk, egg and baking soda in small bowl; mix well. Add to remaining crumb mixture; mix well. Spoon into greased and floured 9x13-inch baking pan. Add walnuts and cinnamon to reserved crumb mixture. Sprinkle over batter. Bake at 350 degrees for 35 to 45 minutes or until coffee cake tests done.

Lois Bentson, Westside #473

Grandmother Tooter's Doughnuts

Yield:
24 servings
Utensil:
deep fryer

2 eggs
7 tablespoons melted
  shortening
1 teaspoon baking
  powder
1 teaspoon baking soda

11/2 cups sugar
1/8 teaspoon salt
11/2 cups buttermilk
3 cups flour
Oil for deep frying

Approx Per
Serving:
Cal 151
Prot 3 g
Carbo 25 g
Fiber <1 g
T Fat 4 g
27% Calories
from Fat
Chol 18 mg
Sod 75 mg

Combine eggs, shortening, baking powder, baking soda, sugar, salt and buttermilk in bowl; mix well. Add flour 1 cup at a time, mixing to form stiff dough. Roll on floured surface; cut out with doughnut cutter. Deep-fry in hot oil until golden brown; drain well.

Nutritional information does not include oil for deep frying.

Tooter Fields, Bear Creek #530

HOLIDAY FRENCH TOAST   (V.I.P.)

Yield:
6 servings
Utensil:
electric skillet

12 1-inch thick slices
  French bread
6 eggs
4 cups milk
1/2 teaspoon salt
1 teaspoon nutmeg

1 teaspoon vanilla extract
2 tablespoons butter
1/2 cup confectioners'
  sugar
1 cup butter
1/2 cup orange juice

**Approx Per
Serving:**
*Cal 732
Prot 19 g
Carbo 56 g
Fiber 1 g
T Fat 48 g
59% Calories
from Fat
Chol 328 mg
Sod 1011 mg*

Arrange bread in single layer in 9x13-inch dish. Combine eggs, milk, salt, nutmeg and vanilla in mixer bowl; mix well. Pour over bread. Chill overnight. Melt 1 tablespoon butter in electric skillet heated to 300 degrees. Brown 6 slices bread on both sides in butter in skillet; keep warm. Repeat with 1 tablespoon butter and remaining bread. Cream confectioners' sugar and 1 cup butter in saucepan until light and fluffy. Mix in orange juice. Heat until butter melts, stirring to mix well. Serve with French toast.

Gene Runyon
Executive Committee California State Grange

FEATHER-LIGHT PANCAKES   ⧖

Yield:
4 servings
Utensil:
griddle

2 egg yolks, slightly
  beaten
1 1/2 cups buttermilk
1 1/2 cups flour
1 1/2 teaspoons baking soda

1 teaspoon salt
1 1/2 tablespoons oil
2 egg whites, stiffly
  beaten

**Approx Per
Serving:**
*Cal 292
Prot 11 g
Carbo 40 g
Fiber 1 g
T Fat 9 g
29% Calories
from Fat
Chol 110 mg
Sod 967 mg*

Combine egg yolks and buttermilk in mixer bowl; mix well. Sift in flour, baking soda and salt. Add oil; mix well. Fold in stiffly beaten egg whites. Spoon onto hot griddle. Bake until golden brown on both sides.

Marilynn Rasp, Rainbow Valley #689

BLUEBERRY CORN BREAD

1 cup fresh blueberries
1½ cups flour
1 cup yellow cornmeal
¼ cup sugar
½ teaspoon salt
4 teaspoons baking
  powder
2 eggs, beaten
2 cups milk
¼ cup melted shortening

Rinse and drain blueberries. Sift flour, cornmeal, sugar, salt and baking powder into bowl. Combine eggs, milk and shortening in bowl; mix well. Add to dry ingredients; beat until smooth. Fold in blueberries. Spoon into greased electric skillet preheated to 250 degrees. Cover with lid with vent open. Bake for 25 to 30 minutes or until bread tests done.

Ruby L. Tait, Costa Mesa #612

MOTHER'S BROWN BREAD

3 cups cornmeal
4 cups graham flour
2 teaspoons (heaping)
  salt
2 cups molasses
2 teaspoons (heaping)
  baking soda
3 cups boiling water

Combine cornmeal, graham flour, salt and molasses in bowl; mix well. Stir in baking soda dissolved in boiling water. Fill 2 greased 3-pound shortening cans ⅔ full; cover with heavy foil. Place in steamer. Steam for 3 hours. Remove to wire rack to cool.

Kermit W. Richardson, National Grange Overseer

HADDON HALL GINGERBREAD

Yield:
9 servings
Utensil:
baking pan

Approx Per
Serving:
Cal 298
Prot 4 g
Carbo 44 g
Fiber 1 g
T Fat 12 g
36% Calories
from Fat
Chol 24 mg
Sod 252 mg

¹/₂ cup shortening
2 tablespoons sugar
1 egg, beaten
1 cup dark molasses
2¹/₄ cups sifted flour

1 teaspoon baking soda
¹/₂ teaspoon salt
1 teaspoon ginger
1 teaspoon cinnamon
1 cup boiling water

Cream shortening in mixer bowl until light. Add sugar 1 tablespoon at a time, beating constantly until fluffy. Beat in egg and molasses. Sift flour, baking soda, salt, ginger and cinnamon together. Add to batter alternately with boiling water, mixing well after each addition. Spoon into 8x8-inch baking pan lined with greased waxed paper or baking parchment. Bake at 325 degrees for 45 minutes. Serve with Lemon Sauce for Gingerbread (below). May also serve with whipped cream if preferred.

Sylvia Clair, Anderson #418

LEMON SAUCE FOR GINGERBREAD

Yield:
9 servings
Utensil:
double boiler

Approx Per
Serving:
Cal 70
Prot 1 g
Carbo 13 g
Fiber <1 g
T Fat 2 g
24% Calories
from Fat
Chol 27 mg
Sod 48 mg

¹/₂ cup sugar
2 tablespoons cornstarch
¹/₄ cup cold water
1 cup boiling water
1 tablespoon butter

1 egg, beaten
Juice and grated rind of
  ¹/₂ lemon
¹/₈ teaspoon nutmeg
¹/₈ teaspoon salt

Mix sugar and cornstarch in double boiler. Stir in cold water. Add boiling water, mixing well. Add butter. Cook for 15 minutes or until thickened, stirring frequently. Stir a small amount of hot mixture into egg; stir egg into hot mixture. Add lemon juice, lemon rind, nutmeg and salt; beat until smooth. Serve hot on gingerbread.

Sylvia Clair, Anderson #418

GRANDMA'S GINGERBREAD

Yield:
6 servings
Utensil:
baking pan

*Approx Per
Serving:*
Cal 179
Prot 5 g
Carbo 34 g
Fiber 1 g
T Fat 3 g
*14% Calories
from Fat*
Chol 74 mg
Sod 32 mg

1 cup flour

1/2 cup sugar

Ginger and salt to taste

2 eggs

1/2 cup (about) milk

Mix flour, sugar, ginger and salt in bowl. Add eggs and enough milk to make of desired consistency, mixing well. Spoon into greased square baking pan. Bake at 350 degrees until gingerbread tests done.

Helen O. Bohn, Orchard City #333

LEMON BREAD

Yield:
12 servings
Utensil:
loaf pan

*Approx Per
Serving:*
Cal 212
Prot 3 g
Carbo 34 g
Fiber <1 g
T Fat 8 g
*31% Calories
from Fat*
Chol 45 mg
Sod 157 mg

1 1/2 cups sifted flour

1 teaspoon baking
  powder

1/2 teaspoon salt

3 tablespoons shortening

3 tablespoons butter,
  softened

1 cup sugar

2 eggs or egg substitute

1/2 cup milk

1/3 cup sugar

2 tablespoons lemon
  juice

Sift flour, baking powder and salt together. Combine shortening, butter, 1 cup sugar and eggs in mixer bowl; beat until light. Add dry ingredients alternately with milk, mixing well after each addition. Spoon into greased 5x9-inch loaf pan. Bake at 350 degrees for 1 hour or until bread tests done. Pour mixture of 1/3 cup sugar and lemon juice over bread. Cool in pan for 10 minutes. Remove to wire rack to cool completely.

Helen L. Brown, Bakersfield #566

POPPY SEED BREAD

Yield:
16 servings
Utensil:
2 loaf pans

Approx Per Serving:
Cal 428
Prot 5 g
Carbo 60 g
Fiber 1 g
T Fat 20 g
40% Calories from Fat
Chol 43 mg
Sod 188 mg

3 cups flour
1½ teaspoons baking powder
1 teaspoon salt
2½ cups sugar
3 eggs
1¼ cups oil
1½ cups milk
1½ tablespoons poppy seed

3 teaspoons vanilla extract
3 teaspoons butter flavoring
3 teaspoons almond extract
¾ cup sugar
¼ cup orange juice

Sift flour, baking powder and salt together. Combine 2½ cups sugar and eggs in mixer bowl; beat until thick and lemon-colored. Add oil; mix well. Add dry ingredients alternately with milk, mixing well after each addition. Stir in poppy seed and half of each flavoring. Spoon into 2 greased 4x8-inch loaf pans. Bake at 350 degrees for 1 hour. Mix ¾ cup sugar with orange juice and remaining flavorings in saucepan. Heat until sugar dissolves, stirring to mix well. Pour over hot bread. Let stand in pans for 15 minutes or until glaze is absorbed. Remove to wire rack to cool.

Daisy Schultz, Pleasant Valley #675

STRAWBERRY-NUT BREAD

Yield:
36 servings
Utensil:
2 loaf pans

Approx Per Serving:
Cal 176
Prot 2 g
Carbo 21 g
Fiber 1 g
T Fat 10 g
48% Calories from Fat
Chol 24 mg
Sod 91 mg

4 eggs
1 cup oil
2 cups sugar
3 cups flour
1 teaspoon baking soda
1 tablespoon cinnamon

1 teaspoon salt
2 10-ounce packages frozen sliced strawberries, thawed
1¼ cups chopped pecans

Beat eggs in mixer bowl until frothy. Add oil and sugar; mix well. Sift in flour, baking soda, cinnamon and salt; mix until smooth. Stir in strawberries and pecans. Spoon into 2 greased and floured 5x9-inch loaf pans. Bake at 350 degrees for 1 hour and 10 minutes or until loaves test done. Cool in pans for 10 minutes. Remove to wire racks to cool completely.

Rose M. Lewis, Rosedale #565

ZUCCHINI BREAD

Yield:
24 servings
Utensil:
2 loaf pans

Approx Per
Serving:
Cal 258
Prot 3 g
Carbo 33 g
Fiber 1 g
T Fat 13 g
45% Calories
from Fat
Chol 27 mg
Sod 169 mg

3 eggs
1 cup oil
1 cup sugar
1 cup packed brown
  sugar
1 teaspoon vanilla extract
3 cups flour
1½ teaspoons baking
  soda

1 teaspoon baking powder
2 teaspoons cinnamon
½ teaspoon nutmeg
1 teaspoon salt
2½ cups coarsely
  shredded unpeeled
  zucchini
1 cup finely chopped
  walnuts

Combine eggs, oil, sugar, brown sugar and vanilla in large mixer bowl; beat at medium speed until light. Sift in flour, baking soda, baking powder, cinnamon, nutmeg and salt, beating at low speed until smooth. Stir in zucchini and walnuts. Spoon into 2 greased and floured 5x9-inch loaf pans. Bake at 350 degrees for 60 to 70 minutes or until loaves test done. Cool in pans for 15 minutes. Remove to wire rack to cool completely. May use egg substitute equivalent to 3 eggs if preferred.

Lois Prosser, Centerville #797

ZUCCHINI-NUT BREAD

Yield:
24 servings
Utensil:
2 loaf pans

Approx Per
Serving:
Cal 231
Prot 3 g
Carbo 30 g
Fiber 1 g
T Fat 12 g
45% Calories
from Fat
Chol 27 mg
Sod 102 mg

3 eggs
1 cup oil
2 cups sugar
2 cups grated zucchini
3 tablespoons vanilla
  extract

3 cups flour
¼ teaspoon baking
  powder
1 teaspoon salt
1 tablespoon cinnamon
½ cup chopped pecans

Beat eggs in mixer bowl until foamy. Add oil, sugar, zucchini and vanilla; mix lightly. Add flour, baking powder, salt and cinnamon; mix until moistened. Stir in pecans. Spoon into 2 greased 5x9-inch loaf pans. Bake at 325 degrees for 1 hour or until loaves test done. Remove to wire rack to cool.

Rita A. Haase, Clearlake #680

PINEAPPLE-ZUCCHINI BREAD

Yield:
24 servings
Utensil:
2 loaf pans

**Approx Per
Serving:**
Cal 244
Prot 3 g
Carbo 30 g
Fiber 1 g
T Fat 13 g
*47% Calories
from Fat*
Chol 27 mg
Sod 181 mg

3 eggs
1 cup oil
1³/4 cups sugar
2 teaspoons vanilla extract
2 cups grated zucchini
3 cups flour
1 teaspoon baking powder

2 teaspoons baking soda
2 teaspoons cinnamon
³/4 teaspoon nutmeg
1 teaspoon salt
1 cup chopped walnuts
1 cup drained crushed
 pineapple

Beat eggs in mixer bowl until light and foamy. Add oil, sugar and vanilla; mix well. Mix in zucchini. Add flour, baking powder, baking soda, cinnamon, nutmeg and salt; mix well. Stir in walnuts and pineapple. Spoon into 2 greased 5x9-inch loaf pans. Bake at 350 degrees for 1 hour. Remove to wire rack to cool.

Phoebe Andreas, Elbow Creek #733

BLACK PEPPER BREAD

Yield:
24 servings
Utensil:
baking sheet

**Approx Per
Serving:**
Cal 173
Prot 5 g
Carbo 30 g
Fiber 1 g
T Fat 3 g
*17% Calories
from Fat*
Chol 25 mg
Sod 204 mg

1¹/2 cups milk
3 tablespoons sugar
¹/4 cup butter
1 teaspoon basil
2 teaspoons cheese salt
2 envelopes rapid-rise
 yeast

³/4 cup warm water
7 cups flour
1 egg
1¹/2 teaspoons pepper
1 egg yolk
2 tablespoons water
Cracked pepper to taste

Scald milk in saucepan; remove from heat. Stir in sugar, butter, basil and cheese salt until butter melts. Cool to lukewarm. Dissolve yeast in ³/4 cup water in large bowl. Add milk mixture, 3 cups flour and egg; beat for 2 minutes. Add remaining flour and 1¹/2 teaspoons pepper gradually, mixing to form dough. Place in greased bowl, turning to coat surface. Let rise, covered, until doubled in bulk. Divide into 6 portions. Roll each into 20-inch rope. Braid three ropes together on greased 11x17-inch baking sheet, making 2 loaves; pinch ends to seal. Let rise, covered, until doubled in bulk. Brush with egg yolk beaten with 2 tablespoons water; sprinkle with cracked pepper. Bake at 375 degrees for 30 to 35 minutes or until brown.

Walter L. Schnitzius, Welcome #791

PORTUGUESE EASTER BREAD

V.I.P.

Yield:
48 servings
Utensil:
4 baking pans

Approx Per
Serving:
Cal 223
Prot 5 g
Carbo 37 g
Fiber 1 g
T Fat 6 g
24% Calories
from Fat
Chol 65 mg
Sod 188 mg

3 cakes yeast
1 cup lukewarm water
12 cups (or more) flour
1 tablespoon salt

2 cups milk
3 cups sugar
12 eggs, beaten
1 cup melted butter

Dissolve yeast in lukewarm water in small bowl. Sift flour and salt into large bowl. Heat milk to lukewarm in saucepan. Add sugar and beaten eggs; mix well. Add to flour mixture with yeast; mix well. Knead until smooth and elastic. Add melted butter, kneading until smooth and adding additional flour if needed for desired consistency. Let rise, covered, until doubled in bulk. Shape into 4 slightly flattened round loaves in buttered round baking pans. Let rise until doubled in bulk. Bake at 350 degrees for 45 minutes. Remove to wire rack to cool. May press uncooked egg in shell into top of each loaf before baking if desired.

Elsie Espinola, Region 7 GWA Director

CALIFORNIA CHILI BREAD

Yield:
12 servings
Utensil:
baking sheet

Approx Per
Serving:
Cal 382
Prot 9 g
Carbo 21 g
Fiber 1 g
T Fat 29 g
69% Calories
from Fat
Chol 49 mg
Sod 623 mg

1 cup mayonnaise
1/2 cup butter, softened
1 8-ounce can chopped
   green chilies, drained

2 cups shredded
   Monterey Jack cheese
1 loaf French bread

Blend mayonnaise and butter in bowl. Add green chilies and cheese; mix well. Cut bread horizontally into halves; place cut side up on baking sheet. Spread with butter mixture; cover loosely with foil. Bake at 350 degrees for 20 minutes or until cheese melts. Slice crosswise to serve.

Lorena Meyer, Millville #443

CALIFORNIA FRESH STRAWBERRIES
Santa Maria, California

CITRUS GROVE
Eastern Kern County, California

CRUSTY IRISH SODA BREAD

Yield:
16 servings
Utensil:
2 baking pans

2 cups raisins
4 cups flour
1 tablespoon baking
  powder
1 teaspoon baking soda
¼ cup sugar

1 teaspoon salt
¼ cup butter
1 egg, slightly beaten
1¾ cups buttermilk
2 teaspoons caraway seed

*Approx Per
Serving:*
Cal 231
Prot 5 g
Carbo 45 g
Fiber 2 g
T Fat 4 g
*15% Calories
from Fat*
Chol 22 mg
Sod 306 mg

Combine raisins with hot water to cover in bowl; let stand for several minutes. Mix flour, baking powder, baking soda, sugar and salt in large bowl. Cut in butter with pastry blender until crumbly. Beat egg with buttermilk in bowl. Stir in caraway seed. Add drained raisins. Add to crumb mixture; mix well with fork. Knead on floured surface for 2 to 3 minutes. Shape into 2 round loaves in 8-inch baking pans, pressing down to fill pans completely. Cut cross ½ inch deep in top of each loaf. Bake at 375 degrees for 35 to 40 minutes or until golden brown. Remove to wire rack to cool. Top with mixture of confectioners' sugar and lemon juice if desired.

Nora J. Hayes, Springfield #523

NO-KNEAD WHOLE WHEAT BREAD

Yield:
48 servings
Utensil:
4 loaf pans

5 pounds whole wheat
  flour
2 cups dry milk
2 tablespoons salt
8 cups warm water

½ cup molasses
½ cup safflower oil
2 envelopes dry yeast
½ cup warm water

*Approx Per
Serving:*
Cal 196
Prot 7 g
Carbo 37 g
Fiber 6 g
T Fat 3 g
*14% Calories
from Fat*
Chol 1 mg
Sod 284 mg

Mix flour, dry milk powder, and salt in bowl. Add 8 cups water, molasses and oil; mix well. Cover with damp towel. Let stand overnight. Dissolve yeast in ½ cup warm water in cup. Add to dough; mix well. Let rise, covered, in warm place for 1½ hours or until doubled in bulk. Punch dough down; shape into 4 loaves. Place in 4 greased loaf pans. Let rise for 30 minutes. Bake at 325 degrees for 1 hour and 10 minutes. Remove to wire rack to cool.

Audrey Frankford, Loomis #638

CAKES

APPLE CAKE

Yield:
15 servings
Utensil:
cake pan

Approx Per
Serving:
Cal 405
Prot 4 g
Carbo 52 g
Fiber 2 g
T Fat 21 g
46% Calories
from Fat
Chol 28 mg
Sod 137 mg

2 cups sugar
2 teaspoons cinnamon
1 cup oil
2 eggs
1/2 teaspoon salt

4 cups grated apples
2¹/2 cups flour
1 cup finely chopped
pecans
1 teaspoon baking soda

Combine sugar, cinnamon, oil, eggs and salt in bowl; mix well. Stir in apples. Let stand for 20 minutes. Add flour, pecans and baking soda; mix well. Pour into greased and floured 10-inch tube pan or 9x13-inch cake pan. Bake at 350 degrees for 1 hour or until cake tests done.

Trinidad J. Graham, Grover City #746

EASY RAW APPLE CAKE

Yield:	
15 servings	
Utensil:	
cake pan	

Approx Per Serving:
Cal 380
Prot 5 g
Carbo 56 g
Fiber 3 g
T Fat 17 g
39% Calories from Fat
Chol 28 mg
Sod 264 mg

4 cups chopped Golden
   Delicious apples
1/2 cup oil
2 eggs
2 cups sugar
2 cups flour

2 teaspoons baking soda
1 teaspoon salt
1 tablespoon cinnamon
1 3/4 cups chopped
   walnuts
1 cup raisins

Mix apples, oil, eggs and sugar in large bowl. Combine flour, baking soda, salt and cinnamon in medium bowl; do not sift. Add flour mixture to apple mixture; mix well. Stir in walnuts and raisins. Pour into greased 9x12-inch cake pan. Bake at 350 degrees for 40 to 45 minutes or until cake tests done.

Zay Little, Fort Bragg #672

FRESH APPLE CAKE

Yield:	
12 servings	
Utensil:	
cake pan	

Approx Per Serving:
Cal 452
Prot 4 g
Carbo 68 g
Fiber 2 g
T Fat 19 g
37% Calories from Fat
Chol 0 mg
Sod 139 mg

4 cups sifted flour
2 teaspoons baking soda
2 cups sugar
2 cups water
1 cup oil

3 1/2 cups chopped apples
2 tablespoons baking
   cocoa
1 tablespoon cinnamon

Combine flour and baking soda in large bowl; mix well. Combine sugar, water, oil, apples, cocoa and cinnamon in saucepan. Bring to a boil. Boil for 4 minutes. Cool to lukewarm. Stir into flour mixture. Pour into greased and floured 9x12-inch cake pan. Bake at 350 degrees for 40 to 45 minutes or until cake tests done. May add 1 cup chopped walnuts to flour mixture.

Laura Curry, Bodega Bay #777

EGGLESS AND SUGARLESS APPLE-RAISIN CAKE

Yield:
12 servings
Utensil:
cake pan

*Approx Per
Serving:*
Cal 259
Prot 4 g
Carbo 32 g
Fiber 2 g
T Fat 14 g
47% Calories
from Fat
Chol 0 mg
Sod 175 mg

1³/₄ cups flour
¹/₂ teaspoon baking
powder
1 teaspoon baking soda
¹/₂ teaspoon cinnamon
¹/₂ teaspoon nutmeg

¹/₄ teaspoon ground cloves
1 cup chopped walnuts
1 cup raisins
2 cups unsweetened
apple juice
¹/₂ cup margarine

Sift flour, baking powder, baking soda, cinnamon, nutmeg and cloves together. Stir in walnuts. Combine raisins, apple juice and margarine in 2-quart saucepan. Bring to a boil. Remove from heat to cool. Add flour mixture all at once; mix well with wooden spoon. Pour into greased 10x10-inch glass cake pan. Bake at 350 degrees for 30 to 35 minutes or until cake tests done. May add ¹/₂ teaspoon salt to flour mixture. May substitute other fruits and juices for raisins and apple juice.

Willie Eastlick, Greenhorn #384

APPLESAUCE CAKES

Yield:
16 servings
Utensil:
2 loaf pans

*Approx Per
Serving:*
Cal 440
Prot 5 g
Carbo 78 g
Fiber 3 g
T Fat 14 g
27% Calories
from Fat
Chol 0 mg
Sod 225 mg

5 cups flour
2 tablespoons baking
cocoa
¹/₂ teaspoon ground cloves
¹/₂ teaspoon cinnamon
1 tablespoon baking
soda

¹/₂ teaspoon salt
2 cups sugar
2 cups water
2 cups raisins
1 cup shortening
2 cups applesauce

Sift flour, cocoa, cloves, cinnamon, baking soda and salt together. Combine sugar, water, raisins and shortening in saucepan. Bring to a boil. Simmer for 10 minutes. Combine boiled mixture and flour mixture in large bowl; mix well. Stir in applesauce. Spoon into 2 waxed paper-lined loaf pans or 1 angel food cake pan. Bake at 250 degrees for 2 hours. May add 1 cup chopped walnuts to batter.

Carol M. Ormsby, Mt. Vernon #453

Butterscotch Chiffon Cake

Yield:
18 servings
Utensil:
tube pan

Approx Per
Serving:
Cal 256
Prot 4 g
Carbo 43 g
Fiber <1 g
T Fat 8 g
27% Calories
from Fat
Chol 59 mg
Sod 206 mg

2¹/₄ cups flour, sifted
1 tablespoon baking
  powder
1 teaspoon salt
2 cups packed brown
  sugar
¹/₂ cup oil

5 egg yolks
³/₄ cup water
2 teaspoons vanilla
  extract
1 cup egg whites
¹/₂ teaspoon cream of
  tartar

Sift flour, baking powder and salt into bowl. Add brown sugar; mix well. Make well in center of flour mixture. Add oil, egg yolks, water and vanilla; beat until smooth. Beat egg whites and cream of tartar in large mixer bowl until stiff peaks form. Pour egg yolk mixture over egg whites gradually, folding in just until blended; do not stir. Pour into ungreased tube pan. Bake for 65 to 70 minutes or until top springs back when lightly touched. Invert onto funnel to cool. Loosen sides with spatula. Invert onto serving plate. Spread with favorite butterscotch frosting or glaze.

Evelyn Ray, San Dimas #658

Butterscotch-Nut Torte

Yield:
12 servings
Utensil:
2 cake pans

Approx Per
Serving:
Cal 567
Prot 7 g
Carbo 69 g
Fiber 1 g
T Fat 31 g
48% Calories
from Fat
Chol 189 mg
Sod 243 mg

6 egg yolks
1¹/₂ cups sugar
1 teaspoon baking
  powder
2 teaspoons vanilla extract
1 teaspoon almond extract
6 egg whites, stiffly beaten
2 cups graham cracker
  crumbs
1 cup chopped pecans

2 cups whipping cream
3 tablespoons
  confectioners' sugar
¹/₄ cup melted butter
¹/₄ cup water
1 cup packed brown sugar
1 tablespoon flour
1 egg, well beaten
¹/₄ cup fresh orange juice
¹/₂ teaspoon vanilla extract

Beat egg yolks in bowl. Beat in sugar gradually. Stir in baking powder, 2 teaspoons vanilla and almond extract. Fold in egg whites. Stir in crumbs and pecans. Pour into 2 greased and waxed paper-lined 9-inch round cake pans. Bake at 325 degrees for 30 to 35 minutes or until layers test done. Cool in pans for several minutes. Remove to wire rack to cool completely. Beat whipping cream in mixer bowl. Stir in confectioners' sugar. Frost cake. Bring butter and remaining ingredients to a boil in saucepan. Simmer until thickened, stirring constantly. Cool. Drizzle over cake.

Eleanor Edgmon, Rohner #509

Swiss Carrot Cakes

Yield:
16 servings
Utensil:
2 loaf pans

Approx Per Serving:
Cal 452
Prot 5 g
Carbo 45 g
Fiber 2 g
T Fat 29 g
56% Calories from Fat
Chol 53 mg
Sod 255 mg

2¹/₂ cups sifted flour
1 teaspoon baking powder
1 teaspoon salt
1¹/₂ teaspoons baking soda
2 teaspoons cinnamon
1¹/₂ cups oil
2 cups sugar
4 eggs
2 cups grated carrots
1   8-ounce can crushed pineapple
1¹/₂ cups chopped walnuts
1 teaspoon vanilla extract

Sift flour, baking powder, salt, baking soda and cinnamon together. Combine oil and sugar in large mixer bowl; beat well. Add eggs 1 at a time, beating well after each addition. Add flour mixture to egg mixture; beat well. Stir in carrots, pineapple, walnuts and vanilla. Spread in 2 greased loaf pans. Bake at 350 degrees for 1 hour or until loaves test done. Cool in pans for 5 minutes. Remove to wire rack to cool completely.

Olive Wallington, Sierra Nevada #454

Pineapple-Carrot Cake

Yield:
15 servings
Utensil:
cake pan

Approx Per Serving:
Cal 444
Prot 3 g
Carbo 57 g
Fiber 1 g
T Fat 24 g
47% Calories from Fat
Chol 63 mg
Sod 181 mg

1 cup oil
2 cups sugar
3 eggs, beaten
1 cup drained crushed pineapple
2 cups grated carrots
2 cups sifted flour
1 teaspoon baking powder
1¹/₂ teaspoons baking soda
2 teaspoons cinnamon
1 teaspoon vanilla extract
¹/₂ cup butter
1 cup sugar
¹/₂ cup sour cream or buttermilk
1 tablespoon dark corn syrup
1 teaspoon vanilla extract

Combine oil, 2 cups sugar and eggs in bowl; mix well. Stir in pineapple and carrots. Add flour, baking powder, baking soda, cinnamon and 1 teaspoon vanilla; mix well. Pour into greased and floured 9x13-inch cake pan. Bake at 350 degrees for 40 minutes or until cake tests done. Combine butter, 1 cup sugar, sour cream and corn syrup in saucepan. Bring to a boil. Simmer for 5 minutes, stirring frequently. Stir in 1 teaspoon vanilla. Pour warm mixture over warm cake.

Leota Barrett, Redwood Valley #382
Elizabeth W. Miller, Redwood Valley #382

CHOCOLATE CAKE

Yield:
12 servings
Utensil:
2 cake pans

Approx Per Serving:
Cal 436
Prot 6 g
Carbo 60 g
Fiber 2 g
T Fat 20 g
41% Calories from Fat
Chol 36 mg
Sod 350 mg

3 cups flour
1/2 cup baking cocoa
2 cups sugar
1 teaspoon salt
2 teaspoons vanilla
  extract

1 cup buttermilk
2 eggs
1 cup oil
1 cup boiling water
2 teaspoons baking soda

Sift flour, baking cocoa, sugar and salt into bowl. Make well in center. Add vanilla, buttermilk, eggs and oil; beat until smooth. Stir in mixture of boiling water and baking soda. Pour into 2 greased and floured 9-inch round cake pans. Bake at 350 degrees for 35 to 45 minutes or until layers test done. Cool in pans for several minutes. Remove to wire rack to cool completely. Spread with favorite frosting.

Ida Maxine Apple, Fair Valley #752

CHOCOLATE-CHERRY CAKE

Yield:
12 servings
Utensil:
2 cake pans

Approx Per Serving:
Cal 358
Prot 5 g
Carbo 55 g
Fiber 2 g
T Fat 15 g
36% Calories from Fat
Chol 36 mg
Sod 289 mg

2 cups flour
2 cups sugar
1/2 cup shortening
3/4 cup water
3/4 cup buttermilk
1 teaspoon baking soda
1 teaspoon salt
1/2 teaspoon baking
  powder

1 teaspoon vanilla extract
1/2 teaspoon almond
  extract
4 ounces chocolate,
  melted, cooled
2 eggs
1/2 cup finely chopped
  drained maraschino
  cherries

Combine flour, sugar, shortening, water, buttermilk, baking soda, salt, baking powder, flavorings, melted chocolate, eggs and cherries in large mixer bowl. Beat at medium speed for 30 seconds or until blended. Beat at high speed for 3 minutes. Pour into 2 greased and floured 9-inch round cake pans. Bake at 350 degrees for 30 to 40 minutes or until layers test done. Cool in pans for several minutes. Remove to wire rack to cool completely. Spread with favorite frosting.

Virginia Taylor, Palermo #493

CLASSIC GERMAN CHOCOLATE CAKE

Yield:
12 servings
Utensil:
3 cake pans

Approx Per
Serving:
Cal 742
Prot 10 g
Carbo 79 g
Fiber 2 g
T Fat 45 g
53% Calories
from Fat
Chol 136 mg
Sod 201 mg

2 cups flour
1 teaspoon baking soda
1/4 teaspoon salt
4 ounces German's
  sweet chocolate
1/2 cup water
2 cups sugar
1 cup shortening
4 egg yolks
2 teaspoons vanilla
  extract

1 cup buttermilk
4 egg whites, stiffly beaten
1 14-ounce can
  sweetened condensed
  milk
3 egg yolks, beaten
1/2 cup shortening
1 1/3 cups flaked coconut
1 cup chopped pecans
1 tablespoon vanilla
  extract

Sift flour, baking soda and salt together. Combine chocolate and water in saucepan. Cook over low heat until chocolate is melted, stirring frequently. Beat sugar and 1 cup shortening in mixer bowl until light and fluffy. Beat in 4 egg yolks and 2 teaspoons vanilla. Stir in chocolate mixture. Add flour mixture and buttermilk alternately to creamed mixture, stirring well after each addition. Fold in egg whites. Spread in 3 greased and floured 9-inch round cake pans. Bake at 350 degrees for 30 minutes or until wooden pick comes out clean. Cool in pans for 15 minutes. Remove to wire rack to cool completely. Combine condensed milk, 3 egg yolks and 1/2 cup shortening in heavy saucepan. Cook for 10 minutes or until thickened, stirring frequently. Stir in coconut, pecans and 1 tablespoon vanilla. Cool slightly. Spread between layers and over top and side of cake.

Fern Whitaker, De Sabla #762

For an easy treat, split 2 chocolate cake layers and fill with a mixture of 16 ounces whipped topping, 8 ounces softened cream cheese, 4 cups confectioners' sugar, 2 cups miniature chocolate chips and 1/2 cup nuts.

CHOCOLATE-MALLO CAKE

Yield:
10 servings
Utensil:
cake pan

*Approx Per
Serving:*
Cal 592
Prot 6 g
Carbo 101 g
Fiber 2 g
T Fat 21 g
*31% Calories
from Fat*
Chol 0 mg
Sod 271 mg

1 2-layer package
   devil's food cake mix
1 cup packed brown
   sugar
1/2 cup baking cocoa

2 cups water
12 marshmallows, cut
   into quarters
1 cup broken pecans

Prepare cake mix using package directions; set aside. Mix brown sugar and baking cocoa in 9x13-inch cake pan. Stir in water. Top with marshmallows. Pour cake batter over all. Sprinkle with pecans. Bake at 350 degrees for 45 to 50 minutes or until cake tests done. May serve with whipped cream if desired.

Eva Spencer, Palermo #493

EARTHQUAKE CAKE

Yield:
15 servings
Utensil:
cake pan

*Approx Per
Serving:*
Cal 530
Prot 4 g
Carbo 68 g
Fiber 1 g
T Fat 28 g
*46% Calories
from Fat*
Chol 61 mg
Sod 453 mg

1 cup chopped pecans
1 cup flaked coconut
1 2-layer package
   German Chocolate
   cake mix
8 ounces cream cheese,
   softened

1/2 cup margarine,
   softened
1 teaspoon vanilla extract
1 1-pound package
   confectioners' sugar

Sprinkle pecans and coconut in 9x13-inch cake pan sprayed with nonstick cooking spray. Prepare cake mix using package directions. Pour into prepared pan. Beat cream cheese, margarine, vanilla and confectioners' sugar in mixer bowl. Spoon over batter. Bake at 350 degrees for 50 minutes; cake will crack.

Virginia Wann, Oakdale #435

MISSISSIPPI MUD CAKE

Yield:
15 servings
Utensil:
cake pan

Approx Per
Serving:
Cal 580
Prot 5 g
Carbo 86 g
Fiber 2 g
T Fat 26 g
39% Calories
from Fat
Chol 107 mg
Sod 185 mg

4 eggs
2 cups sugar
1 cup melted butter
1½ cups flour
⅓ cup baking cocoa
1 teaspoon vanilla extract
1 cup chopped pecans
1   7-ounce jar
   marshmallow creme

½ cup melted butter
6 tablespoons milk
⅓ cup baking cocoa
1 teaspoon vanilla extract
1   1-pound package
   confectioners' sugar

Beat eggs and sugar in bowl. Add 1 cup melted butter, flour, ⅓ cup baking cocoa, 1 teaspoon vanilla and pecans; mix well. Pour into greased and floured 9x13-inch cake pan. Bake at 350 degrees for 30 minutes or until cake tests done. Spread marshmallow creme over hot cake. Combine ½ cup melted butter, milk, ⅓ cup baking cocoa, 1 teaspoon vanilla and confectioners' sugar in bowl; beat well. Spread over cake. Chill thoroughly.

Glynnis Grogan, Estrella #488

OLD-FASHIONED DEVIL'S FOOD CAKE

Yield:
12 servings
Utensil:
3 cake pans

Approx Per
Serving:
Cal 522
Prot 10 g
Carbo 85 g
Fiber 3 g
T Fat 17 g
29% Calories
from Fat
Chol 57 mg
Sod 146 mg

1 cup sugar
¾ cup baking cocoa
1 cup milk
1 egg, beaten
1 cup sugar
¾ cup shortening

2 eggs, beaten
¼ teaspoon salt
6 cups flour
1 teaspoon baking soda
½ cup milk
2 teaspoons vanilla extract

Combine 1 cup sugar, ¾ cup baking cocoa, 1 cup milk and 1 egg in saucepan. Cook until smooth and thickened, stirring frequently. Let stand until cool. Cream 1 cup sugar and shortening in mixer bowl until light and fluffy. Add 2 eggs, salt, flour, baking soda and ½ cup milk; mix well. Stir in vanilla and cocoa mixture. Pour into 3 greased and floured 9-inch round cake pans. Bake at 375 degrees for 20 minutes or until layers test done. Cool in pans for several minutes. Remove to wire rack to cool completely. This very delicious recipe is at least 90 years old. I'm 92, and this is an old recipe of my mother's.

Nina R. Eastlick, Greenhorn #384

TRIPLE CHOCOLATE CAKE   *V.I.P.*

Yield:
18 servings
Utensil:
bundt pan

Approx Per Serving:
Cal 263
Prot 4 g
Carbo 41 g
Fiber 1 g
T Fat 12 g
37% Calories from Fat
Chol 27 mg
Sod 285 mg

1 2-layer package chocolate cake mix
1 4-ounce package chocolate instant pudding mix
2 eggs
1¾ cups milk
2 cups chocolate chips
¼ cup confectioners' sugar

Combine cake mix, pudding mix, eggs, milk and chocolate chips in bowl; mix by hand for 2 minutes. Pour into greased and floured bundt or tube pan. Bake at 350 degrees for 35 to 65 minutes or until cake tests done. Cool in pan for 15 minutes. Invert onto serving plate. Sprinkle with confectioners' sugar. Serve small pieces; this is a very rich cake!

Juanita Runyon, Region 8 GWA Director

EGGLESS-MILKLESS-BUTTERLESS CAKE

Yield:
10 servings
Utensil:
loaf pan

Approx Per Serving:
Cal 323
Prot 3 g
Carbo 64 g
Fiber 2 g
T Fat 7 g
19% Calories from Fat
Chol 0 mg
Sod 302 mg

2 cups flour
5 teaspoons baking powder
1 cup packed brown sugar
2¼ cups water
1 cup raisins
2 ounces citron, finely chopped
⅓ cup shortening
½ teaspoon salt
1 teaspoon nutmeg
1 teaspoon cinnamon

Sift flour and baking powder together. Combine brown sugar, water, raisins, citron, shortening, salt, nutmeg and cinnamon in saucepan. Bring to a boil. Simmer for 3 minutes. Let stand until cool. Stir in flour mixture. Pour into greased 5x9-inch loaf pan. Bake at 350 degrees for 45 minutes or until loaf tests done.

Beata J. Schwartz, Sacramento #12

DARK FRUITCAKES

V.I.P.

Yield:
16 servings
Utensil:
2 loaf pans

Approx Per
Serving:
Cal 366
Prot 4 g
Carbo 70 g
Fiber 2 g
T Fat 9 g
22% Calories
from Fat
Chol 56 mg
Sod 73 mg

1¼ cups flour
⅛ teaspoon baking soda
1 teaspoon cinnamon
½ teaspoon nutmeg
¼ teaspoon allspice
¼ teaspoon cloves
1 6-ounce can frozen
 orange juice
 concentrate, thawed

½ cup molasses
1 15-ounce package
 raisins
1 pound chopped mixed
 candied fruit and peels
½ cup butter, softened
⅔ cup sugar
3 eggs
½ cup chopped walnuts

Line two 3x5-inch loaf pans or one 4x11-inch pan with heavy paper, allowing ½ inch of paper to extend above all sides. Sift first 6 ingredients together. Combine orange juice concentrate, molasses and raisins in saucepan. Bring to a boil over medium heat, stirring occasionally; reduce heat. Simmer for 5 minutes. Remove from heat. Stir in candied fruit and peels. Cream butter in mixer bowl until light and fluffy. Beat in eggs 1 at a time. Add flour mixture; mix well. Stir in cooked mixture. Pour into prepared pans. Bake at 275 degrees for 1½ hours for smaller pans or 2¼ to 2½ hours for larger pan. Cool in pans.

Leona M. Greene, Region 4 GWA Director

FAST FRUIT AND CAKE

Yield:
20 servings
Utensil:
cake pan

Approx Per
Serving:
Cal 170
Prot 2 g
Carbo 28 g
Fiber <1 g
T Fat 6 g
29% Calories
from Fat
Chol 21 mg
Sod 161 mg

¼ cup oil
1 2-layer package white
 cake mix
2 eggs

½ cup water
1 21-ounce can
 blueberry pie filling

Pour oil into 9x13-inch cake pan, making sure oil covers bottom of pan. Combine cake mix, eggs and water in pan; mix by hand for 2 minutes. Spread batter evenly in pan. Spoon pie filling over batter. Swirl with fork to marbelize. Bake at 350 degrees for 35 to 45 minutes or until cake tests done. Cool in pan. Garnish with confectioners' sugar or serve with whipped cream or whipped topping. May substitute any flavor pie filling.

Harriet Wilson, Van Duzen River #517

APPLESAUCE FRUITCAKES

Yield:
30 servings
Utensil:
3 loaf pans

Approx Per
Serving:
Cal 429
Prot 4 g
Carbo 70 g
Fiber 3 g
T Fat 17 g
34% Calories
from Fat
Chol 36 mg
Sod 143 mg

2 cups raisins
3½ cups sifted flour
2 teaspoons baking soda
2 teaspoons nutmeg
1 teaspoon each salt,
　cinnamon and cloves
1½ cups shortening
2 cups sugar
5 eggs
2 cups applesauce
1 cup chopped dates

1 pound chopped dried
　fruit mix
1 cup chopped candied
　pineapple
1 cup candied cherries,
　cut into halves
½ cup chopped candied
　lemon peel
½ cup chopped candied
　orange peel
2 cups chopped pecans

Soak raisins in warm water; drain and pat dry. Sift next 6 ingredients together 3 times. Cream shortening and sugar in mixer bowl until light and fluffy. Beat in eggs 1 at a time. Stir in applesauce. Add flour mixture; mix well. Stir in fruits and pecans. Pour into 3 greased and floured 5x9-inch loaf pans. Bake at 300 degrees for 1 hour or until loaves test done. Cool in pans for several minutes. Remove to wire rack to cool completely.

Barbara Bosio, Lompoc #646

LAZY DAISY CAKE

Yield:
8 servings
Utensil:
cake pan

Approx Per
Serving:
Cal 358
Prot 4 g
Carbo 59 g
Fiber 2 g
T Fat 12 g
30% Calories
from Fat
Chol 76 mg
Sod 192 mg

1 cup flour
¼ teaspoon salt
1 teaspoon baking
　powder
2 eggs
1 cup sugar
1 tablespoon vanilla
　extract
½ cup milk

1 tablespoon butter
2 tablespoons whipping
　cream
3 tablespoons butter,
　softened
10 tablespoons brown
　sugar
1 cup flaked coconut or
　chopped walnuts

Sift flour, salt and baking powder together. Beat eggs in mixer bowl until light and thickened. Beat in sugar and vanilla. Add flour mixture; mix well. Combine milk and 1 tablespoon butter in saucepan. Cook just to the boiling point. Add to beaten mixture; beat well. Pour into greased and floured 9x9-inch cake pan. Bake at 350 degrees for 18 to 20 minutes or until cake tests done. Combine remaining ingredients in bowl; mix well. Spread over cooled cake. Brown under broiler.

Diane Hayes, Montgomery #442

LUCERNE LOST CAKE

Yield:
24 servings
Utensil:
cake roll pan

Approx Per Serving:
Cal 339
Prot 3 g
Carbo 49 g
Fiber 1 g
T Fat 16 g
40% Calories from Fat
Chol 18 mg
Sod 196 mg

2 cups flour
2 cups sugar
1 teaspoon baking soda
1/8 teaspoon salt
1 cup water
1/4 cup baking cocoa
1 cup margarine
1/2 cup plus 1 tablespoon
   buttermilk

2 eggs
1 teaspoon vanilla extract
1/2 cup margarine
3 tablespoons baking cocoa
6 tablespoons buttermilk
1 teaspoon vanilla extract
1   1-pound package
   confectioners' sugar
1 cup chopped pecans

Sift flour, sugar, baking soda and salt together in bowl. Combine water, 1/4 cup baking cocoa and 1 cup margarine in saucepan. Bring to a full boil. Stir into flour mixture; do not rinse saucepan. Add 1/2 cup plus 1 tablespoon buttermilk, eggs and 1 teaspoon vanilla to mixture; beat well. Pour into greased and floured 15x18-inch cake roll pan. Bake at 350 degrees for 15 to 20 minutes or until cake tests done. Combine 1/2 cup margarine, 3 tablespoons baking cocoa, 6 tablespoons buttermilk and 1 teaspoon vanilla in saucepan. Bring to a boil. Remove from heat. Beat in confectioners' sugar. Spread over hot cake. Sprinkle with pecans.

Iona Risler, Lucerne Valley #673

MAYONNAISE CAKE

Yield:
10 servings
Utensil:
cake pan

Approx Per Serving:
Cal 719
Prot 4 g
Carbo 96 g
Fiber 2 g
T Fat 37 g
46% Calories from Fat
Chol 64 mg
Sod 451 mg

2 cups flour
2 teaspoons baking soda
1/4 cup baking cocoa
1 cup sugar
1 cup mayonnaise
1 cup water
1 teaspoon vanilla extract

1 cup butter
1/4 cup baking cocoa
1/2 cup milk
1   1-pound package
   confectioners' sugar
1 teaspoon vanilla extract

Sift flour, baking soda, 1/4 cup baking cocoa and sugar together. Mix mayonnaise, water and 1 teaspoon vanilla in bowl. Add flour mixture; mix well. Pour into lightly greased 8x8-inch cake pan. Bake at 350 degrees for 30 minutes or until cake tests done. Combine butter, 1/4 cup baking cocoa and milk in saucepan. Bring to a boil. Beat in confectioners' sugar and 1 teaspoon vanilla. Spread over cooled cake. May double recipe and bake in 9x13-inch cake pan.

Irene V. Nunn, North Fork #763

MOONSHINE CAKE

Yield:
16 servings
Utensil:
tube pan

Approx Per
Serving:
Cal 125
Prot 3 g
Carbo 23 g
Fiber <1 g
T Fat 2 g
16% Calories
from Fat
Chol 80 mg
Sod 89 mg

1¹/₄ cups flour
¹/₂ teaspoon cream of
tartar
¹/₂ teaspoon salt
6 egg whites

1¹/₄ cups sugar
6 tablespoons water
6 egg yolks, beaten
1 teaspoon vanilla or
lemon extract

Sift flour, cream of tartar and salt together 6 times. Beat egg whites in mixer bowl until stiff peaks form. Combine sugar and water in saucepan. Boil for 2 minutes. Pour over egg whites. Beat until stiff. Add egg yolks and vanilla gradually, beating well after each addition. Add flour mixture; mix well. Pour into ungreased tube pan. Bake at 300 degrees for 1 hour or until cake tests done. Cool in pan for several minutes. Invert onto serving plate.

Barbara Ford, Dows Prairie #505

CRUNCH-TOPPED OATMEAL CAKE

Yield:
15 servings
Utensil:
cake pan

Approx Per
Serving:
Cal 427
Prot 4 g
Carbo 62 g
Fiber 2 g
T Fat 19 g
40% Calories
from Fat
Chol 42 mg
Sod 261 mg

1¹/₃ cups flour
¹/₂ teaspoon salt
1 teaspoon baking soda
1 teaspoon cinnamon
¹/₂ teaspoon nutmeg
1¹/₂ cups boiling water
1 cup oats
¹/₂ cup margarine,
softened
1 cup packed brown sugar
1 cup sugar

1 teaspoon vanilla extract
2 eggs
6 tablespoons butter,
softened
¹/₂ cup sugar
¹/₂ cup packed brown sugar
¹/₄ cup half and half
¹/₄ teaspoon vanilla
extract
1 cup flaked coconut
1 cup chopped pecans

Sift first 5 ingredients together. Mix boiling water with oats in bowl. Cream ¹/₂ cup margarine and next 3 ingredients in mixer bowl until light and fluffy. Beat in eggs 1 at a time. Stir in oats and flour mixture. Pour into greased and floured 9x12-inch cake pan. Bake at 350 degrees for 30 minutes or until cake tests done. Cream 6 tablespoons butter, ¹/₂ cup sugar and ¹/₂ cup brown sugar in mixer bowl. Beat in half and half and ¹/₄ teaspoon vanilla. Stir in coconut and pecans. Spread over warm cake. Broil until bubbly.

Maxine Mattila, Fort Bragg #672

1-2-3-4 Cake

1 cup butter, softened
4 eggs
2 cups sugar
3 cups flour
1 cup milk

1 teaspoon salt
1 tablespoon baking
  powder
1 teaspoon vanilla extract

Cream butter and eggs in mixer bowl until light and fluffy. Add sugar; beat well. Add flour and milk alternately to creamed mixture, beating well after each addition. Stir in salt and baking powder. Beat in vanilla. Pour into greased and floured bundt pan. Bake at 350 degrees for 50 to 60 minutes or until cake tests done. Frost with favorite frosting. May bake in 3 cake pans for 20 to 25 minutes. May add 1 cup chopped walnuts to batter and leave cake unfrosted.

Pat Jarrett, Anderson #418

Orange Kiss-Me Cake

2 cups flour
1 cup sugar
1 teaspoon baking soda
1 teaspoon salt
Pulp and juice of 1
  orange
1 cup raisins
1/3 cup chopped walnuts

1/2 cup shortening
3/4 cup milk
2 eggs
1/3 cup sugar
1/3 cup finely chopped
  walnuts
1 teaspoon cinnamon

Mix flour, 1 cup sugar, baking soda and salt in bowl. Add orange pulp, raisins, 1/3 cup chopped walnuts, shortening, milk and eggs; mix well. Pour into greased bundt pan. Bake at 350 degrees for 40 to 50 minutes or until cake tests done. Cool in pan for several minutes. Invert onto serving plate. Brush with orange juice. Mix 1/3 cup sugar, 1/3 cup finely chopped walnuts and cinnamon in bowl. Sprinkle over cake. I won money and a new kitchen from the Orange Show in 1950.

Frances E. Dick, Hesperia #682

AUNT CHRISTINE'S ORANGE CAKE

Yield:
16 servings
Utensil:
tube pan

Approx Per Serving:
Cal 357
Prot 5 g
Carbo 49 g
Fiber 2 g
T Fat 17 g
42% Calories from Fat
Chol 107 mg
Sod 236 mg

1½ cups whole wheat cake flour
1½ cups cake flour
1 teaspoon baking powder
½ teaspoon salt
1 cup butter, softened
2 cups sugar
½ teaspoon vanilla extract

2 tablespoons grated orange rind
5 eggs
¾ cup milk
¼ cup butter
½ cup sugar
⅓ cup orange juice

Sift flours, baking powder and salt together twice. Cream 1 cup butter and 2 cups sugar in mixer bowl until light and fluffy. Beat in vanilla and orange rind. Beat in eggs 1 at a time. Add flour mixture and milk alternately to creamed mixture, beating well after each addition. Pour into buttered and floured 10-inch tube pan. Bake at 350 degrees for 1 hour or until cake springs back when lightly touched. Combine ¼ cup butter, ½ cup sugar and orange juice in saucepan. Cook over low heat until sugar is dissolved, stirring frequently. Pour over hot cake in pan. Cool in pan. Invert onto serving plate. This recipe was handed down from my husband Jack's great-aunt Christine, a fine Scottish lady.

Kay Hayward, Anderson Valley #669

ORANGE-PINEAPPLE CAKE

Yield:
15 servings
Utensil:
cake pan

Approx Per Serving:
Cal 433
Prot 3 g
Carbo 56 g
Fiber 1 g
T Fat 23 g
46% Calories from Fat
Chol 43 mg
Sod 308 mg

1 2-layer package butter-recipe cake mix
3 eggs
¾ cup oil
1 11-ounce can mandarin oranges
1 16-ounce can crushed pineapple

1 6-ounce package vanilla instant pudding mix
16 ounces whipped topping

Combine cake mix, eggs, oil and oranges with juice in bowl; mix well. Pour into 9x13-inch cake pan sprayed with nonstick cooking spray. Bake at 375 degrees for 30 minutes or until cake tests done. Combine pineapple with juice, pudding mix and whipped topping in mixer bowl. Beat until fluffy and of spreading consistency. Spread over cooled cake.

Irene M. Davis, Centerville #797

ORANGE SLICE CAKE

Yield:
15 servings
Utensil:
cake pan

Approx Per Serving:
Cal 718
Prot 8 g
Carbo 118 g
Fiber 5 g
T Fat 26 g
31% Calories from Fat
Chol 57 mg
Sod 250 mg

1 cup margarine, softened
2 cups sugar
4 eggs
1 teaspoon baking soda
1/2 cup buttermilk
2 tablespoons grated orange rind
3 1/2 cups flour
1 pound dates, chopped
1 15-ounce package orange slice candy, chopped
2 cups chopped walnuts
1 cup flaked coconut
2 cups confectioners' sugar
1/2 cup (or more) orange juice

Cream margarine and sugar in mixer bowl until light and fluffy. Beat in eggs 1 at a time. Dissolve baking soda in buttermilk. Stir into creamed mixture. Add orange rind and flour gradually, beating well after each addition. Add dates, candy, walnuts and coconut; mix well. Spoon into nonstick 9x13-inch cake pan. Bake at 250 degrees for 35 to 40 minutes or until cake tests done. Drizzle mixture of confectioners' sugar and orange juice over warm cake. Cool in pan. Cut into squares.

Ruby B. Evans, Lake Earl #577

PEACHES AND CREAM CAKE

Yield:
15 servings
Utensil:
cake pan

Approx Per Serving:
Cal 184
Prot 3 g
Carbo 26 g
Fiber 1 g
T Fat 8 g
40% Calories from Fat
Chol 32 mg
Sod 154 mg

1 16-ounce can sliced peaches
3/4 cup flour
1 4-ounce package vanilla instant pudding mix
1 teaspoon baking powder
1 egg, beaten
1/2 cup milk
3 tablespoons melted margarine
8 ounces cream cheese, softened
1/2 cup sugar
1/2 teaspoon cinnamon
1 tablespoon sugar

Drain peaches, reserving 1/2 cup juice. Chop peaches finely. Combine flour, pudding mix and baking powder in large bowl; mix well. Mix egg, milk and margarine in bowl. Add to flour mixture; mix well. Spread in greased 9x13-inch cake pan. Top with peaches. Combine cream cheese, 1/2 cup sugar and reserved peach juice in mixer bowl; beat well. Spoon over peaches. Sprinkle with mixture of cinnamon and 1 tablespoon sugar. Bake at 350 degrees for 45 minutes.

Myrna Mohler, Westside #473

FRESH PEAR CAKE

Yield:
16 servings
Utensil:
tube pan

Approx Per
Serving:
Cal 562
Prot 6 g
Carbo 58 g
Fiber 2 g
T Fat 36 g
55% Calories
from Fat
Chol 60 mg
Sod 213 mg

3 cups flour
1/2 teaspoon salt
1 teaspoon baking soda
2 teaspoons cinnamon
3 eggs
2 cups sugar
1 cup oil
2 teaspoons vanilla
extract
1 cup chopped pecans

3 cups finely chopped
fresh pears
1 cup confectioners'
sugar
8 ounces cream cheese,
softened
1/2 cup mayonnaise
1 teaspoon vanilla extract
1 cup chopped pecans

Sift flour, salt, baking soda and cinnamon together. Beat eggs in bowl. Add sugar, oil and 2 teaspoons vanilla; beat well. Stir in flour mixture. Add 1 cup pecans and pears; mix well. Pour into greased and floured tube pan or 9x13-inch cake pan. Bake at 350 degrees for 1 hour or until cake tests done. Combine confectioners' sugar, cream cheese, mayonnaise and 1 teaspoon vanilla in bowl; mix well. Stir in 1 cup pecans. Spread over cooled cake.

Myrtle C. Swegles, Gazelle #380

SPICY PERSIMMON CAKE

Yield:
15 servings
Utensil:
cake pan

Approx Per
Serving:
Cal 212
Prot 2 g
Carbo 32 g
Fiber 1 g
T Fat 9 g
38% Calories
from Fat
Chol 17 mg
Sod 187 mg

1 1/2 cups persimmon
pulp
1 teaspoon baking soda
2 cups flour
2 teaspoons baking
powder
1 teaspoon cinnamon
1/2 teaspoon nutmeg
1/2 teaspoon ground
cloves

1/4 teaspoon salt
1/2 cup butter, softened
1 cup sugar
1/2 cup finely chopped
pecans
1 teaspoon grated
orange peel
1/2 teaspoon grated
lemon peel

Mix persimmon pulp and baking soda in small bowl. Set aside. Sift flour, baking powder, cinnamon, nutmeg, cloves and salt together. Cream butter and sugar in mixer bowl until light and fluffy. Add persimmon mixture and sifted ingredients; mix well. Stir in pecans, orange peel and lemon peel. Spoon into 9x13-inch cake pan. Bake at 350 degrees for 30 minutes or until cake tests done.

Hazel Hillis, Golden State #429

PINEAPPLE CAKE

Yield:
15 servings
Utensil:
cake pan

Approx Per
Serving:
Cal 356
Prot 3 g
Carbo 68 g
Fiber 1 g
T Fat 9 g
21% Calories
from Fat
Chol 35 mg
Sod 180 mg

2 eggs
1 20-ounce can crushed
   pineapple
2 cups flour
1 cup sugar
1 cup packed brown
   sugar
2 teaspoons baking soda

½ cup chopped pecans
3 ounces cream cheese,
   softened
¼ cup margarine,
   softened
1 teaspoon vanilla extract
2 cups confectioners'
   sugar

Beat eggs in large bowl until light and lemon-colored. Add undrained pineapple, flour, sugar, brown sugar, baking soda and pecans in order listed, mixing well after each addition. Spoon into oiled 9x13-inch cake pan. Bake at 350 degrees for 45 minutes or until cake tests done. Cool in pan. Combine cream cheese, margarine, vanilla and confectioners' sugar in mixer bowl. Beat until of desired spreading consistency. Spread over cooled cake.

Linda McCarter, Hornbrook #391

YELLOW CAKE WITH PUDDING FROSTING

Yield:
20 servings
Utensil:
cake pan

Approx Per
Serving:
Cal 270
Prot 3 g
Carbo 48 g
Fiber <1 g
T Fat 8 g
27% Calories
from Fat
Chol 2 mg
Sod 186 mg

1 2-layer package
   yellow cake mix
1 16-ounce can crushed
   pineapple
½ cup packed brown
   sugar

1 4-ounce package
   vanilla instant
   pudding mix
4 ounces whipped
   topping

Prepare and bake cake using package directions for 9x13-inch cake. Poke small round holes in hot cake. Combine undrained pineapple and brown sugar in saucepan; mix well. Cook until heated through. Pour over cake. Let stand until cooled slightly. Prepare pudding mix using package directions. Spread over cake. Chill completely. Spread with whipped topping just before serving. Garnish with chopped walnuts.

Bernice Baldocchi, Dos Palos #541

POPPY SEED CAKE

1 2-layer package white cake mix
1 4-ounce package lemon instant pudding mix
¼ cup poppy seed
1 cup water
½ cup oil
4 eggs

Combine cake mix, pudding mix and poppy seed in large bowl; mix well. Add water and oil; mix well. Add eggs 1 at a time, beating well after each addition. Spoon into greased and floured bundt pan. Bake at 350 degrees for 45 minutes or until cake tests done. Cool in pan for 15 minutes. Invert onto serving plate. May substitute yellow cake mix for white cake mix and may drizzle with glaze made with confectioners' sugar, butter and lemon juice.

Ruth Ballew, Fort Bragg #672

QUICK PRUNE CAKE

2 cups flour
1 tablespoon baking powder
Salt to taste
½ cup shortening
1 cup sugar
2 eggs
1½ cups milk
1 cup chopped cooked prunes

Sift flour, baking powder and salt together several times. Cream shortening, sugar and eggs in mixer bowl until light and fluffy. Add sifted ingredients alternately with milk, mixing well after each addition. Stir in prunes. Spoon into greased 9x13-inch cake pan. Bake at 350 degrees for 45 minutes or until cake tests done.

Lillian Richmond, Westside #473

PUMPKIN CAKE

4 eggs
1 29-ounce can
   pumpkin
3/4 cup sugar
3/4 cup packed brown
   sugar
1/2 teaspoon salt
1/2 teaspoon cinnamon
1/2 teaspoon ground
   ginger
1/2 teaspoon allspice
2 cups milk
1 2-layer package
   yellow cake mix
1 cup chopped pecans
3/4 cup melted butter

Beat eggs in large bowl until frothy. Add pumpkin, sugar, brown sugar, salt, cinnamon, ginger, allspice and milk in order listed, mixing well after each addition. Spoon into ungreased 9x13-inch cake pan. Sprinkle cake mix and pecans over top. Drizzle with butter. Bake at 375 degrees for 40 minutes or until cake tests done.

Olive Orzalli, Sonoma Valley #407

SAVARIN

1 envelope dry yeast
1 cup warm water
3/4 cup margarine
4 eggs, beaten
2 tablespoons sugar
2 cups flour
1 cup sugar
1 cup water
1/4 cup rum
1/2 cup apricot preserves
2 tablespoons sugar

Dissolve yeast in 1 cup warm water in bowl. Add margarine, eggs, 2 tablespoons sugar and half the flour; beat until smooth. Stir in remaining flour until smooth. Knead on floured surface. Spread in ring mold. Bake at 375 degrees for 25 to 30 minutes. Cool in pan for 10 minutes. Remove to wire rack to cool completely. Place on serving plate. Bring 1 cup sugar and 1 cup water to a boil in a saucepan. Simmer for 2 minutes. Let stand until cool. Stir in rum. Drizzle slowly over cooled cake until all liquid is absorbed. Press apricot preserves through strainer. Combine with 2 tablespoons sugar in small saucepan. Bring to a boil, stirring constantly. Simmer for 1 to 2 minutes. Let stand until cool. Spread over cake. May fill center of cake with fresh berries or peaches.

Georgia Quigg, Orchard City #333

SPICE CAKE

Yield:
15 servings
Utensil:
cake pan

2 cups flour
1 teaspoon cinnamon
1/2 teaspoon nutmeg
1/2 teaspoon allspice
Ground cloves to taste
1/2 cup walnuts
1/2 cup raisins
1 cup shortening
2 cups packed brown
   sugar
3 eggs
1 cup sour milk

Approx Per
Serving:
Cal 386
Prot 4 g
Carbo 54 g
Fiber 1 g
T Fat 18 g
41% Calories
from Fat
Chol 45 mg
Sod 38 mg

Sift flour, cinnamon, nutmeg, allspice and cloves together 2 times. Mix a small amount of sifted dry ingredients with walnuts and raisins in small bowl. Cream shortening and brown sugar in mixer bowl until light and fluffy. Add eggs; beat until creamy. Add sifted dry ingredients alternately with sour milk, mixing well with a spoon after each addition. Stir in walnut mixture. Spoon into 9x13-inch cake pan. Bake at 375 degrees for 45 minutes or until cake tests done.

Elaine Brennan, Sonoma Valley #407

DUTCH BOILED SPICE CAKE

Yield:
15 servings
Utensil:
cake pan

1 1/2 cups sugar
2 cups water
1 teaspoon ground cloves
1 teaspoon allspice
1 teaspoon salt
2 teaspoons cinnamon
3/4 cup raisins
1 cup margarine
3 cups flour
2 teaspoons baking soda
1 1/2 cups chopped
   walnuts

Approx Per
Serving:
Cal 378
Prot 5 g
Carbo 48 g
Fiber 2 g
T Fat 20 g
46% Calories
from Fat
Chol 0 mg
Sod 397 mg

Combine sugar, water, cloves, allspice, salt, cinnamon and raisins in saucepan; mix well. Bring to a boil. Remove from heat. Stir in margarine until melted. Let stand until cool. Sift flour and baking soda into bowl. Add raisin mixture; mix well. Spoon into greased and floured 9x12-inch cake pan. Top with walnuts. Bake at 350 degrees for 40 to 50 minutes or until cake tests done.

Polly R. Ornelaz, Lompoc #646

Mom's Sponge Cake

Yield:
16 servings
Utensil:
tube pan

Approx Per
Serving:
Cal 160
Prot 5 g
Carbo 27 g
Fiber <1 g
T Fat 4 g
20% Calories
from Fat
Chol 133 mg
Sod 101 mg

10 egg yolks
1½ cups sugar
½ cup water
1 teaspoon vanilla extract
1½ cups cake flour

10 egg whites
1½ teaspoons baking
powder
¼ teaspoon salt

Beat egg yolks and sugar in mixer bowl until very thick. Add water, vanilla and flour; mix well. Beat egg whites with baking powder and salt in another mixer bowl until stiff peaks form. Fold into egg yolk mixture. Spoon into ungreased tube pan. Bake at 300 degrees for 45 minutes. Increase oven temperature to 325 degrees. Bake for 15 minutes longer. Invert onto funnel to cool completely. Loosen cake from side of pan. Invert onto cake plate.

Gladys Craspay, Estrella #488

Upside-Down Strawberry Shortcake

Yield:
6 servings
Utensil:
cake pan

Approx Per
Serving:
Cal 544
Prot 7 g
Carbo 90 g
Fiber 4 g
T Fat 18 g
30% Calories
from Fat
Chol 58 mg
Sod 446 mg

2 cups flour
1 tablespoon baking
powder
3 tablespoons sugar
½ teaspoon salt
¼ cup shortening

1 egg
⅓ cup milk
2 to 4 cups strawberries
¼ cup melted butter
1 cup packed brown
sugar

Sift flour, baking powder, sugar and salt into bowl. Cut in shortening until crumbly. Beat egg with milk. Add to flour mixture; mix well. Knead lightly on floured surface. Roll ½ inch thick. Arrange strawberries in 9-inch round cake pan. Pour mixture of butter and brown sugar over top. Place dough on top. Bake at 450 degrees for 20 minutes or until golden brown. Serve with whipped cream.

Amy A. Stubbs, Lompoc #646

SURPRISE CAKE

Yield:
16 servings
Utensil:
tube pan

Approx Per
Serving:
Cal 217
Prot 3 g
Carbo 38 g
Fiber 2 g
T Fat 7 g
27% Calories
from Fat
Chol 0 mg
Sod 310 mg

1 teaspoon baking soda
1 10-ounce can tomato
   soup
1 cup sugar
2 tablespoons shortening
1 teaspoon salt
2 cups (scant) flour
1 cup chopped fruit peel
1 cup raisins
1 cup chopped walnuts
1/2 teaspoon nutmeg
1/2 teaspoon cinnamon
1/4 teaspoon ground
   cloves
2 tablespoons brandy

Dissolve baking soda in a small amount of water. Stir into tomato soup. Combine sugar, shortening, salt, flour, fruit peel, raisins, walnuts, soup mixture, nutmeg, cinnamon, cloves and brandy in large bowl in order listed, mixing well after each addition. Spoon into greased and floured tube pan. Bake at 300 degrees for 45 minutes or until cake tests done.

Betty H. Barrett, Chaplain, California State Grange

WINE CAKE

Yield:
16 servings
Utensil:
bundt pan

Approx Per
Serving:
Cal 274
Prot 3 g
Carbo 32 g
Fiber <1 g
T Fat 14 g
48% Calories
from Fat
Chol 53 mg
Sod 250 mg

1 2-layer package
   yellow cake mix
1 4-ounce package
   vanilla instant
   pudding mix
1 teaspoon nutmeg
3/4 cup oil
3/4 cup white wine
4 eggs

Combine cake mix, pudding mix, nutmeg, oil, wine and eggs in large bowl. Beat for 5 minutes. Spoon into un-greased bundt pan. Bake at 350 degrees for 50 minutes or until cake tests done. Cool in pan for 5 minutes. Invert onto serving plate.

Thelma Rains, Fort Bragg #672

ZUCCHINI-PUMPKIN CAKE

Yield:
15 servings
Utensil:
cake pan

**Approx Per
Serving:**
*Cal 422
Prot 6 g
Carbo 55 g
Fiber 2 g
T Fat 21 g
44% Calories
from Fat
Chol 43 mg
Sod 236 mg*

3 eggs
1 cup oil
2 teaspoons vanilla
  extract
2 cups sugar
2 cups shredded
  zucchini, drained
1 cup drained crushed
  pineapple

3 cups flour
1 teaspoon baking
  powder
1 teaspoon salt
1 teaspoon baking soda
1 teaspoon cinnamon
1 cup chopped walnuts
1/2 cup raisins

Beat eggs in large bowl until frothy. Add oil, vanilla, sugar, zucchini and pineapple; mix well. Stir in flour, baking powder, salt, baking soda, cinnamon, walnuts and raisins. Spoon into greased 9x13-inch cake pan. Bake at 350 degrees for 50 minutes or until cake tests done.

June E. Kimbel, Sonoma Valley #407

CHOCOLATE-ZUCCHINI CAKE

Yield:
15 servings
Utensil:
cake pan

**Approx Per
Serving:**
*Cal 367
Prot 5 g
Carbo 47 g
Fiber 2 g
T Fat 19 g
45% Calories
from Fat
Chol 60 mg
Sod 266 mg*

2 1/2 cups flour, sifted
1/2 teaspoon allspice
1/2 teaspoon cinnamon
1/2 teaspoon salt
2 teaspoons baking soda
1/4 cup baking cocoa
1 cup packed brown
  sugar
1/2 cup sugar

1/2 cup butter, softened
1/2 cup oil
3 eggs
1 teaspoon vanilla extract
1/2 cup buttermilk
3 6-inch zucchini,
  shredded
1/2 to 1 cup chocolate
  chips

Sift flour, allspice, cinnamon, salt, baking soda and baking cocoa together. Cream brown sugar, sugar, butter and oil in large bowl until light and fluffy. Stir in eggs, vanilla and buttermilk. Sift in dry ingredients; stir until blended. Stir in zucchini. Spoon into greased and floured 9x13-inch cake pan. Sprinkle with chocolate chips. Bake at 325 degrees for 45 minutes or until cake tests done.

Patricia Ray, Ripon #511

BLACK BOTTOM CUPCAKES

1½ cups flour
1 cup sugar
¼ cup baking cocoa
1 teaspoon baking soda
½ teaspoon salt
1 teaspoon vanilla extract
1 cup cold water
⅓ cup oil
1 teaspoon vinegar

1 cup chocolate chips
⅓ cup sugar
1 egg, slightly beaten
⅛ teaspoon salt
8 ounces cream cheese,
  softened
¼ cup chopped walnuts
2 tablespoons sugar

Mix flour, 1 cup sugar, baking cocoa, baking soda and salt in bowl. Mix vanilla, cold water, oil and vinegar in small bowl. Add to dry ingredients; mix well. Fill paper-lined muffin cups ⅓ full. Mix chocolate chips, sugar, egg, salt and cream cheese in bowl. Spoon 1 tablespoon mixture into each filled muffin cup. Sprinkle each with mixture of walnuts and 2 tablespoons sugar. Bake at 350 degrees for 25 to 30 minutes or until cupcakes test done.

Linda Yancey, Wintersburg #583

GRANDMA'S EASY CUPCAKES

1 cup flour
1 cup sugar
1½ teaspoons baking
  powder
½ teaspoon salt
2 eggs

2 tablespoons vegetable
  oil
⅔ cup (about) milk
1½ teaspoons vanilla
  extract

Mix dry ingredients in bowl. Beat eggs in measuring cup. Add oil and enough milk to measure 1 cup; mix well. Add to dry ingredients; mix well. Beat in vanilla. Spoon into greased or paper-lined muffin cups. Bake at 350 degrees for 25 minutes or until cupcakes test done.

Ruth M. Carr, United Rescue #450

CANDIES & COOKIES

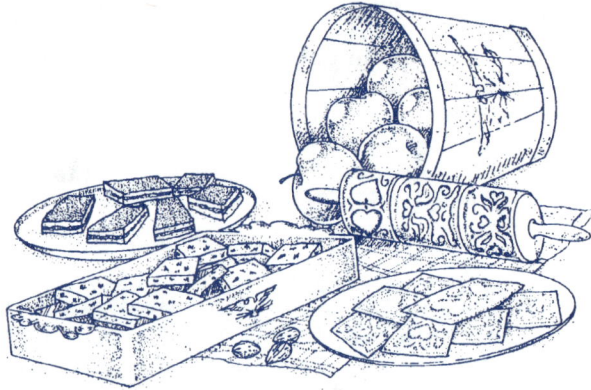

ALMOND ROCA

Yield:
32 servings
Utensil:
baking sheet

Approx Per Serving:
Cal 406
Prot 4 g
Carbo 40 g
Fiber 2 g
T Fat 28 g
59% Calories from Fat
Chol 31 mg
Sod 102 mg

2 cups butter
4 cups superfine sugar
2 cups whole almonds
2 cups semisweet
  chocolate chips

2 cups finely ground
  walnuts
2 cups semisweet
  chocolate chips, melted

Melt butter in heavy saucepan over medium heat. Add sugar, stirring vigorously. Cook until caramel in color or to 270 degrees on candy thermometer, stirring constantly. Add almonds. Cook until medium brown in color or to 290 degrees on candy thermometer, stirring constantly. Pour onto buttered baking sheet. Top with 2 cups chocolate chips, spreading evenly. Sprinkle half the walnuts on top. Chill until set. Turn candy over. Spread with remaining melted chocolate chips. Sprinkle with remaining walnuts. Let stand until set. Break into pieces.

Lois E. Smith, State Youth Director

CATHEDRAL WINDOWS

Yield:
36 servings
Utensil:
saucepan

Approx Per Serving:
Cal 141
Prot 1 g
Carbo 18 g
Fiber 2 g
T Fat 8 g
50% Calories from Fat
Chol 8 mg
Sod 17 mg

1 cup chocolate chips
2 tablespoons butter
1 egg, beaten
1 teaspoon vanilla extract
1 cup confectioners' sugar
1 cup chopped pecans

1 10-ounce package multi-colored miniature marshmallows
1 14-ounce package coconut

Melt chocolate chips and butter in saucepan over low heat. Remove from heat. Add egg, vanilla, confectioners' sugar, pecans and marshmallows in order listed, mixing well after each addition. Divide onto 3 squares of waxed paper. Shape each into a roll. Divide coconut into 3 portions on waxed paper. Coat each roll with coconut. Chill, wrapped in foil, until firm. Cut into 1/4-inch thick slices.

Ethel Brookshire, Santa Cruz-Live Oak #503

CINNAMON NUTS

Yield:
12 servings
Utensil:
saucepan

Approx Per Serving:
Cal 234
Prot 4 g
Carbo 21 g
Fiber 2 g
T Fat 16 g
60% Calories from Fat
Chol 3 mg
Sod 11 mg

1 cup sugar
1/2 cup water
1/8 teaspoon cream of tartar

1/2 teaspoon cinnamon
1 teaspoon vanilla extract
1 tablespoon butter
3 cups walnuts

Combine sugar, water, cream of tartar and cinnamon in saucepan; mix well. Bring to a boil over high heat. Cook to 230 to 234 degrees on candy thermometer, spun thread stage. Remove from heat. Stir in vanilla and butter; mix well. Stir in walnuts. Pour onto baking sheet, spreading evenly. Let stand until set. Break apart.

Elizabeth W. Miller, Redwood Valley #382

CRISPY TREATS

Yield:
48 servings
Utensil:
glass dish

Approx Per
Serving:
Cal 54
Prot <1 g
Carbo 9 g
Fiber <1 g
T Fat 2 g
31% Calories
from Fat
Chol 3 mg
Sod 62 mg

6½ cups crisp rice cereal
⅓ cup butter
1 10-ounce package
  miniature
  marshmallows

1 teaspoon vanilla extract
½ cup miniature
  chocolate chips

Place cereal in large bowl. Melt butter in saucepan over medium heat. Add miniature marshmallows, stirring until melted and smooth. Remove from heat. Stir in vanilla. Pour over cereal; mix well. Stir in chocolate chips. Spoon into 9x12-inch glass dish, patting evenly. Let stand until cool. Cut into squares.

Phyllis Holmes, Palermo #493

NO-COOK DIVINITY

Yield:
60 servings
Utensil:
bowl

Approx Per
Serving:
Cal 70
Prot <1 g
Carbo 14 g
Fiber <1 g
T Fat 2 g
22% Calories
from Fat
Chol 0 mg
Sod 18 mg

1 envelope fluffy white
  frosting mix
½ cup boiling water
⅓ cup light corn syrup

1 teaspoon vanilla extract
1 1-pound package
  confectioners' sugar
1 cup chopped walnuts

Combine frosting mix, boiling water, corn syrup and vanilla in mixer bowl. Beat at high speed for 5 minutes or until stiff peaks form. Add confectioners' sugar, beating constantly at low speed. Stir in walnuts. Drop by teaspoonfuls onto waxed paper. Let stand for 12 hours or longer or until candy is firm and dry. Turn candy over. Let stand until firm and dry. Store in airtight container.

Thelma Steadman, Riverbank #719

PEANUT BRITTLE   *V.I.P.*

Yield:
16 servings
Utensil:
electric skillet

Approx Per
Serving:
Cal 227
Prot 4 g
Carbo 40 g
Fiber 1 g
T Fat 7 g
26% Calories
from Fat
Chol 0 mg
Sod 88 mg

3 cups sugar
1   8-ounce package
    salted peanuts

¹/₂ teaspoon baking soda

Cook sugar in electric skillet over low heat until melted and golden brown, stirring constantly. Add peanuts; mix well. Stir in baking soda. Spread on baking sheet. Let stand until cool. Break into pieces.

Mary L. Jamerson, Region 10 GWA Director

GRAHAM CRACKER FUDGE

Yield:
18 servings
Utensil:
glass dish

Approx Per
Serving:
Cal 187
Prot 4 g
Carbo 23 g
Fiber 1 g
T Fat 10 g
46% Calories
from Fat
Chol 9 mg
Sod 105 mg

2 ounces unsweetened
    chocolate
1   14-ounce can
    sweetened condensed
    milk

¹/₂ teaspoon vanilla extract
1³/₄ cups graham cracker
    crumbs
1 cup chopped pecans
1 tablespoon butter

Melt chocolate in saucepan over low heat. Add condensed milk. Cook for 5 minutes or until mixture thickens, stirring constantly. Add vanilla, graham cracker crumbs, pecans and butter; mix well. Spread into 8x8-inch glass dish. Let stand until cool. Cut into squares.

Natalie Snell, Panama #566

KEVIN'S FAVORITE FUDGE

Yield:
60 servings
Utensil:
glass dish

Approx Per Serving:
Cal 189
Prot 1 g
Carbo 26 g
Fiber 1 g
T Fat 10 g
46% Calories from Fat
Chol 2 mg
Sod 46 mg

1 cup margarine, softened
1   8-ounce jar marshmallow creme
2 cups chopped pecans
4 cups chocolate chips
2 teaspoons vanilla extract
1   12-ounce can evaporated milk
4½ cups sugar

Cream margarine in mixer bowl. Add marshmallow creme, pecans, chocolate chips and vanilla; mix well. Set aside. Combine evaporated milk and sugar in saucepan. Bring mixture to a rolling boil. Boil for 9 minutes, stirring constantly with wooden spoon. Pour over margarine mixture; mix well. Pour into buttered 9x11-inch glass dish. Let stand until cool. Cut into squares. Store in airtight container in refrigerator.

Carol A. Dennis, Garden Grove #613

PEANUT BUTTER FUDGE

Yield:
18 servings
Utensil:
glass dish

Approx Per Serving:
Cal 230
Prot 5 g
Carbo 37 g
Fiber 1 g
T Fat 8 g
30% Calories from Fat
Chol 3 mg
Sod 77 mg

2 cups sugar
2/3 cup evaporated milk
1 cup peanut butter
1 teaspoon vanilla extract
1 cup marshmallow creme

Combine sugar and evaporated milk in saucepan. Bring mixture to a boil over medium heat, stirring constantly. Stir in peanut butter, vanilla and marshmallow creme. Spoon into buttered 8x8-inch glass dish. Let stand until cool. Cut into squares.

Carol Gilliland, Tracy #759

DRYING APRICOTS
Morgan Hill, California

DATES AND CITRUS
Coachella Valley, California

ANGEL FOOD COOKIES

Yield:
24 servings
Utensil:
cookie sheet

Approx Per
Serving:
Cal 169
Prot 1 g
Carbo 19 g
Fiber 1 g
T Fat 10 g
52% Calories
from Fat
Chol 9 mg
Sod 63 mg

1 cup shortening
1/2 cup sugar
1/2 cup packed brown
   sugar
1 egg, beaten
2 cups flour

1 teaspoon baking soda
1 teaspoon cream of
   tartar
1/4 teaspoon salt
1 cup coconut
1 teaspoon vanilla extract

Cream shortening, sugar and brown sugar in mixer bowl until light and fluffy. Beat in egg. Add flour, baking soda, cream of tartar and salt; mix well. Stir in coconut and vanilla. Shape dough into small balls. Dip tops in water; dip in additional sugar. Place 2 inches apart on greased cookie sheet. Bake at 350 degrees for 15 minutes. Cool on wire rack.

Betty Lee Myers, Ceres #520

APPLESAUCE COOKIES

Yield:
60 servings
Utensil:
cookie sheet

Approx Per
Serving:
Cal 68
Prot 1 g
Carbo 10 g
Fiber <1 g
T Fat 3 g
41% Calories
from Fat
Chol 4 mg
Sod 50 mg

1 cup applesauce
1 cup raisins
2 cups sifted flour
1 teaspoon salt
1 teaspoon baking
   powder
1/2 teaspoon baking soda

1 teaspoon cinnamon
1/2 teaspoon nutmeg
1/2 teaspoon ground cloves
1 cup sugar
1/2 cup shortening
1 egg
1 cup chopped pecans

Mix applesauce and raisins in small bowl. Sift flour, salt, baking powder, baking soda, cinnamon, nutmeg and cloves together. Cream sugar, shortening and egg in mixer bowl until light and fluffy. Stir in applesauce mixture. Add sifted ingredients; mix well. Stir in pecans. Drop by spoonfuls 2 inches apart onto greased cookie sheet. Bake at 375 degrees for 12 to 15 minutes. Cool on wire rack. Store in airtight container.

Ann Stowell, Hesperia #682

OLD-FASHIONED BUTTERMILK COOKIES

Yield:
36 servings
Utensil:
cookie sheet

2 eggs
1½ cups sugar
⅔ cup buttermilk
1 teaspoon baking soda
1 cup butter, softened
1 teaspoon lemon extract

1 teaspoon vanilla extract
½ teaspoon ground
nutmeg
1 cup chopped walnuts
4½ cups (about) flour

Approx Per
Serving:
Cal 162
Prot 3 g
Carbo 21 g
Fiber 1 g
T Fat 8 g
42% Calories
from Fat
Chol 26 mg
Sod 75 mg

Beat eggs in mixer bowl until frothy. Add sugar, buttermilk, baking soda and butter in order listed, beating constantly. Stir in flavorings, nutmeg and walnuts. Add enough flour to make an easily handled dough. Roll ¼ inch thick on floured surface; cut with cookie cutter. Place on ungreased cookie sheet. Bake at 400 degrees for 10 minutes. Cool on wire rack.

Virginia Bresciani, Feather River #440

CORNMEAL COOKIES

Yield:
36 servings
Utensil:
cookie sheet

¾ cup margarine,
softened
¾ cup sugar
1 egg
1½ cups flour
½ cup cornmeal

1 teaspoon salt
1 teaspoon baking
powder
1 teaspoon vanilla extract
½ cup raisins

Approx Per
Serving:
Cal 86
Prot 1 g
Carbo 12 g
Fiber <1 g
T Fat 4 g
42% Calories
from Fat
Chol 6 mg
Sod 115 mg

Cream margarine and sugar in large mixer bowl until light and fluffy. Beat in egg. Add flour, cornmeal, salt, baking powder, vanilla and raisins; mix well. Drop by teaspoonfuls onto greased cookie sheet. Bake at 350 degrees for 15 minutes or until lightly browned. Cool on wire rack. May make Chocolate Cornmeal Cookies by adding ¼ cup baking cocoa and ¼ cup milk to cookie dough before baking.

Aiko Pennington, Sierra Nevada #454

CARROT-WALNUT COOKIES

Yield:
24 servings
Utensil:
cookie sheet

*Approx Per
Serving:*
Cal 203
Prot 2 g
Carbo 27 g
Fiber 1 g
T Fat 10 g
44% Calories
from Fat
Chol 9 mg
Sod 140 mg

3/4 cup margarine,
  softened
3/4 cup sugar
1 egg, beaten
1 cup mashed cooked
  carrots
2 cups flour
1 cup chopped walnuts
2 teaspoons baking
  powder
1/4 teaspoon salt

1/2 teaspoon lemon
  extract
1 teaspoon vanilla extract
2 tablespoons
  margarine, softened
2 cups confectioners'
  sugar
2 to 3 tablespoons
  orange juice
Grated rind of 1 orange

Cream 3/4 cup margarine and sugar in mixer bowl until light and fluffy. Beat in egg. Add carrots; mix well. Add flour, walnuts, baking powder, salt and flavorings; mix well. Drop by tablespoonfuls onto greased cookie sheet. Bake at 375 degrees for 12 to 15 minutes. Combine 2 tablespoons margarine, confectioners' sugar , orange juice and orange rind in small bowl; mix until of desired glaze consistency. Spread on hot cookies.

Marna Linzy, Capay #461

CHOCOLATE CHIP COOKIES

Yield:
48 servings
Utensil:
cookie sheet

*Approx Per
Serving:*
Cal 109
Prot 1 g
Carbo 13 g
Fiber <1 g
T Fat 6 g
51% Calories
from Fat
Chol 5 mg
Sod 63 mg

3/4 cup butter-flavored
  shortening
1 1/4 cups packed brown
  sugar
2 tablespoons milk
1 tablespoon vanilla
  extract

1 egg
1 3/4 cups flour
1 teaspoon salt
3/4 teaspoons baking
  soda
1 cup chocolate chips
1 cup pecan pieces

Cream shortening, brown sugar, milk and vanilla in mixer bowl until light and fluffy. Add egg; mix well. Add mixture of flour, salt and baking soda; mix well. Stir in chocolate chips and pecans. Drop by rounded teaspoonfuls 3 inches apart onto ungreased cookie sheet. Bake at 375 degrees for 6 1/2 minutes. Cool on cookie sheet for 2 minutes. Remove to wire rack to cool completely. These cookies won first prize at a state grange baking contest.

Earl S. Harter, Berry Creek #694

DELUXE CHOCOLATE CHIP COOKIES

Yield:
60 servings
Utensil:
cookie sheet

Approx Per Serving:
Cal 77
Prot 1 g
Carbo 12 g
Fiber <1 g
T Fat 3 g
37% Calories from Fat
Chol 7 mg
Sod 34 mg

2 cups flour
1/3 cup baking cocoa
1/2 teaspoon baking powder
1/4 teaspoon salt
1/2 cup margarine, softened
1/2 cup semisweet chocolate chips

1 tablespoon instant coffee granules
3/4 cup sugar
3/4 cup packed brown sugar
2 eggs
2 teaspoons vanilla extract
1 cup semisweet chocolate chips

Blend flour, baking cocoa, baking powder and salt together. Melt margarine and 1/2 cup chocolate chips in saucepan over low heat. Stir in coffee powder. Let stand for 5 minutes. Combine sugar, brown sugar, eggs and vanilla in mixer bowl; beat well. Add melted chocolate mixture; mix well. Add dry ingredients; mix well. Stir in remaining 1 cup chocolate chips. Drop cookies by spoonfuls onto cookie sheet. Bake at 350 degrees for 11 minutes. Cool on cookie sheet for 1 minute. Remove to wire rack to cool completely. May substitute 1 cup peanut butter chips for 1 cup chocolate chips.

Lorna Brown, Grover City #746

MRS. FIELDS CHOCOLATE CHIP COOKIES

Yield:
72 servings
Utensil:
cookie sheet

Approx Per Serving:
Cal 113
Prot 1 g
Carbo 14 g
Fiber 1 g
T Fat 6 g
48% Calories from Fat
Chol 6 mg
Sod 65 mg

2 cups flour
1/2 teaspoon salt
1 teaspoon baking powder
1 teaspoon baking soda
2 cups oats
1/3 cup oat bran
1 cup margarine, softened

1 cup sugar
1 cup packed brown sugar
2 eggs
1 teaspoon vanilla extract
2 cups chocolate chips
1 1/2 cups chopped pecans

Blend flour, salt, baking powder and baking soda together. Combine oats and oat bran in blender container. Process until finely ground. Cream margarine, sugar and brown sugar in mixer bowl until light and fluffy. Add eggs and vanilla; mix well. Add flour mixture and blended oat mixture; mix well. Stir in chocolate chips and pecans. Shape by teaspoonfuls into balls on cookie sheet. Bake at 375 degrees for 8 minutes. This is supposed to be an accurate version of the original Mrs. Fields cookie recipe.

Barbara Fields, Bear Creek #530

CHOCOLATE WAFFLE COOKIES   *U.I.P.*

Yield:
60 servings
Utensil:
waffle iron

Approx Per Serving:
Cal 75
Prot 1 g
Carbo 10 g
Fiber 1 g
T Fat 4 g
43% Calories from Fat
Chol 14 mg
Sod 42 mg

1 cup melted margarine
1 cup baking cocoa
1½ cups sugar
2 teaspoons vanilla extract

4 eggs
2½ cups flour
⅛ teaspoon baking powder

Combine margarine, baking cocoa, sugar, vanilla, eggs, flour and baking powder in bowl; mix well. Drop by teaspoonfuls onto hot waffle iron. Bake for 60 to 75 seconds or until cookies test done.

Donna J. Niles, Flora, California State Grange

GERMAN CHOCOLATE-CREAM BROWNIES   *U.I.P.*

Yield:
12 servings
Utensil:
baking pan

Approx Per Serving:
Cal 297
Prot 4 g
Carbo 29 g
Fiber <1 g
T Fat 19 g
57% Calories from Fat
Chol 87 mg
Sod 217 mg

4 ounces German's sweet chocolate
5 tablespoons butter
8 ounces cream cheese, softened
1¼ cups sugar
3 eggs
1 tablespoon flour

2 teaspoons vanilla extract
½ teaspoon baking powder
½ teaspoon salt
½ cup flour
¼ teaspoon almond extract
½ cup chopped pecans

Melt chocolate and 3 tablespoons butter in saucepan over low heat. Let stand until cool. Beat cream cheese and 2 tablespoons butter in mixer bowl until smooth. Add ¼ cup sugar gradually, mixing constantly. Add 1 egg, flour and ½ teaspoon vanilla; mix well. Beat remaining 2 eggs in bowl until light and lemon-colored. Add ¾ cup sugar. Beat until thickened. Add baking powder, salt and flour; mix well. Stir in chocolate mixture and remaining ingredients. Layer half the chocolate batter, cream cheese mixture and remaining chocolate batter in greased 8x8-inch baking pan. Zigzag layers with knife to marbleize. Bake at 350 degrees for 40 minutes. Cool. Cut into bars.

Jeanne Davies, Executive Committee, National Grange

Magic Cookie Bars

Yield:
24 servings
Utensil:
baking pan

Approx Per
Serving:
Cal 203
Prot 3 g
Carbo 21 g
Fiber 1 g
T Fat 13 g
54% Calories
from Fat
Chol 16 mg
Sod 102 mg

1/2 cup melted butter
1 1/2 cups graham cracker
  crumbs
1 cup chopped walnuts
1 cup semisweet
  chocolate chips

1 3-ounce can flaked
  coconut
1 14-ounce can
  sweetened condensed
  milk

Pour butter in 9x13-inch baking pan. Layer graham cracker crumbs, walnuts, chocolate chips and coconut in prepared pan. Pour condensed milk evenly over top. Bake at 350 degrees for 25 minutes or until golden brown. Cool in pan for 15 minutes. Cut into bars. May substitute butterscotch chips for chocolate chips.

Ethel Plecker, Waterford #553
Christine Kearne, Yucaipa Valley #582

Surprise Meringues

Yield:
30 servings
Utensil:
cookie sheet

Approx Per
Serving:
Cal 59
Prot 1 g
Carbo 9 g
Fiber <1 g
T Fat 3 g
41% Calories
from Fat
Chol 0 mg
Sod 15 mg

3 egg whites
1/8 teaspoon salt
1/8 teaspoon cream of
  tartar

1 teaspoon vanilla extract
3/4 cup sugar
1 cup chocolate chips
1/3 cup chopped walnuts

Beat egg whites with salt, cream of tartar and vanilla in mixer bowl until soft peaks form. Add sugar gradually, beating until stiff peaks form. Fold in chocolate chips and walnuts. Drop by rounded teaspoonfuls onto plain brown paper-lined cookie sheet. Bake at 250 degrees for 25 to 30 minutes.

Betty Van Wyk, Escalon #447

$250.00 COOKIE

Yield:
112 servings
Utensil:
cookie sheet

Approx Per
Serving:
Cal 156
Prot 2 g
Carbo 19 g
Fiber 1 g
T Fat 9 g
47% Calories
from Fat
Chol 17 mg
Sod 69 mg

2 cups butter, softened
2 cups sugar
2 cups packed brown
   sugar
4 eggs
2 teaspoons vanilla
   extract
4 cups flour

5 cups oats
1 teaspoon salt
2 teaspoons baking soda
4 cups chocolate chips
1   8-ounce chocolate
   candy bar, grated
3 cups chopped walnuts

Cream butter, sugar, brown sugar, eggs and vanilla in mixer bowl until light and fluffy. Mix flour, oats, salt and baking soda together. Add to creamed mixture; mix well. Stir in chocolate chips, grated chocolate bar and walnuts. Shape into balls. Place 2 inches apart on cookie sheet. Bake at 375 degrees for 10 minutes. Cool on cookie sheet for 2 minutes. Remove to wire rack to cool completely. Store in airtight container.

Lorraine Mason, Empire #521

ONE DARN GOOD COOKIE

Yield:
60 servings
Utensil:
cookie sheet

Approx Per
Serving:
Cal 117
Prot 1 g
Carbo 16 g
Fiber 1 g
T Fat 6 g
41% Calories
from Fat
Chol 15 mg
Sod 63 mg

1 cup butter, softened
1 cup sugar
1 cup packed brown
   sugar
2 eggs
1 teaspoon vanilla extract

2 cups flour
2$\frac{1}{2}$ cups oats
$\frac{1}{2}$ teaspoon salt
1 teaspoon baking soda
2 cups chocolate chips

Cream butter, sugar and brown sugar in mixer bowl until light and fluffy. Add eggs and vanilla; mix well. Add flour, oats, salt, baking soda and chocolate chips; mix well. Shape into 1$\frac{1}{2}$-inch balls. Place 2 inches apart on cookie sheet. Bake at 375 degrees for 10 minutes. Cool on cookie sheet for 2 minutes. Remove to wire rack to cool completely. May substitute 1$\frac{1}{2}$ cups raisins and 1$\frac{1}{2}$ cups chopped walnuts for 2 cups chocolate chips.

Fred Metzger, Vista #609

DOUBLE CHOCOLATE-OATMEAL COOKIES

Yield:
60 servings
Utensil:
cookie sheet

*Approx Per
Serving:*
Cal 93
Prot 1 g
Carbo 11 g
Fiber 1 g
T Fat 5 g
*48% Calories
from Fat*
Chol 4 mg
Sod 62 mg

1½ cups sugar
1 cup margarine,
  softened
1 egg
1 teaspoon vanilla extract
¼ cup water
1¼ cups flour
½ cup baking cocoa

½ teaspoon baking soda
½ teaspoon salt
¼ to ½ cup chopped
  walnuts
2½ cups quick-cooking
  oats
1 cup chocolate chips

Cream sugar, margarine, egg, vanilla and water in mixer bowl until light and fluffy. Add flour, baking cocoa, baking soda, salt, walnuts, oats and chocolate chips; mix well. Drop by teaspoonfuls onto cookie sheet. Bake at 350 degrees for 8 to 10 minutes or until almost firm. Remove to wire rack to cool completely.

Thelma Jackson, Humboldt #501

FUDGE-OATMEAL COOKIES

Yield:
36 servings
Utensil:
saucepan

*Approx Per
Serving:*
Cal 98
Prot 2 g
Carbo 15 g
Fiber 1 g
T Fat 4 g
*32% Calories
from Fat*
Chol 4 mg
Sod 27 mg

2 cups sugar
½ cup baking cocoa
½ cup milk
¼ cup butter or
  margarine

2 cups quick-cooking
  oats
½ cup peanut butter
1 teaspoon vanilla extract

Combine sugar, baking cocoa, milk and butter in saucepan. Bring to a boil. Boil for 2 minutes. Remove from heat. Stir in oats, peanut butter and vanilla. Drop by teaspoonfuls onto waxed paper. Let stand until cool.

Viola Hoehlke, Hesperia #682

SWEET DREAMS

Yield:
72 servings
Utensil:
cookie sheet

Approx Per
Serving:
Cal 99
Prot 1 g
Carbo 13 g
Fiber <1 g
T Fat 5 g
47% Calories
from Fat
Chol 10 mg
Sod 52 mg

2 cups flour
1 teaspoon baking soda
1/2 teaspoon salt
1 teaspoon cinnamon
1 teaspoon ground
   ginger
1 cup butter, softened

11/2 cups packed brown
   sugar
1 egg
1 teaspoon vanilla extract
1 cup chopped pecans
2 cups chocolate chips
1 cup confectioners' sugar

Blend flour, baking soda, salt, cinnamon and ginger together. Cream butter in mixer bowl. Add brown sugar and egg; mix well. Add dry ingredients and vanilla; mix well. Stir in pecans and chocolate chips. Chill for several hours. Shape into 1-inch balls; roll in confectioners' sugar. Place on cookie sheet. Bake at 375 degrees for 8 to 10 minutes. Remove to wire rack to cool.

Frances Johnson, Bear Creek #530

COCONUT MACAROONS

Yield:
18 servings
Utensil:
cookie sheet

Approx Per
Serving:
Cal 51
Prot 1 g
Carbo 9 g
Fiber 1 g
T Fat 2 g
25% Calories
from Fat
Chol 0 mg
Sod 22 mg

2 egg whites
1/2 teaspoon vanilla
   extract
1/8 teaspoon salt

2/3 cup sugar
1   3-ounce can flaked
   coconut

Beat egg whites with vanilla and salt in mixer bowl until soft peaks form. Add sugar gradually, beating until stiff peaks form. Fold in coconut gently. Drop by rounded teaspoonfuls onto greased cookie sheet. Bake at 325 degrees for 20 minutes. Remove to wire rack to cool.

Beatrice M. Hunt, Millville #443

CRISP COOKIES

Yield:
24 servings
Utensil:
cookie sheet

*Approx Per
Serving:*
Cal 119
Prot 1 g
Carbo 21 g
Fiber 1 g
T Fat 4 g
27% Calories
from Fat
Chol 16 mg
Sod 105 mg

¹/₃ cup butter, softened
1 cup sugar
1 teaspoon coconut or
  almond extract
1 egg, lightly beaten
1 cup baking mix
1¼ cups instant potato
  buds

Combine butter, sugar, flavoring and egg in mixer bowl; mix well. Stir in baking mix and potato buds. Drop by teaspoonfuls onto greased cookie sheet. Bake at 325 degrees for 10 to 15 minutes or until golden brown. Cool on wire rack.

Lauretta Weed, Santa Cruz-Live Oak #503

DATE DAB COOKIES

Yield:
72 servings
Utensil:
cookie sheet

*Approx Per
Serving:*
Cal 96
Prot 1 g
Carbo 16 g
Fiber <1 g
T Fat 3 g
29% Calories
from Fat
Chol 6 mg
Sod 52 mg

1 cup chopped dates
¹/₂ cup sugar
1 cup water
2 tablespoons flour
1¹/₂ teaspoons baking
  soda
¹/₂ cup warm water
1 cup shortening
2 cups packed brown
  sugar
2 eggs
1 teaspoon vanilla extract
1 teaspoon salt
4¹/₄ cups (or more) flour

Combine dates, sugar, 1 cup water and 2 tablespoons flour in saucepan. Bring to a boil. Remove from heat. Let stand until cool. Dissolve baking soda in ¹/₂ cup warm water. Cream shortening, brown sugar, eggs and vanilla in mixer bowl until light and fluffy. Add baking soda mixture, salt and flour; mix well. Drop by teaspoonfuls onto greased cookie sheet, reserving a small amount of dough for cookie tops. Make an indentation in each with floured spoon. Fill with ¹/₂ teaspoon cooled date mixture. Cover with dab of reserved cookie dough. Bake at 375 degrees for 15 to 20 minutes. Cool on wire rack.

Dora Sather, Mt. Vernon #453

Kiwifruit Bars (V.I.P.)

Yield:
40 servings
Utensil:
baking pan

Approx Per
Serving:
Cal 111
Prot 1 g
Carbo 22 g
Fiber 1 g
T Fat 3 g
20% Calories
from Fat
Chol 0 mg
Sod 68 mg

1 pound ripe kiwifruit
1 to 1¹/₂ cups sugar
1 tablespoon potato
  starch or rice flour
¹/₂ cup margarine,
  softened
1 cup packed brown
  sugar

1¹/₂ cups flour
¹/₂ teaspoon salt
¹/₂ teaspoon baking soda
1¹/₂ cups quick-cooking
  oats
¹/₄ cup water

Cut kiwifruit into halves; scoop out pulp. Combine pulp, sugar and potato starch in saucepan. Bring to a boil. Reduce heat to low. Cook until thickened to the consistency of jam. Set aside. Cream margarine and brown sugar in mixer bowl until light and fluffy. Stir in mixture of flour, salt and baking soda. Add oats and water; stir until crumbly. Pat half the crumb mixture into greased 9x13-inch baking pan. Spread with cooled kiwifruit sauce. Sprinkle with remaining crumb mixture. Bake at 350 degrees for 25 minutes or until golden brown. Cool. Cut into bars.

Katie Squire, California State Grange Junior Director

Easy German Christmas Cookies ⌛

Yield:
32 servings
Utensil:
cookie sheet

Approx Per
Serving:
Cal 151
Prot 3 g
Carbo 16 g
Fiber 1 g
T Fat 9 g
52% Calories
from Fat
Chol 13 mg
Sod 77 mg

1¹/₃ cups ground
  almonds
2 cups sifted
  confectioners' sugar
1 cup margarine,
  softened

2 eggs, beaten
2 cups flour
1 teaspoon grated lemon
  rind
3 egg whites
6 tablespoons sugar

Combine almonds and confectioners' sugar in mixer bowl. Add margarine and eggs; mix well. Stir in flour and grated lemon rind. Drop onto nonstick cookie sheet. Beat egg whites in mixer bowl until soft peaks form. Add sugar gradually, beating until stiff peaks form. Spread ¹/₂ tablespoon meringue on each cookie. Bake at 350 degrees for 9 minutes. Cool on wire rack.

Alice J. Capen, American River #172

LEMON FINGERS

Yield:
18 servings
Utensil:
baking pan

Approx Per Serving:
Cal 290
Prot 3 g
Carbo 45 g
Fiber <1 g
T Fat 12 g
35% Calories from Fat
Chol 75 mg
Sod 102 mg

1 cup butter, softened
2 cups flour
1 cup confectioners' sugar
4 eggs

2 cups sugar
1/4 cup flour
1/2 cup lemon juice
1/2 cup confectioners' sugar

Combine butter, 2 cups flour and 1 cup confectioners' sugar in bowl; mix well. Spread in 9x13-inch baking pan, patting evenly. Bake at 350 degrees for 20 minutes. Beat eggs in bowl until frothy. Add sugar, 1/4 cup flour and lemon juice; mix well. Pour over baked layer. Bake for 20 minutes longer. Sprinkle with remaining 1/2 cup confectioners' sugar. Cool. Cut into bars.

Hazel Ivey, Banner #627

GUMDROP COOKIES

Yield:
40 servings
Utensil:
baking pan

Approx Per Serving:
Cal 68
Prot 1 g
Carbo 13 g
Fiber <1 g
T Fat 1 g
20% Calories from Fat
Chol 16 mg
Sod 33 mg

3 eggs
1 1/4 cups sugar
2 teaspoons vanilla extract

1 1/2 cups flour
1/2 teaspoon salt
1/2 cup ground pecans
40 small gumdrops

Beat eggs, sugar and vanilla in mixer bowl until light and lemon-colored. Add flour and salt; beat until smooth. Spoon into greased and floured 9x12-inch baking pan. Sprinkle with pecans. Press gumdrops into batter, allowing 1 gum drop per serving. Bake at 325 degrees for 25 to 30 minutes. Cool in pan for 10 to 15 minutes. Cut into squares. Cool completely.

Constance Baer, Rough and Ready #795

MELT-AWAYS

1 cup margarine,
softened
1 cup small curd cottage
cheese
2 cups flour
1 cup melted butter

1½ cups sugar
Cinnamon to taste
1 cup confectioners'
sugar
2 teaspoons milk

Combine margarine, cottage cheese and flour in bowl; mix well to form soft dough. Chill for several hours to overnight. Divide dough into 6 portions. Roll each portion into ⅛-inch thick circle on floured surface. Brush with melted butter. Sprinkle with sugar and cinnamon. Cut into 8 wedges. Roll as for crescent rolls. Place on cookie sheet. Bake at 350 degrees for 15 to 20 minutes or until golden brown. Cool on cookie sheet for 2 minutes. Drizzle mixture of confectioners' sugar and milk over warm cookies. Remove to wire rack to cool completely.

Hazel Dowd, Sierra Nevada #454

MINCEMEAT BARS

2 cups flour
1 cup sugar
½ teaspoon baking soda
½ teaspoon salt

½ cup oil
¼ cup milk
2 cups mincemeat
1 cup chopped walnuts

Combine flour, sugar, baking soda and salt in large bowl; mix well. Add oil and milk, stirring until moistened and crumbly. Reserve 1 cup mixture for topping. Press remaining mixture into 9x13-inch baking pan coated with nonstick cooking spray. Spread with mincemeat near but not to edge. Sprinkle with walnuts and reserved crumb mixture. Bake at 400 degrees for 20 minutes or until golden brown. Loosen edge of warm layer with knife. Cool. Cut into bars. Store, loosely covered, at room temperature. May use green tomato mincemeat if desired.

Thelma Meyer, Millville #443

MOLASSES COOKIES

¹/₂ cup shortening
³/₄ cup molasses
1 egg
¹/₂ teaspoon salt
¹/₂ teaspoon baking soda
¹/₂ teaspoon baking
  powder
¹/₂ teaspoon ground
  nutmeg
2 teaspoons cinnamon
1¹/₂ cups oats
¹/₂ cup walnuts
1¹/₂ cups flour
¹/₂ cup sugar

Combine shortening, molasses, egg, salt, baking soda, baking powder, nutmeg, cinnamon, oats, walnuts and flour in large bowl; mix well. Chill until firm. Shape dough into log. Roll in sugar. Cut into slices. Place on greased cookie sheet. Bake at 375 degrees for 12 to 15 minutes. Cool on cookie sheet for 2 minutes. Remove to wire rack to cool completely.

Marcia Lamb, Wintersburg #583

FRUITY OATMEAL COOKIES

2¹/₂ cups flour
1 teaspoon baking soda
1 teaspoon salt
1 cup shortening
1 cup packed brown
  sugar
1 cup sugar
1 teaspoon vanilla extract
¹/₄ cup milk
2 eggs, well beaten
1 cup chopped dates
1 cup coconut
¹/₂ cup raisins
1 cup chopped pecans
1 cup oats

Sift flour, baking soda and salt together. Cream shortening, brown sugar, sugar and vanilla in mixer bowl until light and fluffy. Add milk and eggs; mix well. Add sifted ingredients; mix well. Add dates, coconut, raisins, pecans and oats; mix well. Drop by rounded teaspoonfuls onto greased cookie sheet. Bake at 375 degrees for 12 minutes. Cool on cookie sheet for 2 minutes. Remove to wire rack to cool completely.

Caroline B. Kroeker, Region 2 GWA Director

OATMEAL COOKIES

Yield:
60 servings
Utensil:
cookie sheet

*Approx Per
Serving:*
Cal 77
Prot 1 g
Carbo 11 g
Fiber 1 g
T Fat 3 g
*37% Calories
from Fat*
Chol 4 mg
Sod 51 mg

³/₄ cup margarine,
  softened
1 cup packed brown
  sugar
¹/₂ cup sugar
1 teaspoon vanilla extract
1 egg
¹/₄ cup water

³/₄ cup flour
1¹/₂ teaspoons baking
  soda
3 cups quick-cooking
  oats
¹/₂ cup chopped walnuts
¹/₂ cup raisins or dates

Beat margarine, brown sugar, sugar, vanilla, egg and water in mixer bowl until fluffy. Add flour, baking soda and oats; mix well. Stir in walnuts and raisins. Chill overnight. Drop by teaspoonfuls onto cookie sheet. Bake at 375 degrees for 12 to 15 minutes. Cool on cookie sheet for 2 minutes. Remove to wire rack to cool completely.

Helen Nelson, Oakdale #435

PEANUT BUTTER COOKIES

Yield:
30 servings
Utensil:
cookie sheet

*Approx Per
Serving:*
Cal 106
Prot 2 g
Carbo 13 g
Fiber <1 g
T Fat 6 g
*45% Calories
from Fat*
Chol 15 mg
Sod 79 mg

¹/₂ cup butter, softened
¹/₂ cup peanut butter
¹/₂ cup sugar
¹/₂ cup packed brown
  sugar

1 egg
1¹/₂ cups sifted flour
¹/₂ teaspoon baking soda
¹/₄ teaspoon salt

Combine butter, peanut butter, sugar, brown sugar and egg in bowl; mix well. Sift in flour, baking soda and salt; mix well. Chill dough for 1¹/₂ to 2 hours. Shape into 1 inch balls. Place 3 inches apart on cookie sheet. Flatten in crisscross design with fork dipped in flour. Bake at 375 degrees for 6 minutes. Cool on cookie sheet for 2 minutes. Remove to wire rack to cool completely.

Pauline Roberts, Golden State #429

PERSIMMON COOKIES

Yield:
60 servings
Utensil:
cookie sheet

Approx Per Serving:
Cal 63
Prot 1 g
Carbo 9 g
Fiber <1 g
T Fat 3 g
38% Calories from Fat
Chol 4 mg
Sod 51 mg

1/2 cup shortening
1 cup sugar
1 egg, beaten
1 cup persimmon pulp
1 teaspoon lemon extract
2 cups flour
1/2 teaspoon ground cloves
1 teaspoon baking soda
1 teaspoon salt
1 teaspoon cinnamon
1/2 teaspoon nutmeg
1/2 teaspoon ginger
3/4 cup raisins
3/4 cup chopped walnuts

Cream shortening and sugar in mixer bowl until light and fluffy. Add egg; mix well. Add persimmon pulp and flavoring; mix well. Add flour, cloves, baking soda, salt, cinnamon, nutmeg and ginger; mix well. Stir in raisins and walnuts. Drop by spoonfuls onto greased cookie sheet. Bake at 350 degrees for 20 minutes. Cool on cookie sheet for 2 minutes. Remove to wire rack to cool completely.

Dixie Hutchinson, Vacaville #575

PERSIMMON BARS

Yield:
48 servings
Utensil:
baking pan

Approx Per Serving:
Cal 100
Prot 1 g
Carbo 16 g
Fiber 1 g
T Fat 4 g
35% Calories from Fat
Chol 4 mg
Sod 117 mg

2 cups flour
2 tablespoons baking powder
1 tablespoon baking soda
1/2 teaspoon salt
1/2 teaspoon nutmeg
1/2 teaspoon cinnamon
1/2 teaspoon ground cloves
1/2 cup shortening
1 cup sugar
1 egg
2 cups persimmon pulp
1 cup raisins
1 cup chopped pecans
1 cup confectioner's sugar
2 tablespoons lemon juice

Sift flour, baking powder, baking soda, salt, nutmeg, cinnamon and cloves together. Cream shortening in bowl until light and fluffy. Add sugar, egg and persimmon pulp; mix well. Add sifted ingredients; mix well. Stir in raisins and pecans. Spread in greased 14x17-inch baking pan. Bake at 350 degrees for 10 to 20 minutes. Brush warm baked layer with mixture of confectioners' sugar and lemon juice. Cut into bars.

Frauline Sitton, Riverbank #719

POTATO CHIP-BUTTERSCOTCH COOKIES ⌛

Yield:
24 servings
Utensil:
cookie sheet

1 cup butter, softened
1 cup packed brown
  sugar
2 eggs, beaten
2¼ cups flour

1 teaspoon baking soda
2 cups crushed potato
  chips
2 cups butterscotch chips
1 cup chopped pecans

Combine butter, brown sugar, eggs, flour, baking soda, potato chips, butterscotch chips and pecans in bowl in order listed, mixing well after each addition. Drop by teaspoonfuls onto greased cookie sheet. Bake at 325 degrees for 12 to 15 minutes. Cool on cookie sheet for 2 minutes. Remove to wire rack to cool completely.

Eileen Dunn, Orchard City #333

Approx Per
Serving:
Cal 267
Prot 3 g
Carbo 29 g
Fiber 1 g
T Fat 16 g
53% Calories
from Fat
Chol 39 mg
Sod 143 mg

POTATO CHIP COOKIES ⌛

Yield:
108 servings
Utensil:
cookie sheet

1 cup shortening
2 cups packed light
  brown sugar
2 eggs
2 cups flour

1 teaspoon baking soda
1 teaspoon vanilla extract
1 cup crushed potato
  chips
1 cup chopped walnuts

Cream shortening, brown sugar and eggs in bowl until light and fluffy. Add flour, baking soda and vanilla; mix well. Stir in potato chips and walnuts. Drop by teaspoonfuls onto ungreased cookie sheet. Bake at 350 degrees for 10 to 12 minutes. Cool on cookie sheet for 2 minutes. Remove to wire rack to cool completely.

Eva Hiles, Wyandotte #495

Approx Per
Serving:
Cal 56
Prot 1 g
Carbo 7 g
Fiber <1 g
T Fat 3 g
46% Calories
from Fat
Chol 4 mg
Sod 14 mg

RAISIN CREMES

> *Yield:*
> *48 servings*
> *Utensil:*
> *baking pan*

> *Approx Per*
> *Serving:*
> *Cal 140*
> *Prot 2 g*
> *Carbo 19 g*
> *Fiber 1 g*
> *T Fat 7 g*
> *43% Calories*
> *from Fat*
> *Chol 21 mg*
> *Sod 60 mg*

1 cup golden raisins
2 cups water
1 cup butter, softened
2 cups sugar
2 eggs
1 teaspoon cinnamon
1 teaspoon baking soda
2¹/2 cups flour, sifted

1 teaspoon vanilla extract
1 cup chopped walnuts
1 cup confectioners'
  sugar
3 tablespoons butter,
  softened
3 tablespoons milk
¹/4 cup chopped walnuts

Boil raisins and water in saucepan for 10 minutes. Drain, reserving 1 cup liquid. Cream 1 cup butter and sugar in bowl until light and fluffy. Add eggs 1 at a time, beating well after each addition. Add mixture of cinnamon, baking soda and flour alternately with reserved raisin liquid, mixing well after each addition. Stir in vanilla, walnuts and raisins. Spread in 9x13-inch baking pan. Bake at 350 degrees for 25 minutes. Let stand until cool. Beat confectioners' sugar, 3 tablespoons butter and milk in bowl for 3 minutes. Spread on cooled baked layer. Sprinkle with ¹/4 cup walnuts. Cut into bars.

Bertha Webb, Ojai Valley #659

CHRISTMAS TREATS

> *Yield:*
> *36 servings*
> *Utensil:*
> *electric skillet*

> *Approx Per*
> *Serving:*
> *Cal 62*
> *Prot <1 g*
> *Carbo 10 g*
> *Fiber <1 g*
> *T Fat 3 g*
> *36% Calories*
> *from Fat*
> *Chol 0 mg*
> *Sod 72 mg*

¹/2 cup margarine
40 marshmallows
1 tablespoon green food
  coloring

4¹/2 cups cornflakes
1 teaspoon vanilla extract
36 (about) cinnamon red
  hot candies

Melt margarine in electric skillet over low heat. Add marshmallows, stirring until melted. Add food coloring. Stir in cornflakes and vanilla. Drop by teaspoonfuls onto waxed paper. Place 1 cinnamon candy in center of each.

Loretta Ellis, Ceres #520

RICE CRISP SQUARES

Yield:
30 servings
Utensil:
glass dish

Approx Per
Serving:
Cal 93
Prot 1 g
Carbo 14 g
Fiber 1 g
T Fat 4 g
37% Calories
from Fat
Chol 0 mg
Sod 82 mg

¹/₄ cup chocolate chips
¹/₄ cup margarine
4 cups marshmallows
³/₄ cup coconut

¹/₂ cup pecans
¹/₂ cup raisins
5 cups crisp rice cereal

Melt chocolate chips, margarine and marshmallows in top of double boiler over hot water. Stir in coconut, pecans and raisins. Add cereal; mix well. Pat into 6x10-inch glass dish. Chill for 2 hours. Cut into squares.

Gerry Broadbent, Ojai Valley #659

GRANDMOTHER'S SCOTTISH SHORTBREAD

Yield:
48 servings
Utensil:
cookie sheet

Approx Per
Serving:
Cal 65
Prot 1 g
Carbo 7 g
Fiber <1 g
T Fat 4 g
53% Calories
from Fat
Chol 10 mg
Sod 32 mg

1 cup butter, softened
³/₄ cup sugar

2 cups flour

Mix butter and sugar in bowl. Shape into a ball. Add flour, mixing until crumbly. Knead until smooth. Press evenly on cookie sheet. Bake at 300 degrees for 20 to 25 minutes or until light brown. Cut into squares.

Eleanor Bartholomew, Sanger #478

BEST SUGAR COOKIES

Yield:
60 servings
Utensil:
cookie sheet

Approx Per Serving:
Cal 113
Prot 1 g
Carbo 12 g
Fiber <1 g
T Fat 7 g
55% Calories from Fat
Chol 7 mg
Sod 70 mg

1 cup confectioners' sugar
1 cup sugar
1 cup margarine, softened
1 cup oil
2 eggs

1 teaspoon vanilla extract
1/2 teaspoon salt
1 teaspoon baking soda
1 teaspoon cream of tartar
4 cups flour

Cream confectioners' sugar, sugar, margarine and oil in bowl until light and fluffy. Add eggs and vanilla; mix well. Add salt, baking soda, cream of tartar and flour; mix well. Chill dough. Shape into small balls on cookie sheet. Flatten with bottom of small glass. Bake at 375 degrees for 10 minutes. Cool on wire rack.

Irene M. Campbell, Gazelle #380

SOFT SUGAR COOKIES

Yield:
24 servings
Utensil:
cookie sheet

Approx Per Serving:
Cal 97
Prot 1 g
Carbo 15 g
Fiber <1 g
T Fat 4 g
35% Calories from Fat
Chol 12 mg
Sod 76 mg

2 cups sifted flour
1/2 teaspoon baking soda
1/2 teaspoon salt
1/4 cup oil
2 tablespoons butter, softened
1/2 cup sugar

1/4 cup packed brown sugar
1 egg, beaten
1/2 cup plus 1 tablespoon sour milk
1/2 teaspoon vanilla extract

Sift flour, baking soda and salt together. Mix oil and butter in bowl. Add sugar, brown sugar and egg; beat until light and fluffy. Add sifted ingredients alternately with sour milk, mixing well after each addition. Stir in vanilla. Drop by rounded tablespoonfuls 3 inches apart onto greased cookie sheet. Bake at 375 degrees for 15 minutes. Cool on wire rack.

Eunice Adams, Hornbrook #391

SUGAR-FREE FRUIT BARS ☺ V.I.P. ⧗

Yield:
24 servings
Utensil:
baking pan

Approx Per
Serving:
Cal 101
Prot 2 g
Carbo 12 g
Fiber 1 g
T Fat 6 g
48% Calories
from Fat
Chol 9 mg
Sod 39 mg

1 cup raisins
2 apples, peeled,
  chopped
1/4 cup shortening
2 tablespoons liquid
  sweetener
1/4 teaspoon ground
  nutmeg

1 cup water
1 egg
1 teaspoon vanilla extract
1 cup chopped walnuts
1 cup flour
1 teaspoon baking soda
1 teaspoon cinnamon

Combine raisins, apples, shortening, sweetener, nutmeg and water in saucepan. Bring to a boil over medium heat. Boil for 3 minutes, stirring frequently. Remove from heat. Let stand until cool. Beat egg in bowl. Add vanilla, walnuts, flour, baking soda and cinnamon; mix well. Stir in raisin mixture. Spread in greased 9x9-inch baking pan. Bake at 350 degrees for 25 minutes. Cut into bars.

Mary and Don Johnson
National Grange Assistant Steward

SWEDISH HEIRLOOM COOKIES

Yield:
54 servings
Utensil:
cookie sheet

Approx Per
Serving:
Cal 82
Prot 1 g
Carbo 8 g
Fiber 1 g
T Fat 5 g
56% Calories
from Fat
Chol 9 mg
Sod 49 mg

1 cup butter, softened
1 tablespoon vanilla
  extract
1 cup confectioners'
  sugar
1/2 teaspoon salt
2 cups flour

1 1/4 cups almonds, finely
  ground
2 tablespoons sugar
  sprinkles
1/2 cup confectioners'
  sugar
Cinnamon to taste

Cream butter, vanilla, 1 cup confectioners' sugar and salt in bowl until light and fluffy. Add flour and almonds; mix well. Shape by rounded teaspoonfuls into balls. Roll each in sugar sprinkles. Place on ungreased cookie sheet. Bake at 325 degrees for 15 to 18 minutes. Cookies will not brown. Roll warm cookies in mixture of 1/2 cup confectioners' sugar and cinnamon.

Virginia L. Peterson, Ceres #520

TEATIME TASSIES

Yield:
24 servings
Utensil:
muffin pan

Approx Per Serving:
Cal 125
Prot 2 g
Carbo 13 g
Fiber <1 g
T Fat 8 g
55% Calories from Fat
Chol 24 mg
Sod 65 mg

3 ounces cream cheese, softened
1/2 cup butter, softened
1 cup sifted flour
1 egg
3/4 cup packed brown sugar
1 tablespoon butter, softened
1 teaspoon vanilla extract
1/8 teaspoon salt
2/3 cup coarsely broken walnuts

Mix cream cheese and 1/2 cup butter in bowl. Stir in flour. Chill dough for 1 hour. Shape into 1-inch balls. Press over bottoms and sides of ungreased miniature muffin cups. Beat egg, brown sugar, 1 tablespoon butter, vanilla and salt in bowl until smooth. Sprinkle walnuts in muffin cups. Fill with egg mixture. Bake at 325 degrees for 25 minutes or until set.

Beatrice Heine, Rutherford #371

THE ONE

Yield:
96 servings
Utensil:
cookie sheet

Approx Per Serving:
Cal 90
Prot 1 g
Carbo 10 g
Fiber <1 g
T Fat 5 g
54% Calories from Fat
Chol 7 mg
Sod 53 mg

1 cup melted butter
1 cup sugar
1 cup packed brown sugar
1 egg
1 cup oil
1 teaspoon vanilla extract
1 teaspoon salt
1 teaspoon baking soda
1 teaspoon cream of tartar
3 1/2 cups flour
1 cup quick-cooking oats
1 cup crisp rice cereal
1 cup coconut
1 cup chopped pecans

Combine butter, sugar and brown sugar in bowl; mix well. Beat in egg, oil and vanilla. Add salt, baking soda, cream of tartar and flour; mix well. Stir in oats, cereal, coconut and pecans. Chill for several hours. Shape into balls on ungreased cookie sheet. Flatten with glass dipped in additional sugar. Bake at 350 degrees for 12 minutes. Cool on wire rack.

Phyllis McMillen, Garcia #676

WALNUT SQUARES

Yield:
24 servings
Utensil:
baking pan

Approx Per
Serving:
Cal 91
Prot 2 g
Carbo 14 g
Fiber <1 g
T Fat 4 g
34% Calories
from Fat
Chol 18 mg
Sod 11 mg

2 eggs
1 cup packed brown
  sugar
1/2 cup flour
1 teaspoon vanilla extract
1 cup walnut pieces

Beat eggs in bowl until frothy. Beat in brown sugar. Add flour; mix well. Stir in vanilla and walnuts. Spoon into 8x8-inch baking pan coated with nonstick cooking spray. Bake at 250 degrees for 20 to 25 minutes. Let stand until cool. Cut into squares.

Josephine Robertini, Nevada Star #116

SOUR CREAM-COCONUT-WALNUT SQUARES

Yield:
36 servings
Utensil:
baking pan

Approx Per
Serving:
Cal 100
Prot 1 g
Carbo 17 g
Fiber 1 g
T Fat 3 g
28% Calories
from Fat
Chol 12 mg
Sod 22 mg

1 pound brown sugar
2 eggs, beaten
1/2 teaspoon baking soda
2 tablespoons cold water
2 tablespoons sour cream
1 teaspoon vanilla extract
1 cup flour
1 cup chopped walnuts
1 cup coconut
1/4 cup flour
Confectioners' sugar

Combine brown sugar and eggs in bowl. Dissolve baking soda in cold water. Blend with sour cream. Add to brown sugar mixture with vanilla; mix well. Stir in 1 cup flour. Mix walnuts and coconut with 1/4 cup flour. Stir into brown sugar mixture. Spread in greased 9x13-inch baking pan. Bake at 350 degrees for 25 to 30 minutes. Cut into squares while warm. Roll in confectioners' sugar to coat.

Nutritional information does not include confectioners' sugar.

Margaret Davidson, Marshall #451

DESSERTS
(including pies)

OLD ENGLISH APPLE DESSERT

Yield:
10 servings
Utensil:
baking dish

Approx Per Serving:
Cal 232
Prot 4 g
Carbo 42 g
Fiber 3 g
T Fat 7 g
25% Calories from Fat
Chol 43 mg
Sod 83 mg

2 eggs
1 cup honey
1 cup whole wheat flour
2 teaspoons baking
  powder

¾ cup chopped walnuts
2 cups chopped peeled
  cooking apples

Beat eggs in mixer bowl. Beat in honey. Sift in flour and baking powder; mix well. Stir in walnuts and apples. Spoon into greased 9x13-inch baking dish. Bake at 350 degrees for 30 minutes. Cut into squares. Serve warm with cream. May substitute 1½ cups sugar for honey.

Margaret Snyder, Wildflower #663

APPLE DISH

Yield:
12 servings
Utensil:
baking dish

Approx Per
Serving:
Cal 226
Prot 2 g
Carbo 44 g
Fiber 3 g
T Fat 6 g
23% Calories
from Fat
Chol 31 mg
Sod 219 mg

12 apples, peeled, sliced
Nutmeg and cinnamon
  to taste
1 cup flour
1/2 to 1 cup sugar

1 teaspoon baking
  powder
1 egg
1/2 teaspoon salt
1/3 cup melted butter

Spread apples in 9x13-inch baking dish; sprinkle with nutmeg and cinnamon. Combine flour, sugar, baking powder, egg and salt in bowl; mix until crumbly. Sprinkle over apples. Drizzle with butter; sprinkle with additional nutmeg and cinnamon. Bake at 350 degrees for 30 to 40 minutes or until golden brown. Serve with whipped topping or ice cream if desired. May sprinkle tart apples with additional sugar if needed.

Irene Faoro, Rincon Valley #710

BANANA-COOKIE FREEZE

Yield:
12 servings
Utensil:
glass dish

Approx Per
Serving:
Cal 434
Prot 6 g
Carbo 66 g
Fiber 2 g
T Fat 18 g
35% Calories
from Fat
Chol 39 mg
Sod 257 mg

8 bananas, thinly sliced
1/2 gallon vanilla ice
  cream, softened

1 16-ounce package
  Oreo cookies, crushed

Combine bananas and ice cream in bowl; mix gently. Layer half the cookie crumbs, ice cream mixture and remaining cookie crumbs in 9x13-inch glass dish. Freeze until firm. Let stand at room temperature for 10 minutes before serving. Garnish servings with maraschino cherries.

Donald Sharp, Loomis #638

BLACKBERRY COBBLER

6 cups blackberries
1¹/₂ cups oats
1 cup flour
¹/₂ cup grated Parmesan
  cheese

1¹/₂ cups packed brown
  sugar
6 ounces butter, chopped

Spread blackberries in baking dish which has been buttered on the bottom. Mix oats, flour, cheese, brown sugar and butter in bowl until crumbly. Sprinkle over berries. Bake at 370 degrees for 30 minutes or until golden brown. The Parmesan cheese gives a nutty flavor to this cobbler.

Dorothy Reid, Loomis #638

BOSTON CREAM PIE

1²/₃ cups flour
2 teaspoons baking
  powder
¹/₈ teaspoon salt
¹/₂ cup butter, softened
1 cup sugar
2 eggs, beaten
¹/₂ cup milk
1 teaspoon vanilla extract

¹/₂ cup sugar
2¹/₂ tablespoons flour
Salt to taste
1 egg
1 cup milk, scalded
1 teaspoon vanilla extract
1 16-ounce can
  chocolate frosting

Sift first 3 ingredients together. Cream butter and 1 cup sugar in mixer bowl until light and fluffy. Beat in 2 eggs. Beat in sifted dry ingredients alternately with ¹/₂ cup milk and 1 teaspoon vanilla. Spoon into 2 greased and floured round baking pans. Bake at 375 degrees for 25 minutes. Remove to wire rack to cool. Mix ¹/₂ cup sugar and next 3 ingredients in double boiler. Stir in 1 cup scalded milk gradually. Cook for 15 minutes, stirring constantly. Stir in 1 teaspoon vanilla. Split baked layers horizontally. Spread custard between layers. Spread frosting over top of dessert. Store in refrigerator.

Joy Beatie, State Women's Activities Director

Boysenberry Crunch

Yield:
12 servings
Utensil:
baking dish

Approx Per Serving:
Cal 477
Prot 4 g
Carbo 85 g
Fiber 4 g
T Fat 15 g
27% Calories from Fat
Chol 0 mg
Sod 335 mg

8 cups boysenberries
2 cups sugar
1/2 cup tapioca
1   2-layer package white
    cake mix
1/2 cup melted margarine
1/2 cup chopped walnuts

Combine boysenberries, sugar and tapioca in bowl; mix gently. Spread in 9x13-inch baking dish. Combine cake mix, margarine and walnuts in bowl; mix until crumbly. Sprinkle over berries. Bake at 350 degrees for 40 to 50 minutes or until golden brown. Serve with ice cream.

Robin Grogan, Estrella #488

Cherry Dessert

Yield:
12 servings
Utensil:
glass dish

Approx Per Serving:
Cal 341
Prot 2 g
Carbo 57 g
Fiber 1 g
T Fat 13 g
34% Calories from Fat
Chol 22 mg
Sod 215 mg

30 graham crackers,
   crushed
1/2 cup melted butter
1/2 cup sugar
40 marshmallows
1/2 cup milk
2 cups whipped topping
1   21-ounce can cherry
    pie filling

Combine graham cracker crumbs, butter and sugar in bowl; mix well. Press half the mixture over bottom and sides of 9x13-inch glass dish. Melt marshmallows in milk in top of double boiler; cool. Add whipped topping; mix well. Layer half the marshmallow mixture, cherry pie filling, remaining marshmallow mixture and remaining crumb mixture in prepared dish. Chill until serving time.

May Amiot, Lake Francis #745

CANDIED DRIED FIGS

Yield:
40 servings
Utensil:
saucepan

Approx Per
Serving:
Cal 81
Prot <1 g
Carbo 21 g
Fiber 2 g
T Fat <1 g
2% Calories
from Fat
Chol 0 mg
Sod 1 mg

5 pounds figs   **1/2 cup water**
2 cups sugar

Combine figs with water to cover in saucepan. Cook for 1 hour. Cool to room temperature. Chill overnight. Repeat process 2 more times, draining well on third day. Combine sugar and 1/2 cup water in saucepan. Cook until sugar dissolves. Add figs. Cook until syrup is absorbed, shaking pan to keep figs from sticking; do not stir. Spread figs on tray. Let dry in the sun or in a 250 to 300-degree oven. Store in glass jars. Eat as is or mix with orange juice to use as filling for fig newtons. May substitute brown sugar for sugar.

Audrey Frankford, Loomis #638

CROWN JEWEL DESSERT

Yield:
20 servings
Utensil:
glass dish

Approx Per
Serving:
Cal 260
Prot 3 g
Carbo 28 g
Fiber <1 g
T Fat 16 g
53% Calories
from Fat
Chol 51 mg
Sod 151 mg

1 3-ounce package each   **16 graham crackers,**
   cherry, strawberry and   **crushed**
   lime gelatin   **1/4 cup melted butter**
4 cups boiling water   **2 cups whipping cream,**
1 1/2 cups cold water   **whipped**
1 3-ounce package   **8 ounces cream cheese**
   lemon gelatin   **1/3 cup confectioners'**
1/2 cup sugar   **sugar**
1/2 cup pineapple juice   **1 tablespoon milk**

Prepare cherry, strawberry and lime gelatin, dissolving each in 1 cup boiling water and adding 1/2 cup cold water. Pour each into shallow dish. Chill until set. Dissolve lemon gelatin in 1 cup boiling water in bowl. Stir in 1/4 cup sugar and pineapple juice. Chill until partially set. Press mixture of cracker crumbs, 1/4 cup sugar and butter into 10x13-inch glass dish. Fold lemon gelatin into whipped cream. Cut congealed gelatin into cubes. Fold into whipped cream mixture. Spoon into prepared dish. Chill for 5 hours. Spread mixture of remaining ingredients over dessert.

Marjorie M. J. and Woodrow Tucker
High Priest of Demeter

LEMON CURD

Yield:
8 servings
Utensil:
double boiler

6 eggs
2 cups sugar

$^1/_2$ cup lemon juice
$^1/_4$ cup butter

Beat eggs with sugar in double boiler. Add lemon juice and butter; mix well. Cook until thickened, stirring constantly. Spoon into sterilized jars. Store in refrigerator. Use as filling for cake, pie or sweet rolls or as spread for toast or hot breads.

Gladys Bird, Costa Mesa #612

Approx Per
Serving:
Cal 306
Prot 5 g
Carbo 52 g
Fiber <1 g
T Fat 10 g
29% Calories
from Fat
Chol 175 mg
Sod 101 mg

PEACH SURPRISE

Yield:
16 servings
Utensil:
bowl

4 cups frozen cooked
   unsweetened peaches,
   thawed
1   4-ounce pacakge
   butterscotch instant
   pudding mix

4 cups softened French
   vanilla ice cream
1 deep-dish graham
   cracker pie shell

Combine peaches and pudding mix in bowl; mix well. Stir in ice cream. Crumble graham cracker pie shell into peach mixture; mix gently. Freeze, covered, until firm. Let stand at room temperture for several minutes before serving.

Nancy Dreaney, Little Lake #670

Approx Per
Serving:
Cal 266
Prot 3 g
Carbo 44 g
Fiber 1 g
T Fat 10 g
32% Calories
from Fat
Chol 15 mg
Sod 213 mg

PLUM COBBLER

Yield:
6 servings
Utensil:
baking pan

8 to 10 sweet red plums,
  chopped
1/2 cup sugar
2 teaspoons tapioca
1 1/2 teaspoons baking
  powder

1 cup flour
2 teaspoons sugar
1/4 teaspoon salt
1/4 cup shortening
1/3 cup milk

Approx Per
Serving:
Cal 294
Prot 4 g
Carbo 50 g
Fiber 3 g
T Fat 10 g
29% Calories
from Fat
Chol 2 mg
Sod 178 mg

Combine plums, 1/2 cup sugar and tapioca in bowl; mix gently. Mix baking powder, flour, 2 teaspoons sugar and salt in bowl. Cut in shortening until crumbly. Add milk all at once; mix with fork to make dough. Knead lightly 8 times on floured surface. Roll into 14-inch circle. Fit into 8-inch round baking pan. Spoon plum mixture into prepared pan. Fold excess dough over filling, leaving a circle uncovered in center. Bake at 450 degrees for 10 minutes. Reduce oven temperature to 350 degrees. Bake for 10 to 20 minutes longer or until golden brown.

Ellen T. Johnson, Little Lake #670

PRUNE SOUFFLÉ

Yield:
4 servings
Utensil:
baking dish

12 large prunes
3 egg whites

3 tablespoons
  confectioners' sugar

Soak prunes in water to cover in saucepan overnight. Cook until tender; drain. Discard pits and mash well. Beat egg whites in mixer bowl until stiff peaks form. Fold in confectioners' sugar and prunes. Spoon into greased baking dish. Bake at 300 degrees for 30 minutes.

Marie L. Rice, Sacramento #12

Approx Per
Serving:
Cal 94
Prot 3 g
Carbo 22 g
Fiber 2 g
T Fat <1 g
1% Calories
from Fat
Chol 0 mg
Sod 38 mg

STRAWBERRY DEVONSHIRE TART

Yield:
10 servings
Utensil:
flan pan

Approx Per Serving:
Cal 269
Prot 3 g
Carbo 40 g
Fiber 3 g
T Fat 12 g
38% Calories from Fat
Chol 51 mg
Sod 88 mg

1 cup flour
1 tablespoon sugar
1 egg yolk
6 tablespoons butter
1 tablespoon ice water
3 tablespoons sour cream
3 ounces cream cheese, softened

3 pints strawberries, hulled
1 cup sugar
3 tablespoons cornstarch
1/2 cup water
4 or 5 drops of red food coloring

Combine flour, 1 tablespoon sugar and egg yolk in bowl. Cut in butter until crumbly. Add 1 tablespoon ice water gradually, mixing with fork until mixture forms ball. Chill thoroughly. Roll on lightly floured surface. Press dough onto bottom and side of 9-inch fluted flan pan. Bake at 375 degrees for 15 minutes. Beat sour cream and cream cheese in bowl until light and fluffy. Spread in cooled shell. Crush 1 cup strawberries. Combine with 1 cup sugar, cornstarch and 1/2 cup water in saucepan. Cook until mixture boils and is thickened. Stir in food coloring. Arrange remaining strawberries over cream cheese mixture. Pour cooked mixture over all. Serve with whipped cream.

Jean M. Durkee, North Fork #763

FARMERS' DESSERT

Yield:
12 servings
Utensil:
baking dish

Approx Per Serving:
Cal 198
Prot 2 g
Carbo 45 g
Fiber 1 g
T Fat 2 g
7% Calories from Fat
Chol 5 mg
Sod 125 mg

1 tablespoon butter
1/4 cup sugar
1/4 teaspoon salt
3/4 cup milk
1 1/2 cups flour
2 teaspoons baking powder

1/2 cup raisins
1 cup packed brown sugar
1 cup boiling water
1/2 teaspoon vanilla extract

Combine butter, sugar and salt in bowl; mix well. Stir in milk. Add flour, baking powder and raisins; mix well. Spread in greased 8x8-inch baking dish. Mix brown sugar, boiling water and vanilla in bowl. Pour over flour mixture. Bake at 350 degrees until brown and batter rises to top. Serve with ice cream or pour a small amount of milk over individual servings.

Paulette Pfannenstiel, Elk Grove #86

FLOATING ISLANDS

Yield:
8 servings
Utensil:
saucepan

Approx Per
Serving:
Cal 196
Prot 7 g
Carbo 29 g
Fiber <1 g
T Fat 6 g
28% Calories
from Fat
Chol 96 mg
Sod 73 mg

1 quart milk
3 egg yolks
1 egg white
1/2 cup sugar

2 tablespoons flour
1 teaspoon vanilla extract
2 egg whites
6 tablespoons sugar

Scald milk in saucepan. Beat egg yolks, 1 egg white, 1/2 cup sugar and flour in bowl. Stir into milk. Cook until thickened. Stir in vanilla. Pour into dish. Beat 2 egg whites in mixer bowl until soft peaks form. Add 6 tablespoons sugar gradually, beating constantly until stiff peaks form. Spoon meringue carefully onto simmering water in saucepan. Poach for several minutes until set. Remove with slotted spoon; drain. Arrange on custard so that little white "islands" are not touching. This recipe was taken from a 1927 White House cookbook.

Myrtle Stacey, Sonoma Valley #307

FOOD FOR THE GODS

Yield:
12 servings
Utensil:
baking dish

Approx Per
Serving:
Cal 270
Prot 5 g
Carbo 44 g
Fiber 1 g
T Fat 9 g
30% Calories
from Fat
Chol 108 mg
Sod 142 mg

9 tablespoons crushed
  white cracker crumbs
2 teaspoons baking
  powder
1/2 cup chopped dates

1 cup chopped English
  walnuts
2 cups sugar
6 eggs, beaten

Mix cracker crumbs and baking powder in bowl. Add dates, walnuts, sugar and eggs; mix well. Pour into baking dish. Bake at 350 degrees for 20 to 25 minutes or until light brown. Cool in dish. Cut into squares. Serve with whipped cream.

Geneva Dillehay, Lompoc #646

GLADYS' TORTE

Yield:
10 servings
Utensil:
baking sheets

8 egg whites
1½ teaspoons vanilla
    extract
1 teaspoon vinegar

2 cups sugar
2 cups whipping cream
1   8-ounce can crushed
    pineapple, drained

Approx Per
Serving:
Cal 343
Prot 4 g
Carbo 45 g
Fiber <1 g
T Fat 18 g
45% Calories
from Fat
Chol 65 mg
Sod 59 mg

Place two 8-inch waxed paper circles on baking sheets. Beat egg whites in mixer bowl until soft peaks form. Beat in vanilla and vinegar. Add sugar 1 tablespoon at a time, beating constantly until stiff peaks form. Spread over waxed paper. Bake at 300 degrees for 1 hour. Remove waxed paper while hot. Beat whipping cream in mixer bowl until soft peaks form. Stir in pineapple. Spread between layers and over top of torte. Chill for 24 hours before serving.

Carmen Beck, Fort Bragg #672

HEAVENLY RICE

Yield:
8 servings
Utensil:
saucepan

3 cups white rice
9 cups water
1 teaspoon salt
1 teaspoon oil
2 tablespoons
    mayonnaise

1 teaspoon vanilla extract
2 cups crushed
    pineapple with juice
16 ounces whipped
    topping

Approx Per
Serving:
Cal 511
Prot 6 g
Carbo 82 g
Fiber 1 g
T Fat 18 g
32% Calories
from Fat
Chol 2 mg
Sod 305 mg

Combine rice, water, salt and oil in saucepan. Cook until rice is tender. Cool thoroughly. Stir in mayonnaise and vanilla. Add pineapple with juice; mix well. Stir in whipped topping. Chill until serving time. I wanted to make rice more appealing to my husband and 4 sons. I came up with this recipe and have made it for 45 years.

Julia Angelo, Fort Bragg #672

RITZ CRACKER-COCONUT DESSERT

Yield:
28 servings
Utensil:
serving dish

**Approx Per
Serving:**
*Cal 157
Prot 2 g
Carbo 18 g
Fiber <1 g
T Fat 9 g
52% Calories
from Fat
Chol 10 mg
Sod 168 mg*

1½ tubes Ritz crackers,
    crushed
½ cup melted margarine
2   4-ounce packages
    coconut instant
    pudding mix
1½ cups cold milk
1 quart vanilla ice
    cream, softened
8 ounces whipped
    topping

Mix cracker crumbs and melted margarine in bowl;
reserve ¼ of the mixture. Spread remaining mixture in
9x13-inch serving dish. Combine pudding mix and milk
in bowl; mix well. Blend in ice cream. Pour into prepared
dish. Let stand for 10 minutes. Spread with whipped topping. Top with reserved crumb mixture. Chill for 3 hours
or longer.

Marjorie Meadows, Anderson #418

PUDDING CAKE

Yield:
15 servings
Utensil:
serving dish

**Approx Per
Serving:**
*Cal 365
Prot 7 g
Carbo 58 g
Fiber 1 g
T Fat 14 g
32% Calories
from Fat
Chol 8 mg
Sod 408 mg*

2   16-ounce angel food
    loaf cakes
2   4-ounce packages
    banana pudding and
    pie filling mix
1   20-ounce can crushed
    pineapple, drained
12 ounces whipped
    topping
1 cup chopped pecans

Tear angel food cake into bite-sized pieces. Prepare pudding mix using package directions. Mix cooled pudding
with pineapple in bowl. Stir in cake pieces. Spread in
serving dish. Chill thoroughly. Spread with whipped topping. Sprinkle with pecans.

Ruth M. Redings, Cupertino #739

SWEDISH APPLE-BREAD PUDDING

Yield:
6 servings
Utensil:
baking dish

Approx Per Serving:
Cal 414
Prot 8 g
Carbo 60 g
Fiber 4 g
T Fat 17 g
36% Calories from Fat
Chol 111 mg
Sod 304 mg

9 slices bread, cut into halves
1/2 cup half and half
1/2 cup sugar
1/2 cup water
6 tart apples, sliced

2 eggs, slightly beaten
1/2 teaspoon cinnamon
1/4 teaspoon cardamom
1 1/2 cups half and half
2 tablespoons butter

Place half the bread in 2 1/2-quart shallow baking dish. Drizzle with 1/2 cup half and half. Mix sugar and water in saucepan. Bring to a boil. Reduce heat. Simmer, covered, for 5 minutes. Remove from heat. Add 1/3 of the apple slices. Simmer for 3 minutes. Remove with slotted spoon. Repeat with remaining apples. Set aside sugar mixture. Spoon apples over bread in baking dish. Cover with remaining bread. Combine eggs, cinnamon and cardamom in bowl; mix well. Stir in 1 1/2 cups half and half and reserved sugar mixture. Pour over all. Dot with butter. Bake at 350 degrees for 1 hour.

Alice Davenport, Scott Valley #386

BREAD PUDDING

Yield:
8 servings
Utensil:
baking dish

Approx Per Serving:
Cal 227
Prot 8 g
Carbo 30 g
Fiber <1 g
T Fat 9 g
34% Calories from Fat
Chol 127 mg
Sod 264 mg

2 cups dry bread cubes
4 cups scalded milk
1 tablespoon butter
1/4 teaspoon salt
3/4 cup sugar

4 eggs, slightly beaten
1 teaspoon vanilla extract
1/2 teaspoon ground or grated nutmeg

Soak bread cubes in milk for 5 minutes. Add butter, salt and sugar. Pour slowly over eggs in large bowl. Add vanilla; mix well. Pour into greased 2 1/2-quart baking dish. Sprinkle with nutmeg. Place in pan of hot water. Bake at 350 degrees for 50 minutes or until firm. Serve warm or cold with sweetened whipped cream. May add 1/2 cup raisins to batter. This recipe was taken from the 1949 *Better Homes & Gardens Cookbook.*

Marilyn Dupray, Fair Oaks #724

Brownie Pudding

Yield:
12 servings
Utensil:
baking dish

Approx Per Serving:
Cal 233
Prot 2 g
Carbo 44 g
Fiber 1 g
T Fat 7 g
24% Calories from Fat
Chol 1 mg
Sod 248 mg

1 cup flour
2 teaspoons baking
   powder
1 teaspoon salt
2/3 cup sugar
2 tablespoons baking
   cocoa

1/2 cup milk
2 tablespoons oil
1/2 cup chopped pecans
1 cup packed brown
   sugar
1/4 cup baking cocoa
2 cups boiling water

Combine flour, baking powder, salt, sugar, 2 tablespoons baking cocoa, milk, oil and pecans in bowl; mix well. Spread in greased 8x8-inch baking dish. Mix brown sugar and 1/4 cup baking cocoa in bowl. Sprinkle over batter. Pour boiling water over all. Bake at 325 degrees for 30 minutes. Serve plain or with whipped topping, whipped cream, ice cream or milk. This recipe was published in various ladies' magazines in 1957. It's been my family's favorite all these years.

Helen Hencratt, Mt. Lassen #417

Grape Nut-Custard Pudding

Yield:
6 servings
Utensil:
baking dish

Approx Per Serving:
Cal 152
Prot 6 g
Carbo 23 g
Fiber 1 g
T Fat 5 g
27% Calories from Fat
Chol 82 mg
Sod 123 mg

1/2 cup Grape Nuts
2 eggs
1/3 cup sugar

2 cups milk
1 teaspoon vanilla extract

Sprinkle Grape Nuts in greased 1-quart baking dish. Beat eggs in bowl. Add sugar, milk and vanilla; mix well. Pour over Grape Nuts. Place in pan of water. Bake at 375 degrees for 1 hour or until custard is firm.

Teresa Johnson, Fort Bragg #672

GRANDMA'S LEMON PUDDING

Yield:
6 servings
Utensil:
baking dish

Approx Per
Serving:
Cal 270
Prot 5 g
Carbo 41 g
Fiber <1 g
T Fat 10 g
33% Calories
from Fat
Chol 128 mg
Sod 140 mg

3 egg yolks
5 tablespoons lemon
  juice
1 cup sugar
3 tablespoons butter

1 cup milk
5 tablespoons flour
1/8 teaspoon salt
3 egg whites, stiffly
  beaten

Beat egg yolks with lemon juice in bowl. Add sugar, butter, milk, flour and salt; mix well. Fold in egg whites. Pour into buttered 2-quart baking dish. Set in shallow pan of water. Bake at 350 degrees for 25 minutes or until dessert pulls from sides of baking dish.

Lenora Sprock, Whitesboro #766

WILD BLACKBERRY PIE

Yield:
8 servings
Utensil:
pie plate

Approx Per
Serving:
Cal 367
Prot 4 g
Carbo 55 g
Fiber 8 g
T Fat 15 g
37% Calories
from Fat
Chol 4 mg
Sod 321 mg

6 cups fresh wild
  blackberries
3/4 cup sugar
Juice of 1/2 lemon
2 tablespoons brandy
2 tablespoons flour

2 tablespoons cornstarch
1/8 teaspoon salt
1 recipe 2-crust pie
  pastry
1 tablespoon butter
1/4 teaspoon mace

Combine blackberries with sugar, lemon juice, brandy, flour, cornstarch and salt in bowl; mix well. Spoon into pastry-lined 9-inch pie plate. Dot with butter; sprinkle with mace. Top with remaining pastry; seal edge and cut vents. Bake at 450 degrees for 10 minutes. Reduce oven temperature to 350 degrees. Bake for 25 to 30 minutes longer. May substitute rum flavoring for brandy.

LaVerne Thomason, Montgomery #442

GRANDMA FAIRBANKS' BOYSENBERRY PIE

Yield:
8 servings
Utensil:
pie plate

Approx Per Serving:
Cal 365
Prot 4 g
Carbo 59 g
Fiber 5 g
T Fat 14 g
33% Calories from Fat
Chol 0 mg
Sod 278 mg

1 cup sugar
3 to 4 tablespoons tapioca
1/2 teaspoon cinnamon
1/4 teaspoon nutmeg

6 cups boysenberries
1 tablespoon lemon juice
1 recipe 2-crust pie pastry

Mix sugar, tapioca, cinnamon and nutmeg in bowl. Add boysenberries and lemon juice; mix gently. Let stand for 15 minutes, stirring occasionally. Spoon into pastry-lined 9-inch pie plate. Top with remaining pastry; seal edge and cut vents. Bake at 400 degrees on lowest oven rack for 55 to 60 minutes or until golden brown. Serve warm or at room temperature. May cover edge with foil to prevent overbrowning. May substitute blackberries for boysenberries if desired.

Mary Fairbanks, Lompoc #646

BUTTERMILK PIE

Yield:
8 servings
Utensil:
pie plate

Approx Per Serving:
Cal 405
Prot 7 g
Carbo 49 g
Fiber <1 g
T Fat 21 g
45% Calories from Fat
Chol 184 mg
Sod 295 mg

6 tablespoons butter, softened
1 1/2 cups sugar
6 eggs

1 cup buttermilk
1 teaspoon vanilla extract
Cinnamon to taste
1 unbaked 9-inch pie shell

Cream butter and sugar in mixer bowl until light and fluffy. Combine with eggs, buttermilk, vanilla and cinnamon in blender container; process until smooth. Spoon into unbaked pie shell. Bake at 425 degrees for 10 minutes. Reduce oven temperature to 350 degrees. Bake for 30 minutes longer.

Rosemarie E. Garner, Durham #460

MOTHER'S CHOCOLATE PIE

Yield:
8 servings
Utensil:
pie plate

**Approx Per
Serving:**
*Cal 303
Prot 5 g
Carbo 47 g
Fiber 1 g
T Fat 12 g
34% Calories
from Fat
Chol 61 mg
Sod 178 mg*

1 cup sugar
1/4 cup flour
3 tablespoons baking cocoa
1 cup milk
2 egg yolks, slightly
   beaten
1 tablespoon melted
   butter

1 teaspoon vanilla extract
1 baked 9-inch pie shell
2 egg whites
1/4 cup sugar
1/2 teaspoons vanilla
   extract

Mix 1 cup sugar, flour and baking cocoa in bowl. Add milk gradually, mixing until smooth. Add egg yolks. Cook over low heat until thick and smooth. Stir in butter and 1 teaspoon vanilla. Spoon into pie shell. Beat egg whites in bowl until frothy. Add 1/4 cup sugar gradually, beating until stiff peaks form. Beat in 1/2 teaspoon vanilla. Spread over pie, covering 1/3 of crust rim. Bake at 400 degrees for 8 to 10 minutes or until light brown. I added the oven degrees to this recipe, as mother cooked on a kerosene stove. She lived to be 100 years old.

Dorothy Gardner, Ojai Valley #659

COTTAGE CHEESE PIE

Yield:
8 servings
Utensil:
pie plate

**Approx Per
Serving:**
*Cal 339
Prot 8 g
Carbo 33 g
Fiber 2 g
T Fat 21 g
53% Calories
from Fat
Chol 75 mg
Sod 400 mg*

12 ounces large curd
   cottage cheese
1/4 cup melted butter
1/2 cup sugar
1/4 teaspoon salt
1 tablespoon flour

Grated rind of 1 lemon
2 egg yolks
1/2 cup raisins
1/2 cup chopped pecans
1 unbaked 8-inch pie
   shell

Combine cottage cheese, butter, sugar, salt, flour, lemon rind and egg yolks in order listed in bowl, mixing well after each addition. Stir in raisins and pecans. Spoon into pie shell. Bake at 400 degrees for 10 minutes. Reduce oven temperature to 350 degrees. Bake for 30 minutes longer or until filling is set. May substitute cherries, currants or other fruit for raisins.

Beata J. Schwartz, Sacramento #12

CREAM PIE AS-YOU-LIKE-IT

Yield:
8 servings
Utensil:
pie plate

Approx Per Serving:
Cal 273
Prot 5 g
Carbo 36 g
Fiber 1 g
T Fat 12 g
41% Calories from Fat
Chol 62 mg
Sod 264 mg

3/4 cup sugar
1/3 cup flour
1/4 teaspoon salt
2 eggs

2 cups milk
1 tablespoon margarine
1 teaspoon vanilla extract
1 baked 9-inch pie shell

Mix sugar, flour and salt in glass bowl. Whisk in eggs and milk. Microwave on High for 8 minutes, whisking every 2 minutes. Add margarine and vanilla; mix well. Spoon into pie shell. May substitute 3 egg yolks for eggs.

Banana Cream Pie: Slice 2 or 3 large bananas into baked pie shell before adding cooled custard. Serve with whipped topping.

Chocolate Cream Pie: Stir 1/2 cup semisweet chocolate chips into hot custard until melted. Serve with whipped topping.

Coconut Cream Pie: Add 1 cup flaked coconut to cooled custard. Serve with whipped topping.

Nutritional information is for basic Cream Pie only.

Joy Beatie, State Women's Activities Director

EGG CUSTARD PIE

Yield:
8 servings
Utensil:
pie plate

Approx Per Serving:
Cal 247
Prot 7 g
Carbo 26 g
Fiber <1 g
T Fat 13 g
47% Calories from Fat
Chol 117 mg
Sod 337 mg

4 eggs
1/2 cup sugar
2 1/2 cups milk
1/2 teaspoon salt

1 teaspoon vanilla extract
1 unbaked 9-inch pie shell
1/2 teaspoon nutmeg

Beat eggs in mixer bowl until frothy. Add sugar, milk, salt and vanilla; beat until smooth. Spoon into unbaked pie shell; sprinkle with nutmeg. Bake at 425 degrees for 20 minutes. Reduce oven temperature to 325 degrees. Bake for 30 to 40 minutes longer or until knife inserted in center comes out clean.

Donna D. Wiles
National Grange Lady Assistant Steward

LEMON PIE

Yield:
8 servings
Utensil:
pie plate

Approx Per
Serving:
Cal 430
Prot 4 g
Carbo 82 g
Fiber 1 g
T Fat 11 g
22% Calories
from Fat
Chol 83 mg
Sod 256 mg

1¹/₂ cups sugar
1¹/₂ cups plus 1 teaspoon
   cornstarch
Salt to taste
Grated rind of 1 lemon
2 cups boiling water
1¹/₃ cups plus 2
   teaspoons lemon juice
2 teaspoons butter

3 egg yolks, slightly beaten
1 baked 9-inch pie shell
3 egg whites
¹/₄ teaspoon salt
¹/₂ teaspoon baking
   powder
6 tablespoons sugar
¹/₂ teaspoon vanilla
   extract

Mix first 7 ingredients in saucepan. Cook over low heat for 7 minutes, stirring constantly. Stir a small amount of hot mixture into egg yolks; stir egg yolks into hot mixture. Cook for 5 minutes longer. Cool slightly. Spoon into pie shell. Beat egg whites with ¹/₄ teaspoon salt in mixer bowl until foamy. Add baking powder; mix well. Beat in 6 tablespoons sugar 1 tablespoon at a time, beating until stiff. Mix in vanilla. Spread on pie, sealing to edge. Bake at 400 degrees for 2 to 3 minutes or until light brown.

Florence Taneyhill, Hessel #750

LEMON CREAM PIE

Yield:
6 servings
Utensil:
pie plate

Approx Per
Serving:
Cal 398
Prot 4 g
Carbo 66 g
Fiber 1 g
T Fat 14 g
31% Calories
from Fat
Chol 76 mg
Sod 309 mg

1 cup sugar
2 tablespoons flour
2 tablespoons cornstarch
¹/₄ teaspoon salt
1¹/₂ cups boiling water
2 egg yolks, beaten
¹/₃ cup lemon juice
Grated rind of 1 lemon

1 tablespoon butter
1 baked 9-inch pie shell
6 tablespoons sugar
1 tablespoon cornstarch
¹/₂ cup water
Salt to taste
1 teaspoon vanilla extract
2 egg whites

Mix first 4 ingredients in bowl. Stir into 1¹/₂ cups boiling water in saucepan. Cook until thickened, stirring constantly. Stir a small amount of hot mixture into egg yolks; stir egg yolks into hot mixture. Cook for 2 minutes, stirring constantly. Stir in lemon juice, lemon rind and butter. Cool. Spoon into pie shell. Mix next 4 ingredients in saucepan. Cook until thickened and clear, stirring constantly. Stir in vanilla. Cool. Beat egg whites in mixer bowl until frothy. Add cooled mixture gradually, beating constantly at low speed. Beat for 5 minutes longer. Spread over pie, sealing to edge. Bake at 350 degrees until golden brown.

Gerry M. Langford, Manton #732

Fresh Peach Pie

Yield:
8 servings
Utensil:
pie plate

1 cup sugar
1/4 cup cornstarch
1/2 3-ounce package
    peach gelatin
1 cup water
6 cups sliced peaches
1 graham cracker pie
    shell

Mix sugar, cornstarch and gelatin in saucepan. Stir in water. Cook until slightly thickened, stirring constantly. Pour over peaches in pie shell. Cool to room temperature. Serve with whipped topping. May substitute apricots, strawberries or nectarines for peaches; use flavor of gelatin to complement fruit.

Pauline Consoli, Escalon #447

*Approx Per
Serving:*
Cal 390
Prot 3 g
Carbo 73 g
Fiber 3 g
T Fat 11 g
*25% Calories
from Fat*
Chol 0 mg
Sod 276 mg

Peanut Butter Pie

Yield:
8 servings
Utensil:
pie plate

1 cup peanut butter
8 ounces cream cheese,
    softened
1 cup sugar
2 tablespoons melted
    butter
8 ounces whipped
    topping
1 teaspoon vanilla extract
1 9-inch graham
    cracker pie shell

Cream peanut butter, cream cheese and sugar in mixer bowl until light and fluffy. Add butter, whipped topping and vanilla; mix well. Spoon into pie shell. Chill for 4 hours or until set.

Doris Georgino, Goat Mountain #818

*Approx Per
Serving:*
Cal 706
Prot 13 g
Carbo 63 g
Fiber 3 g
T Fat 47 g
*58% Calories
from Fat*
Chol 39 mg
Sod 485 mg

Easy Pumpkin Pie

⏳

Yield:
8 servings
Utensil:
pie plate

Approx Per Serving:
Cal 228
Prot 3 g
Carbo 34 g
Fiber 2 g
T Fat 10 g
38% Calories from Fat
Chol 0 mg
Sod 227 mg

2³/4 cups miniature
  marshmallows
1 20-ounce can pumpkin
1 teaspoon pumpkin pie
  spice
1/4 teaspoon salt
1 cup whipped topping
1 baked 9-inch pie shell

Combine marshmallows, pumpkin, pumpkin pie spice and salt in saucepan. Cook over low heat until marshmallows melt, stirring constantly to blend well. Cool to room temperature. Fold in whipped topping. Spoon into pie shell. Chill for 3 hours or until firm. May substitute coconut-crumb pie shell for baked pie shell or whipped cream for whipped topping.

Erol Vickery, San Dimas #658

Sour Cream-Raisin Pie

Yield:
8 servings
Utensil:
pie plate

Approx Per Serving:
Cal 566
Prot 6 g
Carbo 70 g
Fiber 2 g
T Fat 31 g
48% Calories from Fat
Chol 78 mg
Sod 299 mg

1 cup raisins
1 cup sour cream
1 cup sugar
2 eggs
1/2 teaspoon cinnamon
1/4 teaspoon ground
  cloves
1/4 teaspoon salt
1 tablespoon margarine
3 ounces cream cheese,
  softened
1/2 cup confectioners'
  sugar
12 ounces whipped
  topping
1 baked 8 or 9-inch pie
  shell

Combine raisins, sour cream, sugar, eggs, cinnamon, cloves and salt in saucepan; mix well. Cook over medium heat until bubbly, stirring constantly; remove from heat. Stir in margarine. Place saucepan in larger container of cold water to cool. Beat cream cheese and confectioners' sugar in mixer bowl until smooth. Add 1 cup whipped topping; mix well. Add to cooled mixture; mix well. Spoon into pie shell. Top with remaining whipped topping. Chill until serving time.

Josephine Woody, Waterford #553

RHUBARB CUSTARD PIE

Yield:
8 servings
Utensil:
pie plate

3½ cups coarsely
  chopped rhubarb
1½ cups sugar
3 eggs, slightly beaten
¼ cup half and half

⅛ teaspoon salt
1 tablespoon flour
1 unbaked 8-inch pie
  plate

Combine rhubarb, sugar, eggs, half and half and salt in large bowl; mix well. Sprinkle flour evenly into pie shell. Spoon rhubarb mixture into prepared pie shell. Bake at 375 degrees on rack in lower third of oven for 1 hour or until set.

Alice Cerfoglio, Nevada Star #16

Approx Per
Serving:
Cal 299
Prot 4 g
Carbo 50 g
Fiber 2 g
T Fat 10 g
29% Calories
from Fat
Chol 83 mg
Sod 188 mg

FRESH STRAWBERRY PIE

Yield:
8 servings
Utensil:
pie plate

¾ cup sifted flour
½ teaspoon salt
⅓ cup oats
⅓ cup shortening
3 tablespoons cold water

¾ cup sugar
2 tablespoons cornstarch
1 quart fresh
  strawberries
⅓ cup water

Sift flour and salt into bowl. Stir in oats. Cut in shortening until crumbly. Add 3 tablespoons cold water 1 tablespoon at a time, mixing with fork to form dough. Let stand for 5 minutes. Roll on floured surface. Fit into 9-inch pie plate. Trim edge and prick with fork. Bake at 375 degrees until golden brown. Mix sugar and cornstarch in saucepan. Mash 1 cup strawberries with ⅓ cup water in bowl. Add to saucepan. Cook over low heat until thickened, stirring constantly. Reduce heat to low. Cook for 10 minutes, stirring frequently. Cool for 5 minutes. Arrange remaining strawberries in pie shell. Pour cooled glaze over strawberries. Chill until serving time. Serve with whipped cream.

Harriet Sawyer, Musician, California State Grange

Approx Per
Serving:
Cal 229
Prot 2 g
Carbo 36 g
Fiber 3 g
T Fat 9 g
35% Calories
from Fat
Chol 0 mg
Sod 135 mg

STRAWBERRY PIE ⧗

2 quarts strawberries
1 baked 8-inch pie shell
²/₃ cup sugar
3 tablespoons cornstarch
Salt to taste
1 tablespoon butter
1 teaspoon lemon juice
2 or 3 drops of red food
coloring

Arrange best strawberries stem end down in pie shell. Mash remaining berries in 2-cup measure. Add enough water to measure 2 cups. Cook in saucepan until strawberries lose bright color. Press through sieve into saucepan. Add mixture of sugar, cornstarch and salt; mix well. Cook for 5 to 8 minutes or until thickened, stirring constantly. Stir in butter, lemon juice and food coloring. Cool completely. Spoon over strawberries in pie shell. Chill until serving time. Garnish with dollops of whipped cream or whipped topping.

Ida Sordello, Mt. Hamilton #469

GREEN TOMATO PIE

¹/₂ cup flour
1 cup sugar
¹/₂ teaspoon cinnamon
¹/₂ teaspoon nutmeg
¹/₂ teaspoon ground
cloves
6 green tomatoes,
peeled, sliced ¹/₂ inch
thick
¹/₄ cup raisins
1 teaspoon finely grated
lemon rind
1 recipe 2-crust pie
pastry
2 tablespoons unsalted
butter

Mix flour, sugar, cinnamon, nutmeg and cloves in bowl. Add tomatoes, raisins and lemon rind; mix gently. Spoon into pastry-lined pie plate. Dot with butter. Top with remaining pastry. Trim edge and cut vents. Chill for 10 minutes. Bake at 425 degrees for 15 minutes. Reduce oven temperature to 350 degrees. Bake for 50 minutes longer or until golden brown. Serve warm or cool.

H. Marie Smith, Riverbank #719

ZUCCHINI CRUMB PIES

Yield:
16 servings
Utensil:
2 pie plates

4 cups flour
1¹⁄₃ cups sugar
½ teaspoon salt
1½ cups margarine
12 cups chopped, seeded
   peeled zucchini

1 cup lemon juice
1½ cups sugar
1 teaspoon cinnamon
½ teaspoon nutmeg
1 teaspoon cinnamon

*Approx Per
Serving:
Cal 421
Prot 5 g
Carbo 63 g
Fiber 2 g
T Fat 18 g
37% Calories
from Fat
Chol 0 mg
Sod 271 mg*

Mix flour, 1¹⁄₃ cups sugar and salt in bowl. Cut in margarine until crumbly. Reserve ¾ cup mixture. Press remaining mixture into two 10-inch pie plates. Bake at 350 to 375 degrees for 15 minutes. Combine zucchini and lemon juice in saucepan. Cook for 15 minutes. Add 1½ cups sugar, 1 teaspoon cinnamon and nutmeg. Simmer for several minutes. Spoon into hot pie shells. Add 1 teaspoon cinnamon to reserved crumbs; sprinkle over pies. Bake for 30 minutes. Serve with ice cream or whipped topping.

Nina Lobaugh, Grover City #746

ZUCCHINI CUSTARD PIES

Yield:
16 servings
Utensil:
2 pie plates

2 large zucchini, peeled,
   seeded, chopped
¾ cup sugar
2 tablespoons cornstarch
1 teaspoon nutmeg

½ teaspoon salt
3 eggs, beaten
2 cups hot milk
2 deep-dish 9-inch pie
   shells

*Approx Per
Serving:
Cal 202
Prot 4 g
Carbo 24 g
Fiber 1 g
T Fat 10 g
46% Calories
from Fat
Chol 44 mg
Sod 245 mg*

Cook zucchini in water in saucepan until tender; drain. Mash in bowl. Add mixture of sugar, cornstarch, nutmeg and salt; mix well. Beat in eggs and milk. Spoon into pie shells. Bake at 425 degrees for 15 minutes. Reduce oven temperature to 350 degrees. Cook for 30 minutes longer.

Ida Bellezza, Gilroy #398

ZUCCHINI (MOCK APPLE) PIE

Yield:
8 servings
Utensil:
pie plate

1 medium zucchini
1 recipe 2-crust pie
   pastry
1 cup sugar
2 tablespoons flour

1/4 teaspoon cinnamon
1/4 teaspoon allspice
1/4 teaspoon nutmeg
1 1/4 teaspoons cream of
   tartar

Approx Per
Serving:
Cal 309
Prot 3 g
Carbo 45 g
Fiber 1 g
T Fat 13 g
39% Calories
from Fat
Chol 0 mg
Sod 276 mg

Peel and seed zucchini. Slice to yield 3 cups sliced zucchini. Parboil just until tender; drain. Place in pastry-lined pie plate. Sprinkle with mixture of sugar, flour, spices and cream of tartar. Top with remaining pastry, sealing edge and cutting vents. Bake at 450 degrees for 10 minutes. Reduce temperature to 350 degrees. Bake for 40 minutes or until golden brown. Serve warm and everyone will think it is apple pie.

LaVern Albaugh, Mt. Lassen #417

EXTRA-TENDER PASTRY

V.I.P.

Yield:
16 servings
Utensil:
2 pie plates

1/2 cup shortening
2 cups flour
1/4 teaspoon salt
1 egg, beaten

1 tablespoon white
   vinegar
3 tablespoons water

Approx Per
Serving:
Cal 119
Prot 2 g
Carbo 12 g
Fiber <1 g
T Fat 7 g
53% Calories
from Fat
Chol 13 mg
Sod 38 mg

Cut shortening into flour and salt in bowl. Beat egg with vinegar and water in bowl. Add just enough egg mixture to flour mixture to make an easily handled dough. Knead lightly once or twice on floured surface. Divide into 2 portions. Roll to fit pie plates. Fill or bake as desired.

Lillian J. D. Booth, California Grange First Lady

MEATS

PRIME RIB ROAST

Yield:
12 servings
Utensil:
roasting pan

Approx Per Serving:
Cal 428
Prot 49 g
Carbo 0 g
Fiber 0 g
T Fat 25 g
53% Calories from Fat
Chol 143 mg
Sod 132 mg

1 8-pound prime rib roast
Onion powder to taste
Garlic salt to taste
Ground pepper to taste

Sprinkle roast on all sides with onion powder. Coat generously with garlic salt and pepper. Place on rack in roasting pan. Add enough water to just cover bottom of pan. Roast at 400 degrees for 30 minutes. Reduce oven temperature to 260 degrees. Roast to 135 degrees on meat thermometer or for 24 minutes per pound for medium-rare. Use seasonings generously, adding onion salt and garlic powder during roasting time if desired.

Julia Holderbein, Chico #486

PEACH BLOSSOMS
Merced, California

CATTLE RANCH
San Luis Obispo, California

SPANISH ROUND STEAK

<table>
<tr><td>

Yield:
10 servings
Utensil:
baking dish

</td><td>

4 pounds round steak
Salt and pepper to taste
1 cup flour
3 tablespoons oil
2 carrots, chopped
1 onion, chopped

</td><td>

1 green bell pepper,
  chopped
1 canned pimento,
  chopped
2 cups chopped tomatoes

</td></tr>
</table>

*Approx Per
Serving:*
Cal 342
Prot 36 g
Carbo 14 g
Fiber 2 g
T Fat 15 g
40% Calories
from Fat
Chol 102 mg
Sod 64 mg

Cut steak into serving pieces; sprinkle with salt and pepper. Pound flour into steak with meat mallet. Brown on both sides in hot oil in skillet; remove to 2-quart baking dish. Add carrots, onion, green pepper, pimento and tomatoes. Bake at 325 degrees for 2 hours or until tender. May add other seasonings, peas or celery if desired.

Alice M. McKay, Dorris #393

BARBECUED SHORT RIBS

<table>
<tr><td>

Yield:
6 servings
Utensil:
roasting pan

</td><td>

3 pounds beef short ribs
1 onion, finely chopped
1/4 cup vinegar
2 tablespoons brown
  sugar
1 cup catsup

</td><td>

1/2 cup water
3 tablespoons
  Worcestershire sauce
1 teaspoon prepared
  mustard
2 teaspoons salt

</td></tr>
</table>

*Approx Per
Serving:*
Cal 425
Prot 26 g
Carbo 20 g
Fiber 1 g
T Fat 26 g
56% Calories
from Fat
Chol 104 mg
Sod 1352 mg

Cut short ribs into serving pieces. Brown slowly on all sides in heavy nonstick skillet, turning frequently; drain. Remove to roasting pan. Combine onion, vinegar, brown sugar, catsup, water, Worcestershire sauce, mustard and salt in bowl; mix well. Spoon over ribs. Roast, covered, at 325 degrees for 1 1/2 to 2 hours or until tender.

Rose Schuyler, Lompoc #646

HAWAIIAN SHORT RIBS

Yield:
8 servings
Utensil:
baking pan

3 tablespoons sesame
  seed
4 pounds beef short ribs
1 medium onion, sliced
1/2 cup soy sauce
1/4 cup packed brown
  sugar

1 clove of garlic, minced
2 chili peppers, chopped
1 1/2 cups water
1/4 teaspoon ginger
1/4 teaspoon pepper
1 teaspoon cornstarch

*Approx Per
Serving:*
Cal 417
Prot 27 g
Carbo 13 g
Fiber 1 g
T Fat 28 g
*61% Calories
from Fat*
Chol 104 mg
Sod 1116 mg

Sprinkle sesame seed in baking pan. Toast at 400 degrees until brown. Arrange ribs and onion over sesame seed. Combine soy sauce, brown sugar, garlic, chili peppers, 1 1/2 cups water, ginger and pepper in bowl; mix well. Pour over ribs. Bake, covered, at 400 degrees for 2 1/2 hours, stirring occasionally. Remove ribs to serving platter. Skim sauce. Blend cornstarch with a small amount of water. Combine with sauce in saucepan. Cook until thickened, stirring constantly. Serve with ribs.

Lois Galli, Orchard City #333

TERIYAKI STEAK

Yield:
5 servings
Utensil:
grill

1/2 cup soy sauce
1 clove of garlic, minced
Artificial sweetener to
  equal 2 tablespoons
  sugar

1 tablespoon lemon juice
2 tablespoons
  Worcestershire sauce
1/2 teaspoon ginger
1 1/2 pounds flank steak

*Approx Per
Serving:*
Cal 202
Prot 27 g
Carbo 5 g
Fiber <1 g
T Fat 8 g
*36% Calories
from Fat*
Chol 77 mg
Sod 1749 mg

Combine soy sauce, garlic, artificial sweetener, lemon juice, Worcestershire sauce and ginger in shallow dish or plastic bag. Add flank steak. Marinate in refrigerator for 6 to 24 hours, turning occasionally; drain. Grill or broil 2 inches from heat source for 5 minutes on each side. Cut cross grain into thin slices to serve.

Nutritional information includes the entire amount of marinade.

Dorothy A. Sagaser, Clovis #536

SWEET-AND-SOUR BEEF

Yield:
6 servings
Utensil:
skillet

Approx Per
Serving:
Cal 420
Prot 25 g
Carbo 47 g
Fiber 3 g
T Fat 15 g
32% Calories
from Fat
Chol 64 mg
Sod 667 mg

1¹/₂ pounds lean beef
1 cup flour
¹/₄ cup (about) shortening
3 medium carrots, thinly
    sliced
1 medium onion, thinly
    sliced
1   8-ounce can tomato
    sauce
1 tablespoon
    Worcestershire sauce
¹/₄ cup packed brown
    sugar
¹/₄ cup vinegar
1 teaspoon salt
¹/₄ cup water

Cut beef into thin strips. Coat with flour. Brown in a small amount of shortening in skillet. Add carrots, onion, tomato sauce, Worcestershire sauce, brown sugar, vinegar, salt and water, stirring to deglaze skillet. Cook to desired degree of doneness.

Linda Spoon, Mt. Lassen #417

EASY BEEF STROGANOFF

Yield:
6 servings
Utensil:
skillet

Approx Per
Serving:
Cal 269
Prot 23 g
Carbo 3 g
Fiber <1 g
T Fat 18 g
62% Calories
from Fat
Chol 92 mg
Sod 99 mg

1¹/₂ pounds round or
    sirloin steak
¹/₂ cup chopped onion
3 tablespoons butter
Salt and pepper to taste
1 cup mushrooms
³/₄ cup sour cream

Cut beef into strips. Sauté onion in butter in heavy skillet. Add beef. Cook for 5 minutes or until evenly browned on both sides. Add salt, pepper, mushrooms and sour cream. Cook just until heated through. Serve with hot cooked noodles or rice.

Jeanne Davies, Executive Committee, National Grange

CHEDDAR-BEEF PIE

Yield:
6 servings
Utensil:
pie plate

Approx Per Serving:
Cal 371
Prot 24 g
Carbo 13 g
Fiber 1 g
T Fat 25 g
61% Calories from Fat
Chol 115 mg
Sod 902 mg

1 pound ground beef
1 egg
1/3 cup chopped onion
3/4 cup cornflake crumbs
2 tablespoons barbecue sauce
1 teaspoon salt
Pepper to taste
1/2 cup sliced celery
1 tablespoon margarine
1 1/2 cups shredded Cheddar cheese
1 4-ounce can mushrooms, drained
1/4 cup cornflake crumbs
1 tablespoon melted margarine

Combine ground beef, egg, onion, 3/4 cup cornflake crumbs, barbecue sauce, salt and pepper in bowl; mix well. Press over bottom and side of pie plate to form shell. Bake at 400 degrees for 15 minutes; drain. Reduce oven temperature to 350 degrees. Sauté celery in 1 tablespoon margarine in skillet. Add cheese and mushrooms; toss lightly. Spoon into prepared shell. Toss 1/4 cup cornflake crumbs with 1 tablespoon melted margarine in bowl. Sprinkle over pie. Bake at 350 degrees for 10 minutes. May substitute ground turkey or chicken for ground beef or use egg substitute.

Ed Barrett, Paradise #490

GROUND BEEF CASSEROLE

Yield:
6 servings
Utensil:
baking dish

Approx Per Serving:
Cal 402
Prot 20 g
Carbo 33 g
Fiber 4 g
T Fat 22 g
48% Calories from Fat
Chol 53 mg
Sod 1031 mg

1 pound ground beef
1 10-ounce package frozen peas
1 10-ounce can cream of chicken soup
Salt and pepper to taste
1 16-ounce package frozen Tater Tots

Brown ground beef in skillet, stirring until crumbly; drain. Add peas; mix gently. Spoon into 9x13-inch baking dish. Spread with soup; sprinkle with salt and pepper. Top with Tater Tots. Bake at 350 degrees for 25 minutes. May substitute corn or mixed vegetables for peas.

Ruth Carr, United Rescue #450

Beefy Cajun Polenta

Yield:
8 servings
Utensil:
baking dish

Approx Per Serving:
Cal 403
Prot 28 g
Carbo 27 g
Fiber 2 g
T Fat 21 g
46% Calories from Fat
Chol 90 mg
Sod 279 mg

1 large onion, chopped
1 green bell pepper, chopped
2 pounds ground round
2 cups milk
1 cup (scant) cornmeal
1 16-ounce can whole kernel corn
1 teaspoon chili powder
1/2 cup shredded Cheddar cheese
Salt and pepper to taste

Sauté onion and green pepper in saucepan sprayed with nonstick cooking spray. Add ground round. Cook until ground beef is brown and crumbly; drain. Add milk; stir in cornmeal. Cook until thickened, stirring frequently; remove from heat. Add corn, chili powder, cheese, salt and pepper; mix well. Spoon into 9x13-inch baking dish. Bake at 350 degrees for 50 minutes.

Theresa Heuschkel, Jacinto #431

Beefy French Rolls

Yield:
6 servings
Utensil:
baking dish

Approx Per Serving:
Cal 370
Prot 20 g
Carbo 37 g
Fiber 2 g
T Fat 16 g
38% Calories from Fat
Chol 49 mg
Sod 812 mg

4 stalks celery, chopped
1 green bell pepper, chopped
1 medium onion, chopped
2 tablespoons oil
1 pound ground beef
2 8-ounce cans tomato sauce
Salt and pepper to taste
6 large French rolls

Sauté celery, green pepper and onion in oil in skillet. Add ground beef. Cook until ground beef is brown and crumbly, stirring constantly; drain. Add tomato sauce, salt and pepper; mix well. Cut 1/2 inch from end of each French roll, reserving ends. Remove soft insides of rolls with fork; do not puncture sides of rolls. Spoon ground beef filling into rolls; replace ends and secure with wooden picks. Place in baking dish. Bake at 375 degrees for 10 minutes or until heated through.

Dorothy N. Bolton, L.A. Metro #826

Ground Beef-Potato Dish

V.I.P.

Yield:
12 servings
Utensil:
baking pan

Approx Per
Serving:
Cal 399
Prot 20 g
Carbo 47 g
Fiber 3 g
T Fat 15 g
34% Calories
from Fat
Chol 53 mg
Sod 445 mg

2 pounds ground beef
2 large onions, chopped
2 10-ounce cans cream
   of mushroom soup

1 cup milk
Salt and pepper to taste
5 pounds potatoes,
   peeled, sliced

Brown ground beef lightly in skillet, stirring until crumbly. Add onions. Sauté until tender; drain. Add soup and milk; mix well. Cook for 5 minutes. Stir in salt and pepper. Alternate layers of potatoes and ground beef mixture in large baking pan, ending with ground beef mixture and covering potatoes completely. Bake at 350 degrees until potatoes are tender.

Beulah L. Winter
National Grange Deaf Activities Director

Ground Beef-Tater Tot Casserole

Yield:
10 servings
Utensil:
baking dish

Approx Per
Serving:
Cal 225
Prot 11 g
Carbo 17 g
Fiber 1 g
T Fat 13 g
53% Calories
from Fat
Chol 30 mg
Sod 594 mg

1 pound ground beef
Salt and pepper to taste
1/2 medium onion,
   chopped

1 10-ounce can cream
   of mushroom soup
1 16-ounce package
   frozen Tater Tots

Crumble ground beef into 9x13-inch baking dish; sprinkle with salt, pepper and onion. Spread soup over top; do not mix. Top with Tater Tots. Bake at 350 degrees for 1 hour.

Iona E. Sargent, San Luis Obispo #639

SLOW-COOKER DINNER

Yield:
10 servings
Utensil:
slow cooker

Approx Per
Serving:
Cal 394
Prot 22 g
Carbo 41 g
Fiber 12 g
T Fat 15 g
34% Calories
from Fat
Chol 47 mg
Sod 1355 mg

1 pound ground beef
1 pound bacon, chopped
1 cup chopped onion
2 15-ounce cans pork
   and beans
1 15-ounce can red
   kidney beans, drained
1 15-ounce can lima
   beans, drained

1 15-ounce can tomato
   sauce
1/4 cup sugar
1 cup Rhine wine
1 cup cold water
1 1/2 teaspoons salt
1/2 teaspoon dried red
   pepper

Brown ground beef and bacon with onion in skillet, stirring until ground beef is crumbly and bacon is crisp; drain. Combine with pork and beans, kidney beans, lima beans, tomato sauce, sugar, wine, water, salt and red pepper in slow cooker; mix well. Cook on Low for 9 to 10 hours. Serve with hot cooked rice.

John C. Swegles, Gazelle #380

BARBECUED MEATBALLS

Yield:
10 servings
Utensil:
baking dish

Approx Per
Serving:
Cal 510
Prot 26 g
Carbo 56 g
Fiber 2 g
T Fat 20 g
36% Calories
from Fat
Chol 125 mg
Sod 1228 mg

3 pounds ground beef
1 12-ounce can
   evaporated milk
1 cup oats
1 cup cracker crumbs
2 eggs
1/2 cup chopped onion
1/2 teaspoon garlic
   powder
2 teaspoons chili powder

2 teaspoons salt
1/2 teaspoon pepper
2 cups catsup
1 cup packed brown
   sugar
1/4 cup chopped onion
1/2 teaspoon garlic
   powder
1/2 teaspoon liquid
   smoke

Combine ground beef, evaporated milk, oats, cracker crumbs, eggs, 1/2 cup onion, 1/2 teaspoon garlic powder, chili powder, salt and pepper in bowl; mix well. Shape into 1 1/2-inch balls. Place meatballs on waxed paper-lined tray. Freeze until firm. Store in plastic bag in freezer until needed. Combine catsup, brown sugar, 1/4 cup onion, 1/2 teaspoon garlic powder and liquid smoke in bowl; mix until brown sugar dissolves. Arrange meatballs in 9x13-inch baking dish. Pour sauce over meatballs. Bake at 350 degrees for 1 hour.

Hazel Thompson, Hessel #750

California Meat Loaf

Yield:
6 servings
Utensil:
loaf pan

Approx Per Serving:
Cal 403
Prot 28 g
Carbo 21 g
Fiber 3 g
T Fat 24 g
52% Calories from Fat
Chol 125 mg
Sod 1263 mg

1½ pounds ground beef
½ cup pork sausage
1 egg
½ cup cornmeal
½ cup chopped onion
¼ cup chopped green
   bell pepper
1 8-ounce can
   cream-style corn
1 16-ounce can
   chopped tomatoes
2 teaspoons salt
¼ teaspoon pepper

Combine ground beef, sausage, egg, cornmeal, onion, green pepper, corn, tomatoes, salt and pepper in bowl; mix well. Shape into loaf in 5x9-inch loaf pan. Bake at 350 degrees for 1½ hours.

Jean Grogan, Estrella #488

Glazed Meat Loaf

Yield:
8 servings
Utensil:
baking dish

Approx Per Serving:
Cal 286
Prot 22 g
Carbo 9 g
Fiber <1 g
T Fat 17 g
55% Calories from Fat
Chol 102 mg
Sod 613 mg

2 pounds ground chuck
2 tablespoons quick-
   cooking cream of rice
   cereal
1 egg
⅓ cup milk
2 teaspoons salt
½ teaspoon pepper
¼ cup apple jelly
1 tablespoon dry sherry
½ teaspoon browning
   sauce
⅛ teaspoon ginger
Garlic powder to taste

Combine ground chuck, cereal, egg, milk, salt and pepper in bowl; mix lightly. Shape into 4x9-inch loaf in shallow baking dish. Bake at 350 degrees for 30 minutes. Combine jelly, wine, browning sauce, ginger and garlic powder in small saucepan. Cook over low heat until jelly melts, stirring frequently. Cut eight 1-inch deep slices in meat loaf. Brush with sauce. Bake for 30 minutes longer, brushing with glaze 2 or 3 times.

Barbara Carden, Gazelle #380

MEAT LOAF

Yield:
8 servings
Utensil:
baking dish

Approx Per
Serving:
Cal 296
Prot 22 g
Carbo 14 g
Fiber 1 g
T Fat 17 g
51% Calories
from Fat
Chol 77 mg
Sod 644 mg

2 pounds ground beef
1/2 onion, chopped
3/4 cup cracker crumbs
Worcestershire sauce to
   taste
1 teaspoon parsley flakes
1/2 teaspoon salt

2 8-ounce cans tomato
   sauce
2 tablespoons brown
   sugar
1/2 teaspoon dry mustard
1/2 teaspoon nutmeg

Combine ground beef, onion, cracker crumbs, Worcestershire sauce, parsley flakes and salt in bowl; mix well.
Shape into loaf in greased 2-quart baking dish. Bake at 250
degrees for 40 minutes; drain. Combine tomato sauce,
brown sugar, dry mustard and nutmeg in bowl; mix well.
Spoon over meat loaf. Bake for 20 minutes longer.

Orma Albaugh, Lookout #415

SHENANIGAN PIE

Yield:
8 servings
Utensil:
baking dish

Approx Per
Serving:
Cal 593
Prot 29 g
Carbo 58 g
Fiber 5 g
T Fat 28 g
42% Calories
from Fat
Chol 76 mg
Sod 1195 mg

3 quarts water
2 tablespoons canola oil
1 16-ounce package
   elbow or cut macaroni
1 large yellow onion,
   chopped
1 1/4 pounds ground
   chuck
1 cup shredded Cheddar
   cheese

2 8-ounce cans tomato
   sauce
1 10-ounce can red chili
   sauce
1 cup chopped black
   olives
Salt to taste
1 cup shredded Cheddar
   cheese

Bring water and canola oil to a boil in large saucepan. Add
pasta. Cook for 20 minutes or until tender; drain and rinse.
Sauté onion in skillet sprayed with nonstick cooking
spray. Add ground chuck. Cook until brown and crumbly,
stirring frequently; drain. Add pasta, 1 cup cheese, tomato
sauce, chili sauce, olives and salt; mix well. Spoon into
2-quart baking dish; top with 1 cup cheese. Bake at 350
degrees for 1 to 2 hours or until done to taste.

Frances Lindeleaf, Gilroy #398

SWEDISH CABBAGE ROLLS

Yield:
4 servings
Utensil:
Dutch oven

1 large head cabbage
1/2 slice bread
1/2 cup milk
8 ounces sausage
1 pound ground beef
1 egg

2 tablespoons oats
2 crackers, crumbled
1/3 cup uncooked rice, cooked
Salt and pepper to taste

Approx Per Serving:
Cal 465
Prot 31 g
Carbo 22 g
Fiber 2 g
T Fat 27 g
53% Calories from Fat
Chol 154 mg
Sod 493 mg

Cook cabbage in water in saucepan until leaves are tender, removing leaves as they cook; drain cabbage leaves and reserve cooking liquid. Soak bread in milk in bowl. Add sausage, ground beef, egg, oats, cracker crumbs, rice, salt and pepper; mix well. Spoon mixture onto cabbage leaves; roll cabbage to enclose filling. Place in Dutch oven. Add reserved cooking liquid. Simmer, tightly covered, for 2 hours. Bake at 350 degrees until cabbage rolls are light brown and liquid is absorbed.

Helen M. Bloss, Westside #473

BAKED ENCHILADAS

Yield:
6 servings
Utensil:
glass dish

12 corn tortillas
Oil for frying
3 tablespoons flour
1/4 teaspoon paprika
1/2 teaspoon salt
1 1/2 cups milk
1   10-ounce can mild enchilada sauce
1/2 cup sliced black olives

1 cup shredded Cheddar cheese
12 ounces ground beef
1/2 cup chopped onion
1   10-ounce can jalapeño bean dip
1/2 teaspoon salt
1/8 teaspoon pepper
3/4 cup chopped tomato

Approx Per Serving:
Cal 520
Prot 26 g
Carbo 49 g
Fiber 6 g
T Fat 26 g
44% Calories from Fat
Chol 67 mg
Sod 1507 mg

Fry tortillas 1 at a time in oil in skillet for 5 to 10 seconds or just until softened; drain. Mix next 5 ingredients in 4-cup glass measure. Microwave on High for 2 minutes; stir. Microwave for 5 minutes or until bubbly, stirring after each minute. Stir in olives and cheese. Mix ground beef and onion in glass bowl. Microwave, covered, on High for 5 minutes or until cooked through, stirring several times; drain. Stir in bean dip, 1/2 teaspoon salt and pepper. Spoon 1/3 cup beef mixture and 1 tablespoon tomato onto each tortilla; roll up. Place seam side down in 8x12-inch glass dish. Top with cheese sauce. Microwave on High for 10 minutes.

Dot Sackett, North Fork #763

ENCHILADA CASSEROLE

Yield:
12 servings
Utensil:
baking dish

Approx Per Serving:
Cal 343
Prot 20 g
Carbo 24 g
Fiber 1 g
T Fat 19 g
50% Calories from Fat
Chol 57 mg
Sod 785 mg

2 pounds ground beef
1 medium onion, chopped
1 clove of garlic, crushed
1 16-ounce can chili beans
1 10-ounce can mild enchilada sauce
Salt and pepper to taste
1 7-ounce package tortilla chips, crushed
1 10-ounce can cream of chicken soup
1/2 soup can milk
1/2 cup shredded mozzarella cheese

Brown ground beef with onion and garlic in 12-inch skillet, stirring until ground beef is crumbly; drain. Stir in beans, enchilada sauce, salt and pepper. Simmer until of desired consistency. Layer half the crushed tortilla chips, meat sauce and remaining tortilla chips in 9x13-inch baking dish. Top with mixture of soup and milk; sprinkle with cheese. Bake at 300 degrees for 20 to 25 minutes or until heated through.

Delma Cross, Dorris #393

MEXICAN CASSEROLE

Yield:
8 servings
Utensil:
baking dish

Approx Per Serving:
Cal 433
Prot 23 g
Carbo 34 g
Fiber 4 g
T Fat 24 g
48% Calories from Fat
Chol 71 mg
Sod 1192 mg

1 pound ground beef
1 medium onion, chopped
1 10-ounce can tomato soup
1 10-ounce can cream of mushroom soup
1 cup milk
1 envelope taco seasoning mix
12 corn tortillas, torn
8 ounces Cheddar cheese, shredded

Brown ground beef with onion in skillet, stirring until ground beef is crumbly; drain. Add mixture of soups, milk and taco seasoning mix; mix well. Alternate layers of tortillas, meat sauce and cheese in baking dish until all ingredients are used. Bake at 350 degrees for 45 minutes or until heated through.

Laurie Ann Sanderson, Rainbow Valley #689

MEXICAN PIE

Yield:
8 servings
Utensil:
baking dish

Approx Per Serving:
Cal 758
Prot 29 g
Carbo 28 g
Fiber 1 g
T Fat 60 g
70% Calories from Fat
Chol 113 mg
Sod 1132 mg

1 pound ground beef
2 teaspoons chili powder
2 8-count cans crescent rolls
2 medium tomatoes, chopped
1 4-ounce can chopped green chilies
1 cup sour cream
2/3 cup mayonnaise
1/2 cup chopped onion
1 4-ounce can chopped black olives
16 ounces Monterey Jack cheese, shredded

Brown ground beef with chili powder in skillet, stirring until crumbly; drain. Spray 9x13-inch baking dish with nonstick cooking spray; line bottom and sides with crescent roll dough. Layer ground beef, tomatoes and green chilies in prepared dish. Combine sour cream, mayonnaise, onion and olives in bowl; mix well. Spread over layers; top with cheese. Bake at 350 degrees for 30 to 35 minutes or until heated through. May substitute ground turkey for ground beef.

Betty K. Creason, Three Forks #449

TACO CASSEROLE

Yield:
8 servings
Utensil:
baking dish

Approx Per Serving:
Cal 766
Prot 47 g
Carbo 57 g
Fiber 14 g
T Fat 41 g
47% Calories from Fat
Chol 134 mg
Sod 2001 mg

12 corn tortillas, quartered
Oil for frying
2 pounds ground round
1 large onion, chopped
1 clove of garlic, crushed
1/2 teaspoon cumin
Salt and pepper to taste
1 cup tomato sauce
1 30-ounce can refried beans, heated
1 10-ounce can chopped green chilies
16 ounces Cheddar cheese, shredded
2 cups enchilada sauce
2 tablespoons chopped onion

Fry tortillas in oil in skillet until crisp; drain. Brown ground round with next 5 ingredients in skillet, stirring frequently; drain. Stir in tomato sauce. Layer 1/3 of the beans, half the meat mixture, half the tortillas, all the chilies, half the remaining beans, remaining meat mixture, remaining tortillas, half the cheese, remaining beans, enchilada sauce, remaining cheese and 2 tablespoons onion in 9x13-inch baking dish. Bake at 350 degrees for 45 minutes. This is my granddaughter's recipe.

Nutritional information does not include oil for frying.

Vivian Chapin, United Rescue #450

FAVORITE TAMALE PIE

Yield:
8 servings
Utensil:
baking dish

Approx Per
Serving:
Cal 400
Prot 20 g
Carbo 18 g
Fiber 2 g
T Fat 28 g
62% Calories
from Fat
Chol 62 mg
Sod 223 mg

1 clove of garlic, minced
1 onion, chopped
1 green bell pepper,
    finely chopped
1/2 cup oil
1 pound lean ground beef
4 ounces ground pork
1/4 teaspoon
    Worcestershire sauce
1   16-ounce can tomatoes
Chili powder, salt and
    pepper to taste
1 cup shredded Cheddar
    cheese
1 cup cornmeal
3 cups boiling water
Paprika to taste

Sauté first 3 ingredients in oil in skillet. Add meat. Cook until brown, stirring frequently. Add next 5 ingredients; mix well. Simmer for 1 hour or until thickened to desired consistency. Stir in 1/2 cup cheese until melted. Stir cornmeal into boiling water in saucepan. Cook until of consistency of mush. Spoon 2/3 of the mixture into 9x13-inch baking dish, shaping to form shell. Spoon ground beef mixture into prepared dish. Top with remaining cornmeal mixture. Sprinkle with 1/2 cup cheese and paprika. Bake at 350 degrees for 20 minutes.

Norene E. Anderson, Sonoma Valley #407

TORTILLA CASSEROLE

Yield:
6 servings
Utensil:
baking dish

Approx Per
Serving:
Cal 561
Prot 29 g
Carbo 36 g
Fiber 7 g
T Fat 36 g
55% Calories
from Fat
Chol 89 mg
Sod 914 mg

1   28-ounce can tomatoes
1 onion, chopped
1 clove of garlic
1   4-ounce can chopped
    green chilies
1/2 teaspoon cumin
1/2 teaspoon oregano
1/2 teaspoon salt
3 tablespoons corn oil
1 pound lean ground beef
12 corn tortillas
2 cups shredded
    Cheddar cheese
3 green onions, finely
    chopped
1/2 cup sliced black olives

Process first 7 ingredients in blender for 1 minute. Mix with oil in saucepan. Cook over medium heat for 25 minutes. Brown ground beef in skillet, stirring until crumbly; drain. Add 1 cup tomato mixture; mix well. Cut tortillas into halves. Dip tortillas into remaining tomato mixture. Overlap 1/3 of the tortillas in 9x13-inch baking dish. Layer meat sauce, 1 1/3 cups cheese, green onions, olives and remaining tortillas 1/2 at a time in prepared dish. Top with remaining tomato mixture and remaining cheese. Bake at 350 degrees for 35 minutes.

Nancy R. Trempe, L.A. Metro #826

PORCUPINES

½ cup chopped onion
1 clove of garlic, minced
¼ cup chopped green
    bell pepper
¼ cup chopped celery
1 tablespoon oil
1 cup uncooked long
    grain rice

1 pound ground beef
1   8-ounce can tomato
    sauce
¼ cup catsup
Salt and pepper to taste

Sauté onion, garlic, green pepper and celery in oil in skillet until tender. Combine with rice and ground beef in bowl; mix well. Shape into 2-inch meatballs. Combine meatballs, tomato sauce, catsup, salt and pepper in large skillet; mix gently. Simmer for 45 minutes or until meatballs are cooked through, adding water if needed for desired consistency.

Wava Moore, Tulare #198

SEVEN-LAYER CASSEROLE

1 cup uncooked rice
1 cup drained whole
    kernel corn
Salt and pepper to taste
1   8-ounce can tomato
    sauce
½ cup water
½ cup finely chopped
    onion

½ cup finely chopped
    green bell pepper
12 ounces ground beef
1   8-ounce can tomato
    sauce
¼ cup water
4 slices bacon, cut into
    halves

Layer rice and corn in 2-quart baking dish; sprinkle with salt and pepper. Spread mixture of 1 can tomato sauce and ½ cup water over top. Add layers of onion and green pepper. Place ground beef in flattened layer over green pepper; sprinkle with salt and pepper. Spread with mixture of 1 can tomato sauce and ¼ cup water. Top with bacon. Bake, covered, at 350 degrees for 1 hour. Bake, uncovered, for 30 minutes longer or until bacon is crisp.

Mildred C. Hunter, Garden Grove #613

SPAGHETTI PIE

Yield:
6 servings
Utensil:
pie plate

Approx Per
Serving:
Cal 430
Prot 30 g
Carbo 33 g
Fiber 3 g
T Fat 20 g
42% Calories
from Fat
Chol 138 mg
Sod 696 mg

6 ounces uncooked
  spaghetti
2 teaspoons margarine
1/2 cup grated Parmesan
  cheese
2 eggs, beaten
1 cup cottage cheese
1 pound ground beef
1/4 cup chopped green
  bell pepper

1/2 cup chopped onion
1 8-ounce can stewed
  tomatoes
1 6-ounce can tomato
  paste
Sugar to taste
1 teaspoon oregano
1/2 teaspoon garlic salt
1/2 cup shredded
  mozzarella cheese

Cook spaghetti using package directions; drain. Add margarine, Parmesan cheese and eggs; mix well. Shape into shell in oiled 10-inch pie plate. Spread cottage cheese in spaghetti shell. Brown ground beef with green pepper and onion in skillet, stirring until ground beef is crumbly; drain. Add tomatoes, tomato paste, sugar, oregano and garlic salt; mix well. Spoon into prepared pie plate. Bake at 350 degrees for 20 minutes. Sprinkle with mozzarella cheese. Bake for 5 minutes longer.

Verna Webb, Greenhorn #384

STUFFED SPANISH ROLLS

Yield:
12 servings
Utensil:
baking sheet

Approx Per
Serving:
Cal 675
Prot 39 g
Carbo 45 g
Fiber 1 g
T Fat 39 g
51% Calories
from Fat
Chol 129 mg
Sod 1540 mg

2 pounds ground beef
1 large onion, chopped
3 cloves of garlic, crushed
1 4-ounce can chopped
  black olives
1 4-ounce can chopped
  green chilies

1 19-ounce can red chili
  sauce
Salt and pepper to taste
2 pounds Cheddar
  cheese, shredded
12 French rolls

Brown ground beef with onion and garlic in skillet, stirring until ground beef is crumbly. Add olives, green chilies, red chili sauce, salt and pepper; mix well. Simmer until of desired consistency. Cool to room temperature or chill overnight. Stir in cheese. Cut tops from French rolls; scoop out insides, reserving shells. Spoon ground beef filling into rolls; replace tops. Wrap with foil; place on baking sheet. Bake at 300 degrees until heated through. Las Palmas red chili sauce is recommended; vary amounts to suit individual taste.

Phyllis Anderson, Lompoc #646

NOODLE STROGANOFF

Yield:
12 servings
Utensil:
electric skillet

Approx Per Serving:
Cal 356
Prot 19 g
Carbo 10 g
Fiber <1 g
T Fat 27 g
68% Calories from Fat
Chol 104 mg
Sod 731 mg

½ cup chopped onion
1 cup sliced mushrooms
¼ teaspoon garlic powder
½ cup butter
2 pounds ground chuck
¼ cup lemon juice
2 10-ounce cans beef consommé
2 teaspoons salt
½ teaspoon pepper
4 cups uncooked noodles
2 cups sour cream
Parsley to taste

Sauté onion and mushrooms with garlic powder and butter in electric skillet until onion is light brown. Add ground chuck. Cook until brown and crumbly. Add lemon juice, consommé, salt, pepper and noodles. Bring to a boil; reduce heat. Simmer, covered, at 200 degrees for 10 to 15 minutes or until noodles are tender. Stir in sour cream; sprinkle with parsley. Serve immediately.

Audrey V. Butz, Mt. Vernon #453

EASY NOODLE STROGANOFF

Yield:
8 servings
Utensil:
skillet

Approx Per Serving:
Cal 303
Prot 16 g
Carbo 14 g
Fiber 1 g
T Fat 21 g
61% Calories from Fat
Chol 75 mg
Sod 659 mg

1 pound ground beef
¼ cup chopped onion
1 clove of garlic, minced
¼ cup margarine
3 tablespoons lemon juice
1 10-ounce can consommé
3 tablespoons Burgundy
1 6-ounce can mushroom pieces
1 teaspoon salt
¼ teaspoon pepper
4 ounces uncooked noodles
1 cup sour cream

Brown ground beef with onion and garlic in margarine in 10-inch skillet; drain. Add lemon juice, consommé, wine, undrained mushrooms, salt and pepper; mix well. Sprinkle noodles over top. Simmer, covered, for 25 to 30 minutes or until noodles are tender, adding water if needed for desired consistency; remove from heat. Stir in sour cream. Simmer for 2 to 3 minutes. Garnish with parsley. May substitute yogurt for sour cream.

Claire L. Carr, Rincon Valley #710

TAGLIARINI

<table>
<tr><td>

Yield:
6 servings
Utensil:
baking dish

</td></tr>
</table>

<table>
<tr><td>

Approx Per
Serving:
Cal 443
Prot 24 g
Carbo 29 g
Fiber 4 g
T Fat 29 g
55% Calories
from Fat
Chol 94 mg
Sod 1085 mg

</td></tr>
</table>

3 cups uncooked noodles
4 to 6 cups water
1 medium onion,
    chopped
1 clove of garlic, minced
1 tablespoon oil
1 pound ground beef
Chili powder, salt and
    pepper to taste

2 8-ounce cans tomato
    sauce
1 15-ounce can whole
    kernel corn
1 8-ounce can black
    olives
1 cup shredded Cheddar
    cheese

Cook noodles in salted water in saucepan using package directions; drain. Sauté onion and garlic in oil in skillet until tender. Add ground beef, chili powder, salt and pepper. Cook until ground beef is brown, stirring until crumbly; drain. Add tomato sauce, corn and olives; mix well. Add noodles; mix gently. Spoon into greased 3 to 4-quart baking dish. Sprinkle with cheese. Bake at 350 degrees for 30 to 40 minutes or until bubbly.

Marjorie Lemon, Happy Camp #395

ONE-TWO-THREE BAKED HASH

<table>
<tr><td>

Yield:
4 servings
Utensil:
baking dish

</td></tr>
</table>

<table>
<tr><td>

Approx Per
Serving:
Cal 335
Prot 26 g
Carbo 28 g
Fiber 2 g
T Fat 13 g
35% Calories
from Fat
Chol 73 mg
Sod 862 mg

</td></tr>
</table>

3 large potatoes,
    coarsely grated
1 onion, grated

1 12-ounce can corned
    beef

Combine potatoes, onion and corned beef in bowl. Add enough water to make of desired consistency. Spoon into 2-quart baking dish. Bake at 350 degrees for 30 minutes or until heated through.

Vivian Depue, Cherry Valley #586

BREADED ROAST LAMB

Yield:
8 servings
Utensil:
roasting pan

Approx Per Serving:
Cal 386
Prot 38 g
Carbo 9 g
Fiber 1 g
T Fat 20 g
49% Calories from Fat
Chol 120 mg
Sod 502 mg

1 cup bread crumbs
1 tablespoon chopped parsley
2 teaspoons grated lemon rind
1 clove of garlic, minced
2 tablespoons margarine

1 tablespoon oregano
1 teaspoon basil
1 teaspoon rosemary
1 teaspoon salt
1/8 teaspoon pepper
1 4-pound lamb roast

Combine bread crumbs, parsley, lemon rind, garlic, margarine, oregano, basil, rosemary, salt and pepper in bowl; mix well. Press onto roast; place in roasting pan. Roast at 350 degrees for 20 minutes per pound or until done to taste. May also use for beef roast.

Leah "Cricket" Johnson, Fort Bragg #672

GRANDFATHER'S SWEDISH PORK CHOPS

Yield:
4 servings
Utensil:
skillet

Approx Per Serving:
Cal 303
Prot 32 g
Carbo 3 g
Fiber <1 g
T Fat 17 g
53% Calories from Fat
Chol 98 mg
Sod 610 mg

2 tablespoons flour
1/2 teaspoon ginger
1 teaspoon salt
1/2 teaspoon pepper

4 1/2-inch thick loin pork chops
2 tablespoons oil

Mix flour, ginger, salt and pepper in bowl. Coat pork chops with mixture. Brown lightly on both sides in hot oil in heavy skillet. Reduce heat. Simmer for 10 minutes on each side or until done to taste.

Vesper Zelei-Waston, Westside #473

GLAZED SPARERIBS

Yield:
6 servings
Utensil:
baking dish

5 pounds spareribs
1/2 teaspoon garlic salt
1 1/2 teaspoons salt
1   30-ounce can sliced
    pineapple

1/2 cup apple jelly
1/4 cup honey
1 tablespoon soy sauce
1/2 teaspoon ginger
1 cup catsup

Approx Per
Serving:
Cal 840
Prot 43 g
Carbo 69 g
Fiber 2 g
T Fat 44 g
47% Calories
from Fat
Chol 174 mg
Sod 1491 mg

Cut ribs into 3 or 4-rib portions. Sprinkle with mixture of garlic salt and salt. Place in 9x13-inch baking dish. Bake at 350 degrees until nearly tender. Drain pineapple, reserving 1/2 cup juice. Combine reserved juice with jelly, honey, soy sauce and ginger in saucepan. Simmer for 5 minutes. Stir in catsup. Spoon over ribs, turning to coat well. Bake until very tender, turning several times to coat again with sauce. Top with pineapple slices. May substitute plum jelly for apple jelly.

Beulah Branchaud, Millville #443

SAVORY ITALIAN SAUSAGE-RICE BAKE

Yield:
8 servings
Utensil:
baking dish

1 pound Italian sausage
1/2 cup chopped onion
1 clove of garlic, minced
3 small zucchini, sliced
    1/4 inch thick
1 1/2 cups spaghetti sauce
1/2 teaspoon basil

1   10-ounce package
    chicken-flavored
    Rice-A-Roni, prepared
2 cups shredded
    mozzarella cheese
1 cup spaghetti sauce

Approx Per
Serving:
Cal 383
Prot 15 g
Carbo 39 g
Fiber 2 g
T Fat 18 g
43% Calories
from Fat
Chol 43 mg
Sod 1146 mg

Remove sausage from casing; crumble into 12-inch skillet. Add onion and garlic. Cook until sausage is brown, stirring frequently. Remove sausage mixture from skillet with slotted spoon. Drain skillet, reserving 1 tablespoon drippings. Add zucchini to drippings in skillet. Cook over medium-high heat for 1 minute. Cook, covered, over low heat for 2 minutes longer. Combine sausage with 1 1/2 cups spaghetti sauce, basil and Rice-A-Roni in bowl; mix well. Spoon into 9x13-inch baking dish. Sprinkle with 1 cup cheese; top with zucchini. Pour 1 cup spaghetti sauce over top; sprinkle with 1 cup cheese. Bake at 350 degrees for 25 to 30 minutes or until heated through. Let stand for 5 minutes before serving.

Lila Sanderson, Rainbow Valley #689

SPAGHETTI PIZZA

Yield:
8 servings
Utensil:
pizza pan

*Approx Per
Serving:*
Cal 467
Prot 22 g
Carbo 29 g
Fiber 3 g
T Fat 29 g
*56% Calories
from Fat*
Chol 82 mg
Sod 1427 mg

8 ounces sausage
1/2 cup milk
1 egg, beaten
1/2 teaspoon salt
8 ounces spaghetti,
cooked, drained
1 15-ounce can tomato
sauce
1/2 teaspoon oregano
1/4 teaspoon pepper

8 ounces sliced
pepperoni
1 small red or green bell
pepper, sliced
1 cup sliced fresh
mushrooms
1/2 cup sliced black olives
2/3 cup ricotta cheese
8 ounces mozzarella
cheese, shredded

Cook sausage in skillet, stirring until crumbly; drain. Combine milk, egg and salt in bowl. Add spaghetti; mix well. Spread evenly in greased 14-inch pizza pan or 9x13-inch baking pan. Combine tomato sauce, oregano and pepper in bowl; mix well. Spread over spaghetti. Sprinkle pepperoni, sausage, bell pepper, mushrooms and olives over top. Spread with ricotta cheese; sprinkle with mozzarella cheese. Bake at 350 degrees for 25 to 30 minutes or until bubbly. Let stand for 5 minutes before serving.

Luella Crandall, Region 11 GWA Director

SPAGHETTI SAUCE WITH SAUSAGE

Yield:
8 servings
Utensil:
saucepan

*Approx Per
Serving:*
Cal 213
Prot 12 g
Carbo 13 g
Fiber 3 g
T Fat 10 g
*43% Calories
from Fat*
Chol 35 mg
Sod 394 mg

1 pound sweet or hot
Italian bulk sausage
8 ounces ground beef
1 large onion, finely
chopped
8 ounces fresh
mushrooms, sliced
1/2 green bell pepper,
chopped
4 cloves of garlic, minced

1 28-ounce can whole
peeled tomatoes
1 6-ounce can tomato
paste
1 1/2 cups dry red wine
1 tablespoon basil
1 teaspoon marjoram
1 bay leaf
Salt and freshly ground
pepper to taste

Brown sausage and ground beef in large heavy saucepan, stirring until crumbly; drain. Add onion, mushrooms, green pepper and garlic. Cook over medium heat for 8 minutes or until vegetables are tender, stirring frequently. Add tomatoes, crushing with spoon. Stir in remaining ingredients. Bring to a boil; reduce heat. Simmer for 2 1/2 to 3 hours or until thickened to desired consistency, stirring occasionally. Discard bay leaf.

Lillian Stilson, Sacramento #12

LASAGNA

Yield:
8 servings
Utensil:
baking dish

Approx Per
Serving:
Cal 581
Prot 35 g
Carbo 42 g
Fiber 3 g
T Fat 31 g
48% Calories
from Fat
Chol 153 mg
Sod 1092 mg

1 pound Italian sausage
1 clove of garlic, minced
1   16-ounce can tomatoes
2   6-ounce cans tomato
   paste
1 teaspoon Italian
   seasoning
3/4 teaspoon salt
10 ounces uncooked
   lasagna noodles
1 cup chopped cooked
   spinach

2 cups ricotta cheese
1/2 cup grated Parmesan
   cheese
2 eggs, beaten
2 tablespoons parsley
   flakes
1/2 teaspoon salt
1/2 teaspoon pepper
1 pound mozzarella
   cheese, thinly sliced

Brown sausage in skillet over low heat, stirring frequently; drain. Stir in next 5 ingredients. Simmer for 30 minutes, stirring occasionally. Cook noodles using package directions; rinse and drain. Squeeze spinach to remove excess moisture. Mix with next 6 ingredients in bowl. Layer noodles, ricotta cheese mixture, mozzarella cheese and meat sauce 1/2 at a time in 9x13-inch baking dish. Bake at 375 degrees for 30 minutes. Let stand for 10 minutes.

Clara A. Harris, Orangevale #354

KIELBASA WITH SAUERKRAUT AND NEW POTATOES

Yield:
6 servings
Utensil:
skillet

Approx Per
Serving:
Cal 317
Prot 9 g
Carbo 31 g
Fiber 4 g
T Fat 17 g
49% Calories
from Fat
Chol 39 mg
Sod 1270 mg

1 large onion, chopped
3 tablespoons butter
1   16-ounce can
   sauerkraut, drained,
   rinsed
1/2 cup dry white wine
1 cup chicken broth
2 tablespoons brown
   sugar

2 tablespoons wine
   vinegar
1 bay leaf
Salt and pepper to taste
1 pound new red
   potatoes, chopped
1 pound kielbasa, sliced
2 to 3 tablespoons Dijon
   mustard

Sauté onion in butter in skillet until golden brown. Add sauerkraut, wine, chicken broth, brown sugar, vinegar, bay leaf, salt and pepper. Bring to a boil; reduce heat. Simmer for 15 minutes. Add potatoes, sausage and mustard; mix well. Simmer for 15 minutes or until potatoes are tender. Discard bay leaf.

Pearl Helmuth, Sanger #478

CREAMY VEAL AND MUSHROOMS

Yield:
6 servings
Utensil:
skillet

Approx Per Serving:
Cal 536
Prot 36 g
Carbo 25 g
Fiber 2 g
T Fat 32 g
54% Calories from Fat
Chol 187 mg
Sod 229 mg

2 pounds veal steak
6 tablespoons butter
Salt and pepper to taste
2 cloves of garlic, chopped
4 shallots, finely chopped
1 pound button mushrooms
1/2 cup dry white wine
2 cups sour cream
2 tablespoons chopped parsley

Trim veal; cut into 1/2x3-inch strips. Sauté in butter in skillet over medium-high heat for 6 minutes or until golden brown. Season with salt and pepper. Remove with slotted spoon to warm bowl. Add garlic, shallots and mushrooms to drippings in skillet. Sauté for 5 minutes. Stir in wine, sour cream and parsley. Cook until heated through. Add veal; mix gently. Cook until heated through. Serve over hot buttered noodles with green vegetable and favorite salad.

Julie Woodard, Orchard City #333

CREOLE WIENERS

Yield:
5 servings
Utensil:
skillet

Approx Per Serving:
Cal 418
Prot 16 g
Carbo 17 g
Fiber 3 g
T Fat 32 g
68% Calories from Fat
Chol 55 mg
Sod 1581 mg

8 slices bacon, finely chopped
3 large onions, finely chopped
1/4 teaspoon salt
2 16-ounce cans tomatoes
1/4 teaspoon pepper
1 pound wieners

Fry bacon with onions in 10-inch skillet until bacon is crisp and onions are tender. Drain, reserving 2 tablespoons drippings. Stir in salt, undrained tomatoes and pepper. Bring to a boil; reduce heat. Simmer for 15 minutes, stirring occasionally. Add wieners. Simmer, covered, for 15 minutes. Serve with hot cooked rice or noodles. May substitute ham for bacon.

Dolly Dightman, Ukiah #410

POULTRY
(& Seafood)

BASQUE CHICKEN AND RICE

1 5-pound chicken, cut up, skinned
2/3 cup uncooked rice
3 cloves of garlic, chopped
1 cup chopped onion
2 tablespoons oil
4 cups canned tomatoes
3 tablespoons chili powder
1 teaspoon marjoram
1 teaspoon salt
1/4 teaspoon pepper

Rinse chicken and pat dry. Arrange chicken in 3-quart casserole. Brown rice, garlic and onion in oil in skillet over low heat, stirring constantly. Add tomatoes, chili powder, marjoram, salt and pepper; mix well. Pour over chicken. Bake, covered, at 350 degrees for 1 hour or until chicken is tender.

Margaret Daley, Wyandotte #495

HONEY CHICKEN

Yield:
4 servings
Utensil:
baking dish

*Approx Per
Serving:*
Cal 540
Prot 50 g
Carbo 36 g
Fiber <1 g
T Fat 22 g
*36% Calories
from Fat*
Chol 175 mg
Sod 949 mg

3 tablespoons melted
  butter
¼ cup prepared mustard
½ cup honey
1 teaspoon curry powder
1 teaspoon salt
1 3-pound chicken,
  cut up

Combine butter, mustard, honey, curry powder and salt in bowl; mix well. Rinse chicken and pat dry. Dip in honey mixture, turning to coat. Place in 9x13-inch baking dish. Bake at 350 degrees for 1¼ hours, basting occasionally with pan drippings.

Marion L. Jones, Happy Camp #395

ITALIAN CHICKEN IN FOIL

Yield:
4 servings
Utensil:
baking sheet

*Approx Per
Serving:*
Cal 427
Prot 51 g
Carbo 9 g
Fiber 3 g
T Fat 20 g
*43% Calories
from Fat*
Chol 152 mg
Sod 250 mg

1 3-pound chicken, cut
  into quarters
Lemon juice or wine to
  taste
2 tablespoons olive oil
1 large onion, chopped
2 cloves of garlic, minced
4 large tomatoes, chopped
4 large green olives,
  chopped
Basil, oregano, salt and
  pepper to taste
4 bay leaves

Rinse chicken with lemon juice and pat dry. Dot 4 squares foil with olive oil. Place chicken quarter in center of each piece of foil. Combine onion, garlic, tomatoes, olives, basil, oregano, salt and pepper in small bowl; mix well. Spoon equal portion on each chicken quarter. Top each with bay leaf. Fold up foil to enclose chicken. Place on baking sheet. Bake at 425 degrees for 40 minutes. Remove bay leaves. Serve from foil packet.

Lisa Alotta, Clearlake #680

ORANGE CHICKEN

Yield:
4 servings
Utensil:
baking dish

Approx Per
Serving:
Cal 422
Prot 51 g
Carbo 23 g
Fiber 3 g
T Fat 13 g
28% Calories
from Fat
Chol 152 mg
Sod 785 mg

1 3-pound chicken,
  cut up
1/2 cup chopped onion
1/4 cup chopped green
  bell pepper
1/3 cup fresh orange juice
1/2 cup catsup
2 tablespoons flour

1 teaspoon prepared
  mustard
1/2 teaspoon salt
1/2 teaspoon garlic
  powder
1/4 teaspoon pepper
2 oranges, sliced

Rinse chicken and pat dry. Arrange skin side down with thicker side to the outside in a 2-quart glass baking dish. Sprinkle with onion and green pepper. Combine orange juice, catsup, flour, mustard, salt, garlic powder and pepper in small bowl; mix well. Pour over chicken. Cover with plastic wrap. Microwave on High for 20 minutes. Remove plastic wrap and turn chicken; place orange slices on top. Microwave for 8 minutes longer or until tender. Let stand for 5 minutes before serving. May also bake in 350-degree oven for 40 minutes.

Mary Kevorkian, Moro #27

ORANGE-HONEY CHICKEN

Yield:
8 servings
Utensil:
baking dish

Approx Per
Serving:
Cal 598
Prot 51 g
Carbo 35 g
Fiber 3 g
T Fat 29 g
43% Calories
from Fat
Chol 183 mg
Sod 1472 mg

2 3-pound chickens,
  cut up
1/2 cup butter
4 teaspoons salt
1/2 teaspoon pepper
2 teaspoons paprika
4 medium onions, sliced
1/2 cup honey
1/4 cup lemon juice

1 6-ounce can frozen
  orange juice
  concentrate, thawed
2 teaspoons ginger
1 teaspoon nutmeg
1 6-ounce can sliced
  black olives, drained
1 cup seedless orange
  sections

Rinse chicken and pat dry. Brown in butter in skillet on all sides. Season with salt, pepper and paprika. Place in 9x12-inch baking dish. Sauté onions in skillet until tender. Layer over chicken. Combine honey, lemon juice, orange juice, ginger and nutmeg in skillet; mix well. Bring to a boil, stirring constantly. Pour over chicken. Sprinkle with olive slices. Bake, covered, at 350 degrees for 1 hour. Arrange orange sections over top. Bake for 10 minutes longer.

Bonnie Peppers, Napa #307

PEACH BARBECUED CHICKEN

Yield:
4 servings
Utensil:
skillet

Approx Per
Serving:
Cal 619
Prot 52 g
Carbo 59 g
Fiber 2 g
T Fat 19 g
28% Calories
from Fat
Chol 152 mg
Sod 1124 mg

1 3-pound chicken,
   cut up
¼ cup flour
¼ teaspoon salt
Pepper to taste
2 tablespoons margarine
1 9-ounce jar peach jam
½ cup chopped onion

½ cup prepared
   barbecue sauce
2 tablespoons soy sauce
½ cup sliced water
   chestnuts, drained
1 green bell pepper, cut
   into julienne strips

Rinse chicken and pat dry. Dust with flour; season with salt and pepper. Brown in margarine in skillet on all sides; drain off excess pan drippings. Combine jam, onion, barbecue sauce and soy sauce in small bowl; mix well. Pour over chicken in skillet. Simmer, covered, for 30 minutes or until chicken is tender. Add water chestnuts and green pepper. Cook for 10 minutes longer. Serve with hot cooked rice.

Betty-Jane Gardiner, National Grange WA Director

HAWAIIAN KABOBS

Yield:
6 servings
Utensil:
grill

Approx Per
Serving:
Cal 329
Prot 31 g
Carbo 24 g
Fiber 3 g
T Fat 13 g
34% Calories
from Fat
Chol 72 mg
Sod 1100 mg

½ cup reduced-sodium
   soy sauce
½ cup unsweetened
   pineapple juice
¼ cup oil
1 tablespoon brown sugar
1 teaspoon garlic powder
2 teaspoons ground
   ginger
¼ teaspoon freshly
   ground pepper

1 teaspoon dry mustard
1½ pounds chicken
   breast filets, cut into
   1-inch chunks
1 20-ounce can
   pineapple chunks,
   drained
1 large green bell pepper,
   cut into 1-inch pieces
12 medium mushrooms
18 cherry tomatoes

Combine soy sauce, pineapple juice, oil, brown sugar, garlic powder, ginger, pepper and mustard in saucepan; mix well. Bring to a boil; remove from heat. Pour into shallow dish. Add chicken, tossing to coat. Marinate in refrigerator for 1 hour, stirring occasionally. Drain, reserving marinade. Alternate pieces of chicken, pineapple, green pepper, mushrooms and tomatoes on 12 skewers. Grill over hot coals for 15 to 20 minutes, basting frequently with reserved marinade. Serve with hot cooked rice.

Marilynn Rasp, Rainbow Valley #689

LEMON-BUTTER-GARLIC CHICKEN

V.I.P.

Yield:
4 servings
Utensil:
baking dish

**Approx Per
Serving:**
*Cal 247
Prot 27 g
Carbo 2 g
Fiber <1 g
T Fat 15 g
54% Calories
from Fat
Chol 103 mg
Sod 496 mg*

4 chicken breast filets
¼ cup lemon juice
¼ teaspoon salt
¼ teaspoon pepper

1 teaspoon lemon-
pepper seasoning
Garlic to taste
¼ cup melted butter

Rinse chicken and pat dry. Place in greased 9x12-inch baking dish. Pour lemon juice over chicken. Sprinkle with mixture of salt, pepper, lemon-pepper and garlic. Drizzle with melted butter. Bake at 350 degrees for 40 minutes or until tender.

**Patricia Avila
California State Grange Director of Information**

LEMON CHICKEN WITH THYME

☺ ⌛

Yield:
4 servings
Utensil:
skillet

**Approx Per
Serving:**
*Cal 274
Prot 29 g
Carbo 9 g
Fiber 1 g
T Fat 13 g
44% Calories
from Fat
Chol 72 mg
Sod 559 mg*

3 tablespoons flour
½ teaspoon salt
¼ teaspoon pepper
1 pound chicken breast
filets
2 tablespoons olive oil
1 tablespoon margarine

1 medium onion, chopped
1 cup chicken broth
3 tablespoons lemon
juice
½ teaspoon thyme
2 tablespoons chopped
parsley

Combine flour, salt and pepper in plastic bag. Rinse chicken and pat dry. Place in bag; shake to coat. Reserve remaining flour mixture. Brown chicken for 5 minutes on one side in 1 tablespoon olive oil in skillet. Brown on other side in remaining oil for 5 minutes. Remove to warm platter. Add margarine to skillet. Sauté onion until tender. Stir in reserved flour mixture. Cook for 1 minute, stirring constantly. Add broth, 2 tablespoons lemon juice and thyme. Bring to a boil, stirring constantly. Return chicken to skillet; reduce heat to medium-low. Cook, covered, for 5 minutes or until tender. Place chicken on individual serving plates. Stir remaining lemon juice into sauce mixture. Pour over chicken. Sprinkle with parsley.

Bette McKinnon, Feather River #440

MEXICAN CHICKEN CASSEROLE

Yield:
4 servings
Utensil:
baking dish

Approx Per
Serving:
Cal 932
Prot 65 g
Carbo 55 g
Fiber 7 g
T Fat 53 g
50% Calories
from Fat
Chol 187 mg
Sod 2211 mg

1 10-ounce can cream
of mushroom soup
1 10-ounce can cream
of chicken soup
2 4-ounce cans green
chili salsa
1/2 cup milk

1 onion, chopped
4 chicken breasts,
cooked, chopped
1 10-count package
corn tortillas
16 ounces Monterey Jack
cheese, shredded

Combine soups, salsa, milk and onion in saucepan. Bring to a boil, stirring constantly; remove from heat. Stir in chicken. Cut tortillas into strips. Layer tortilla strips, chicken mixture and cheese 1/3 at a time in greased 3-quart baking dish. Chill, covered, overnight. Bake, covered, at 350 degrees for 1 hour. Bake, uncovered, for 30 minutes longer.

Rhonda Toole, Estrella #488

PARMESAN CHICKEN

Yield:
6 servings
Utensil:
baking dish

Approx Per
Serving:
Cal 325
Prot 32 g
Carbo 10 g
Fiber <1 g
T Fat 18 g
49% Calories
from Fat
Chol 101 mg
Sod 457 mg

1 cup crushed butter
crackers
3/4 cup grated Parmesan
cheese
2 tablespoons parsley
flakes

1/2 teaspoon garlic
powder
1/8 teaspoon pepper
1/4 cup butter
6 chicken breast filets

Combine cracker crumbs, Parmesan cheese, parsley, garlic and pepper in bowl; mix well. Reserve 1 tablespoon butter. Melt remaining butter in 9x13-inch baking dish. Rinse chicken and pat dry. Roll in butter; coat with crumb mixture. Arrange in baking dish. Sprinkle with remaining crumbs. Dot with reserved butter. Cover with foil. Bake at 325 degrees for 40 minutes or until tender.

Jan Hartz, CSG Staff-Production Manager
L.A. Metro #826

CHICKEN PICCATA

Yield:
4 servings
Utensil:
skillet

*Approx Per
Serving:*
Cal 420
Prot 28 g
Carbo 9 g
Fiber 1 g
T Fat 31 g
*65% Calories
from Fat*
Chol 119 mg
Sod 210 mg

4 chicken breast filets
2 to 4 tablespoons flour
6 tablespoons butter
3 tablespoons olive oil
Salt and pepper to taste
¼ cup lemon juice

1 teaspoon tarragon
2 tablespoons parsley
8 thin slices lemon
2 tablespoons capers
  with juice

Rinse chicken and pat dry. Dust with flour. Sauté in butter and oil in skillet until golden brown. Remove chicken to warm platter. Season with salt and pepper. Stir lemon juice, tarragon, parsley, lemon slices and capers with juice into pan drippings. Cook over medium heat until heated through, stirring constantly. Pour sauce over chicken; serve immediately.

Nutritional information does not include capers with juice.

Myrtle Gutierrez, Morgan Hill #408

SALT-FREE CRISPY CHICKEN

Yield:
10 servings
Utensil:
2 baking pans

*Approx Per
Serving:*
Cal 322
Prot 33 g
Carbo 30 g
Fiber 2 g
T Fat 7 g
*19% Calories
from Fat*
Chol 117 mg
Sod 461 mg

³/₄ cup flour
2 teaspoons paprika
1 teaspoon Mrs. Dash
  seasoning
1 teaspoon pepper
2 eggs, beaten
¼ cup milk

¼ cup Dijon mustard
1½ teaspoons chopped
  rosemary
10 chicken breasts,
  skinned
3 cups dry bread crumbs
¼ cup parsley

Combine flour, paprika, seasoning and pepper in plastic bag. Beat eggs with milk, mustard and rosemary. Place chicken in bag with flour mixture, shaking to coat. Dip in egg mixture. Coat with mixture of bread crumbs and parsley. Place in 2 greased 9x13-inch baking pans. Let stand for 30 minutes. Bake at 425 degrees for 10 minutes. Reduce oven temperature to 375 degrees. Bake for 25 minutes longer or until chicken is tender. May use egg substitute for eggs.

Bernardine Webster, Rainbow Valley #689

CHICKEN SOLO

Yield:
1 serving
Utensil:
baking dish

Approx Per
Serving:
Cal 279
Prot 29 g
Carbo 14 g
Fiber 1 g
T Fat 11 g
37% Calories
from Fat
Chol 79 mg
Sod 253 mg

1 chicken breast
2 to 3 tablespoons bread
  crumbs

2 teaspoons light
  mayonnaise

Rinse chicken and pat dry; discard skin. Sprinkle under-side of chicken with bread crumbs. Place in baking dish, crumb side down. Spread mayonnaise on top side. Sprinkle with remaining bread crumbs. Bake at 375 degrees for 1 hour or until tender.

Doris Murphy, Van Duzen River #517

BLACK WINGS

Yield:
6 servings
Utensil:
saucepan

Approx Per
Serving:
Cal 720
Prot 53 g
Carbo 6 g
Fiber 0 g
T Fat 52 g
67% Calories
from Fat
Chol 161 mg
Sod 3097 mg

5 pounds chicken wings
1/2 cup margarine
4 ounces browning sauce
3 1/2 ounces liquid smoke

1 cup soy sauce
1 1/2 tablespoons garlic
  powder

Rinse chicken and pat dry. Disjoint wings, discarding tips. Melt margarine in large saucepan. Stir in browning sauce, liquid smoke, soy sauce and garlic powder. Add chicken wings. Cook over medium heat for 30 minutes, stirring often. Marinate, covered, in refrigerator for 4 hours, stirring occasionally. Return to stove. Cook for 30 minutes over medium heat until warmed through. Messy but delicious.

Nutritional information does not include liquid smoke and includes the entire amount of marinade.

Marge Potthoff, Lockeford District #579

HOMESTYLE CHICKEN AND DUMPLINGS

Yield:
6 servings
Utensil:
baking pan

Approx Per
Serving:
Cal 257
Prot 20 g
Carbo 26 g
Fiber 2 g
T Fat 7 g
26% Calories
from Fat
Chol 57 mg
Sod 701 mg

2 tablespoons flour
1 envelope chicken
  gravy mix
1/4 teaspoon garlic
  powder
1 1/2 cups water

4 medium carrots, sliced
2 stalks celery, sliced
8 chicken drumsticks
Salt and pepper to taste
1   10-count can biscuits

Shake flour in large oven cooking bag. Place in 9x13-inch baking pan. Add gravy mix, garlic powder and water. Shake bag to mix ingredients. Place carrots and celery in layer in bag. Rinse drumsticks and pat dry. Season with salt and pepper. Place over vegetables. Arrange biscuits around chicken. Seal bag closed, cutting six 1/2-inch slits in top. Bake at 350 degrees for 50 to 55 minutes. Spoon into serving dish.

Alice Mason, Morgan Hill #408

CHICKEN-BROCCOLI ORIENTAL

Yield:
4 servings
Utensil:
skillet

Approx Per
Serving:
Cal 366
Prot 18 g
Carbo 24 g
Fiber 1 g
T Fat 22 g
55% Calories
from Fat
Chol 53 mg
Sod 2282 mg

1 pound boneless
  chicken thighs, cut
  into strips
1 tablespoon oil
1 medium green or red
  bell pepper, cut into
  1-inch pieces

1 small onion, cut into
  1-inch pieces
1   10-ounce can cream
  of broccoli soup
3 tablespoons water
1 tablespoon soy sauce

Brown chicken in hot oil in skillet. Add bell pepper and onion. Cook for 5 minutes or until vegetables are tender-crisp. Stir in soup, water and soy sauce. Bring to a boil; reduce heat. Simmer, covered, for 5 minutes or until vegetables are tender. Serve with hot cooked rice.

Bertha Kellogg, Bear Creek #530

BAKED CHICKEN SANDWICHES ⌛

Yield:
12 servings
Utensil:
baking sheet

Approx Per
Serving:
Cal 276
Prot 13 g
Carbo 23 g
Fiber 1 g
T Fat 15 g
48% Calories
from Fat
Chol 92 mg
Sod 501 mg

24 slices bread, crusts
  trimmed
2 tablespoons butter
2 cups chopped cooked
  chicken
1 cup chopped celery
3 hard-boiled eggs,
  chopped
1/8 teaspoon salt
1/8 teaspoon pepper
2 to 3 tablespoons
  mayonnaise
1 10-ounce can cream
  of chicken soup
1 cup sour cream

Spread bread slices with butter; set aside. Combine chicken, celery, eggs, salt and pepper in bowl. Add enough mayonnaise to hold mixture together; mix well. Spread onto half the prepared bread; top with remaining slices. Place on greased baking sheet. Mix soup and sour cream in small bowl. Spread over sandwiches. Bake at 350 degrees for 20 minutes. Serve immediately.

Senia Wirta, Fort Bragg #672

CHICKEN BORDELAISE ⌛

Yield:
4 servings
Utensil:
saucepan

Approx Per
Serving:
Cal 289
Prot 23 g
Carbo 6 g
Fiber 1 g
T Fat 17 g
57% Calories
from Fat
Chol 99 mg
Sod 323 mg

2 tablespoons butter
2 tablespoons flour
1 cup chicken stock
1 teaspoon
  Worcestershire sauce
1 clove garlic, mashed
Salt and pepper to taste
12 large mushroom caps
1/4 cup sherry or Madeira
2 cups chopped cooked
  chicken
1/4 cup heavy cream

Melt butter in 2-quart saucepan. Blend in flour and chicken stock. Cook over medium heat until thickened, stirring frequently. Add Worcestershire sauce, garlic, salt and pepper. Stir in mushrooms and sherry. Simmer for 5 minutes, stirring often. Add chicken. Simmer until heated through. Stir in cream. Remove from heat. Serve over hot cooked rice, toast or patty shells.

Joanne Struthers, Alturas #406

CHICKEN-BREAD PUDDING

V.I.P.

Yield:
8 servings
Utensil:
baking dish

Approx Per Serving:
Cal 370
Prot 19 g
Carbo 21 g
Fiber 2 g
T Fat 24 g
57% Calories from Fat
Chol 127 mg
Sod 894 mg

6 slices white bread, crusts trimmed
2 cups chopped cooked chicken
2 tablespoons butter
4 ounces sliced mushrooms
1 8-ounce can sliced water chestnuts, drained
1/4 cup mayonnaise
1 cup shredded Cheddar cheese

1 cup milk
1 10-ounce can cream of celery soup
2 eggs, beaten
2 tablespoons chopped pimento
1 teaspoon salt
1/4 teaspoon freshly ground pepper
1/2 cup bread crumbs
2 tablespoons butter

Line bottom of buttered 9x13-inch baking dish with bread slices, cutting to fit. Top with chicken. Melt 2 tablespoons butter in skillet. Sauté mushrooms in butter until browned; remove from heat. Stir in water chestnuts and mayonnaise. Spoon over chicken layer. Sprinkle with cheese. Combine next 6 ingredients in bowl; mix well. Pour over cheese layer. Bake at 350 degrees for 1 hour or until set. Sprinkle with bread crumbs; dot with remaining 2 tablespoons butter. Bake for 10 minutes longer or until crumbs are browned.

Emily Felder, Lecturer, California State Grange

CHICKEN CASSEROLE

Yield:
8 servings
Utensil:
baking dish

Approx Per Serving:
Cal 361
Prot 19 g
Carbo 17 g
Fiber 1 g
T Fat 24 g
60% Calories from Fat
Chol 112 mg
Sod 688 mg

2 tablespoons butter
6 slices bread
2 cups chopped cooked chicken
1/2 cup chopped celery
1 4-ounce can mushrooms, drained
1/2 cup finely chopped onion

1 cup milk
1/2 cup mayonnaise
2 eggs, beaten
1 10-ounce can cream of mushroom soup
1 cup shredded Cheddar cheese

Butter both sides of bread. Place 3 slices in 9x13-inch baking dish. Layer with chicken, celery, mushrooms and onion; top with remaining 3 slices bread. Combine milk, mayonnaise and eggs in bowl; mix well. Pour over top layer. Chill, covered, in refrigerator overnight. Spoon soup over top; sprinkle with cheese. Bake at 350 degrees for 30 to 45 minutes or until bubbly.

Mrs. Rollo Guthridge, Bayside #500

CHICKEN AND SPAGHETTI

Yield:
6 servings
Utensil:
baking dish

Approx Per
Serving:
Cal 510
Prot 38 g
Carbo 39 g
Fiber 2 g
T Fat 22 g
39% Calories
from Fat
Chol 104 mg
Sod 1035 mg

1 8-ounce package thin
   spaghetti, cooked
1/4 cup chopped onion
2 tablespoons margarine
2 tablespoons flour
1 chicken bouillon cube
1 teaspoon salt
1/2 teaspoon pepper
1 teaspoon dry mustard
1 12-ounce can
   evaporated milk

1 4-ounce can sliced
   mushrooms, drained
2 whole pimentos,
   chopped
3 cups chopped cooked
   chicken
1 cup shredded sharp
   Cheddar cheese
1/2 cup grated Parmesan
   cheese

Place spaghetti in buttered 9x11-inch baking dish. Sauté onion in margarine in skillet until tender. Stir in next 5 ingredients. Add evaporated milk, mushrooms and enough water to make of desired consistency. Cook over low heat until thickened, stirring constantly. Boil for 1 minute; remove from heat. Stir in pimentos. Stir about 2 cups of sauce into spaghetti. Mix chicken with remaining sauce. Pour over spaghetti; sprinkle with cheeses. Bake at 450 degrees for 20 minutes or until brown.

Dolores Rawson, Palermo #493

MACARONI AND CHICKEN

Yield:
6 servings
Utensil:
baking pan

Approx Per
Serving:
Cal 953
Prot 30 g
Carbo 75 g
Fiber 3 g
T Fat 58 g
55% Calories
from Fat
Chol 107 mg
Sod 2388 mg

2 cups uncooked
   macaroni
2 cups chopped cooked
   chicken
1 small onion, chopped
3/4 cup cubed mild
   Cheddar cheese
1 10-ounce can cream
   of chicken soup

1 10-ounce can cream
   of mushroom soup
1 10-ounce can cream
   of celery soup
4 cups milk
4 cups crushed saltine
   crackers
1 cup melted margarine

Spread macaroni in nonstick baking pan. Top with chicken, onion and cheese. Combine soups and milk in bowl; mix well. Pour over top layer. Chill, covered, in refrigerator for several hours to overnight. Spread cracker crumbs over top; drizzle with melted margarine. Bake at 350 degrees for 1 hour.

Dagmar Way, Centerville #797

OVERNIGHT CHICKEN

Yield:
9 servings
Utensil:
baking dish

Approx Per
Serving:
Cal 367
Prot 25 g
Carbo 26 g
Fiber 2 g
T Fat 18 g
44% Calories
from Fat
Chol 76 mg
Sod 1098 mg

1 7-ounce package
  macaroni
3 cups chopped cooked
  chicken
2 cups milk
1 10-ounce can cream
  of chicken soup
1 10-ounce can cream
  of mushroom soup
1 4-ounce can
  mushrooms, drained
8 ounces American
  cheese, shredded
1 small onion, chopped
1/2 teaspoon salt
1 tablespoon chopped
  pimento

Combine macaroni, chicken, milk, soups, mushrooms, cheese, onion, salt and pimento in large bowl; mix well. Spoon into buttered 9x12-inch baking dish. Chill, covered, in refrigerator overnight. Bake at 350 degrees for 1 hour.

Arlene Huckins, Lompoc #646

SKILLET CHICKEN 'N BISCUIT PIE ☺

Yield:
6 servings
Utensil:
skillet

Approx Per
Serving:
Cal 204
Prot 9 g
Carbo 29 g
Fiber 2 g
T Fat 7 g
29% Calories
from Fat
Chol 14 mg
Sod 400 mg

2 tablespoons
  reduced-calorie
  margarine
3 tablespoons flour
1 10-ounce can low-
  sodium chicken broth
1/4 teaspoon pepper
1/4 cup low-fat sour
  cream
1 16-ounce package
  frozen mixed broccoli,
  cauliflower and carrots
1/2 cup chopped cooked
  chicken
1/2 cup chopped onion
1 10-count can multi-
  grain biscuits

Melt margarine in ovenproof skillet. Blend in flour. Cook over medium heat for 1 minute or until smooth and bubbly, stirring constantly. Stir in chicken broth gradually. Cook until mixture begins to boil and thicken, stirring constantly. Stir in pepper, sour cream, mixed vegetables, chicken and onion. Simmer for 5 minutes, stirring frequently. Separate biscuits. Place on top of chicken mixture. Bake at 350 degrees for 25 to 30 minutes or until biscuits are golden brown.

Jenny Johnson, Los Molinos #471

SONORA CHICKEN

Yield:
8 servings
Utensil:
baking pan

Approx Per
Serving:
Cal 590
Prot 42 g
Carbo 25 g
Fiber 3 g
T Fat 36 g
55% Calories
from Fat
Chol 127 mg
Sod 1387 mg

1   15-ounce can prepared chili
1   10-ounce can cream of chicken soup
1   10-ounce can cream of celery soup
1 onion, chopped
½ cup milk
1   4-ounce can chopped green chilies, drained
1   8-count package corn tortillas, cut into 1-inch strips
4 cups chopped cooked chicken
2 cups shredded Cheddar cheese
2 cups shredded Monterey Jack cheese

Combine chili, soups, onion, milk and green chilies in bowl; mix well. Alternate layers of chili sauce, tortillas, chicken and cheeses in 9x13-inch baking pan sprayed with nonstick cooking spray, ending with cheese. Bake at 350 degrees for 30 to 35 minutes or until brown.

Julie Woodard, Orchard City #333

STUFFED CORNISH GAME HENS

Yield:
4 servings
Utensil:
skillets

Approx Per
Serving:
Cal 626
Prot 70 g
Carbo 22 g
Fiber 3 g
T Fat 27 g
40% Calories
from Fat
Chol 213 mg
Sod 511 mg

4 large mushrooms, minced
1 tablespoon butter
1 clove of garlic, crushed
½ cup chicken broth
1 medium carrot, julienned
½ cup cooked white rice
1½ tablespoons sunflower oil
Salt and pepper to taste
1 teaspoon parsley flakes
1 teaspoon butter
4 slices wheat bread
4 Cornish game hens

Sauté mushrooms in 1 tablespoon butter in large skillet for 2 minutes. Add garlic. Sauté for 1 minute longer. Cover skillet and remove from heat. Combine chicken broth and carrot in 8-inch skillet. Cook until carrot is tender. Pour into mushroom mixture; set aside. Heat rice in oil in skillet until warmed through. Stir in salt, pepper and parsley. Stir into mushroom mixture. Butter bread on 1 side. Place buttered side down in skillet over medium heat. Heat until butter is melted. Spoon mushroom mixture into center of each bread slice. Place inside cavity of Cornish hens. Place Cornish hens on rack in roasting pan. Bake at 350 degrees for 1 hour or until tender.

Leslie S. Smith, CSG Staff-Bookkeeper, Fair Oaks #724

SWEDISH TURKEY MEATBALLS ☺

Yield:
6 servings
Utensil:
skillet

Approx Per
Serving:
Cal 337
Prot 26 g
Carbo 11 g
Fiber 1 g
T Fat 21 g
55% Calories
from Fat
Chol 77 mg
Sod 911 mg

1½ cups soft bread crumbs
1 cup milk
½ cup chopped onion
1 tablespoon margarine
1½ pounds ground turkey
2 egg whites, slightly
beaten
¼ cup chopped parsley
1½ teaspoons salt
¼ teaspoon ground ginger

Nutmeg and pepper to
taste
2 to 3 tablespoons
margarine
2 tablespoons flour
¾ cup condensed beef
broth
¼ cup water
½ teaspoon instant
coffee powder

Soak bread crumbs in milk in bowl for 5 minutes. Sauté onion in 1 tablespoon margarine in skillet until tender. Combine with next 7 ingredient in bowl; beat until fluffy. Shape into 1½-inch balls. Brown in 2 to 3 tablespoons margarine in skillet. Remove meatballs with slotted spoon to paper towel. Blend flour into pan drippings. Stir in broth, water and coffee powder. Cook over medium heat until thickened, stirring frequently. Place meatballs in sauce. Simmer over low heat for 30 minutes.

Dawn Kimberlin, Westside #473

TERRIFIC TURKEY CASSEROLE

Yield:
6 servings
Utensil:
baking dish

Approx Per
Serving:
Cal 776
Prot 33 g
Carbo 24 g
Fiber 3 g
T Fat 63 g
71% Calories
from Fat
Chol 99 mg
Sod 1213 mg

3 cups chopped cooked
turkey
1 cup chopped celery
1 tablespoon minced
onion
1½ cups chopped
cashews
1 10-ounce can cream
of chicken soup

1 teaspoon salt
¼ teaspoon pepper
1 tablespoon lemon juice
1 cup mayonnaise
1 cup shredded Cheddar
cheese
2 cups crushed potato
chips

Combine turkey, celery, onion, cashews, soup, salt, pepper, lemon juice and mayonnaise in large bowl; mix well. Spoon into buttered 7x11-inch baking dish. Top with cheese and crushed potato chips. Bake at 375 degrees for 25 minutes. Let stand for 5 minutes before cutting into squares. May substitute chopped walnuts for cashews.

Mary Lanzi, Jacinto #431

TURKEY MEAT LOAF

Yield:
6 servings
Utensil:
baking pan

Approx Per Serving:
Cal 385
Prot 35 g
Carbo 18 g
Fiber 2 g
T Fat 19 g
44% Calories from Fat
Chol 170 mg
Sod 681 mg

2 eggs
2 tablespoons milk
2 pounds ground turkey
1 cup bread crumbs
1 medium onion, finely chopped
3/4 cup chopped celery
1 large apple, peeled, chopped
1 teaspoon poultry seasoning
1 teaspoon salt
1/2 teaspoon pepper
2 slices bacon

Beat eggs with milk in large bowl. Add turkey, bread crumbs, onion, celery, apple, poultry seasoning, salt and pepper; mix well. Shape into roll; place in shallow baking pan. Lay bacon slices over top. Bake at 350 degrees for 1 hour. Let stand to cool slightly before slicing.

Ruby R. Gimblin, North Fork #763

CLAM SPAGHETTI

V.I.P.

Yield:
6 servings
Utensil:
skillet

Approx Per Serving:
Cal 472
Prot 17 g
Carbo 70 g
Fiber 8 g
T Fat 16 g
30% Calories from Fat
Chol 41 mg
Sod 63 mg

6 cloves of garlic, chopped
2 large onions, chopped
1/4 cup olive oil
1 tablespoon basil
Ground pepper to taste
1 tablespoon butter
1 tablespoon oregano
2   6-ounce cans minced clams
1/2 cup dry white wine
1 large bunch parsley, chopped
8 ounces fresh mushrooms, sliced
2 bunches green onions, chopped
1   16-ounce package spaghetti
Grated Parmesan cheese to taste

Sauté garlic and onions with oregano, basil and ground pepper in olive oil and butter in large skillet over low heat for 30 minutes or until onions are tender. Drain clams, reserving juice. Add reserved juice and wine to onion mixture. Simmer for 10 to 15 minutes. Add clams, parsley, mushrooms and green onions; mix well. Cook spaghetti using package directions; drain. Add spaghetti and Parmesan cheese to sauce. Cook over low heat for 5 minutes, tossing to coat spaghetti. Serve immediately.

Rosemary Hansen
California State Grange Executive Committee

PRAWNS FETTUCINI ALFREDO

Yield:
2 servings
Utensil:
skillet

2 tablespoons olive oil
7 ounces peeled medium
  prawns
Garlic to taste
2 tablespoons clarified
  butter

½ cup heavy cream
¼ cup grated Parmesan
  cheese
8 ounces fettucini,
  cooked *al dente*
Salt and pepper to taste

Approx Per
Serving:
Cal 676
Prot 26 g
Carbo 28 g
Fiber 2 g
T Fat 51 g
68% Calories
from Fat
Chol 275 mg
Sod 486 mg

Heat olive oil over high heat in skillet. Add prawns; reduce heat to medium. Add garlic and butter. Cook until shrimp turn pink. Add cream, stirring well. Stir in Parmesan cheese. Cook over medium-low heat until thickened. Add fettucini, salt and pepper, tossing lightly to coat with sauce. Arrange on serving plates. Garnish with lemon wedges and freshly chopped parsley. May add 1 cup broccoli to creamed mixture if desired.

Lizabeth Peralta, Rio Linda #403

SHRIMP PROVENÇALE

Yield:
1 serving
Utensil:
wok

1 ounce butter
5 large shrimp, peeled
1 large clove garlic,
  minced

1 tablespoon chopped
  parsley
Salt and pepper to taste
1 tablespoon Pernod

Approx Per
Serving:
Cal 377
Prot 24 g
Carbo 9 g
Fiber <1 g
T Fat 24 g
62% Calories
from Fat
Chol 279 mg
Sod 446 mg

Heat butter in wok. Add shrimp. Stir-fry until pink. Sprinkle with garlic, parsley, salt and pepper. Stir-fry until heated through. Stir in Pernod and serve immediately.

Bea Aker, Garcia #676

PAELLA

Yield:
12 servings
Utensil:
skillet

Approx Per
Serving:
Cal 592
Prot 69 g
Carbo 32 g
Fiber 2 g
T Fat 19 g
29% Calories
from Fat
Chol 259 mg
Sod 1282 mg

16 ounces Italian
  sausage, sliced
1/4 cup olive oil
2 cloves of garlic
1 teaspoon oregano
2 peppercorns
1 1/2 teaspoons salt
1 teaspoon vinegar
3 pounds boned
  chicken, cut into
  bite-sized pieces
4 cups chicken stock
2 cups uncooked rice
2 pounds whitefish
  filets, cubed
1 teaspoon saffron
1 pound baby shrimp

1 pound lobster meat,
  shredded
1 pound crab meat,
  shredded
2 cups frozen peas,
  thawed
1 cup chopped onion
12 small clams
12 mussels
1 2-ounce jar chopped
  pimento, drained
1 green bell pepper,
  chopped
1/2 cup small pitted
  black olives
2 ounces ham, cut into
  thin strips

Brown sausage in large deep skillet, stirring frequently; drain sausage on paper towels. Combine olive oil, garlic, oregano, peppercorns, salt and vinegar in bowl; crush with spoon. Rub into chicken pieces. Sauté in pan drippings. Add chicken stock, rice and whitefish. Simmer for 20 minutes. Stir in saffron. Add sausage, shrimp, lobster, crab meat, peas and onion. Simmer for 5 minutes or until shrimp turn pink, stirring frequently. Steam clams and mussels in saucepan until opened. Spoon rice mixture onto serving platter. Top with pimento, green pepper, olives and ham. Arrange clams and mussels on top. May also serve directly from skillet.

Val Picotte, Berry Creek #694

Paella is one of the national dishes of Spain and derives its name from the two-eared dish in which it is cooked and served. It is a saffron-flavored stew containing chicken, seafood, rice and various vegetables and should be cooked uncovered from beginning to end.

Easy Paella

⧖

<table>
<tr><td>

Yield:
6 servings
Utensil:
skillet

Approx Per
Serving:
Cal 358
Prot 32 g
Carbo 45 g
Fiber 4 g
T Fat 7 g
17% Calories
from Fat
Chol 151 mg
Sod 716 mg

</td><td>

12 ounces peeled shrimp
1 7-ounce can minced
   clams
2 cups chopped, cooked
   chicken
1 16-ounce can
   tomatoes, drained
1 10-ounce package
   frozen peas
1/2 cup water

</td><td>

2 1/2 cups uncooked
   instant rice
3 tablespoons minced
   onion flakes
1 teaspoon paprika
2 chicken bouillon cubes
1/4 teaspoon cayenne
   pepper
1/8 teaspoon saffron

</td></tr>
</table>

Combine shrimp, clams, chicken, tomatoes, peas, water, rice, onion, paprika, bouillon, cayenne pepper and saffron in large skillet. Bring to a boil; reduce heat. Simmer for 5 minutes, stirring occasionally. Remove from heat; cover. Let stand for 10 minutes before serving.

Tamara Crowell, Anderson #418

Baked Salmon

<table>
<tr><td>

Yield:
6 servings
Utensil:
baking pan

Approx Per
Serving:
Cal 981
Prot 100 g
Carbo 14 g
Fiber 1 g
T Fat 56 g
53% Calories
from Fat
Chol 316 mg
Sod 843 mg

</td><td>

1 6-pound salmon, cut
   into filets
1 large dill pickle, sliced
1 lemon, sliced

</td><td>

1 medium onion, sliced
1 cup Catalina salad
   dressing

</td></tr>
</table>

Arrange salmon in 10x14-inch baking pan. Place pickle, lemon and onion in cavity. Pour salad dressing over top. Bake at 350 degrees for 1 hour. Serve immediately.

Fay Smith, Fort Bragg #672

TUNA ON-A-SHOESTRING

Yield:
4 servings
Utensil:
bowl

1 6-ounce can tuna,
   drained
1 cup shredded carrots
1 cup sliced celery
1/4 cup minced onion

3/4 cup mayonnaise
1 4-ounce can
   shoestring potatoes
1 head crisp lettuce

Approx Per
Serving:
Cal 533
Prot 16 g
Carbo 21 g
Fiber 2 g
T Fat 44 g
72% Calories
from Fat
Chol 48 mg
Sod 473 mg

Combine tuna, carrots, celery, onion and mayonnaise in bowl; mix well. Chill, covered, until serving time. Fold in potatoes just before serving. Serve on lettuce-lined plates.

Elvida Bruns, Escalon #447

EASY POTLUCK NOODLE 'N TUNA FLORENTINE

Yield:
10 servings
Utensil:
skillet

4 cups uncooked noodles
2/3 cup finely chopped
   onion
3 tablespoons margarine
1/3 cup cornstarch
1 1/2 teaspoons seasoned
   salt
1/8 teaspoon pepper
1/8 teaspoon dried thyme
3 cups milk

2/3 cup mayonnaise
2 10-ounce packages
   frozen chopped
   spinach, thawed,
   drained
2 12-ounce cans tuna,
   drained
Grated Parmesan cheese
   to taste

Approx Per
Serving:
Cal 348
Prot 26 g
Carbo 19 g
Fiber 2 g
T Fat 19 g
48% Calories
from Fat
Chol 77 mg
Sod 641 mg

Cook noodles using package directions; drain. Sauté onion in margarine in skillet until tender. Stir in cornstarch, seasoned salt, pepper, thyme, milk and mayonnaise. Simmer over low heat until thickened, stirring frequently. Stir in spinach, tuna and noodles. Simmer until heated through. Spoon into serving dish. Top with cheese.

Grace E. Capen, American River #172

SALADS

BUTTERMILK-APRICOT GELATIN SALAD ⌛

Yield:
20 servings
Utensil:
serving dish

**Approx Per
Serving:**
Cal 95
Prot 2 g
Carbo 16 g
Fiber <1 g
T Fat 3 g
28% Calories
from Fat
Chol 1 mg
Sod 56 mg

1 16-ounce can crushed
   pineapple
1 6-ounce package
   apricot gelatin

2 cups buttermilk
8 ounces whipped
   topping

Bring undrained pineapple to a boil in saucepan over medium heat. Stir in gelatin until dissolved. Remove from heat. Chill until partially set. Stir in buttermilk. Chill until partially set. Stir in whipped topping. Spoon into 10x18-inch serving dish. Chill until set. Cut into squares. Serve with crackers.

Josie Manfrina, Lompoc #646

CRANBERRY SALAD

Yield:
6 servings
Utensil:
salad mold

Approx Per
Serving:
Cal 184
Prot 2 g
Carbo 45 g
Fiber 2 g
T Fat <1 g
1% Calories
from Fat
Chol 0 mg
Sod 90 mg

1 large package
   sugar-free raspberry
   gelatin
1½ cups boiling water

1 16-ounce can whole
   cranberry sauce
1 16-ounce can crushed
   pineapple

Dissolve gelatin in boiling water in bowl. Stir in cranberry sauce until sauce melts. Stir in undrained pineapple. Spoon into 4-cup salad mold. Chill until set. Unmold onto serving plate.

Josephine Long, Westside #473

HOLIDAY CRANBERRY SALAD

Yield:
12 servings
Utensil:
salad mold

Approx Per
Serving:
Cal 122
Prot 2 g
Carbo 30 g
Fiber 1 g
T Fat <1 g
1% Calories
from Fat
Chol 0 mg
Sod 61 mg

2 3-ounce packages
   orange gelatin
1½ cups boiling water
2 teaspoons grated
   orange rind
1 16-ounce can jellied
   cranberry sauce

1 8-ounce can
   juice-pack crushed
   pineapple
½ cup chopped celery

Dissolve gelatin in boiling water in large bowl. Stir in orange rind and cranberry sauce. Chill until partially set. Stir in undrained pineapple and celery. Spoon into 6-cup salad mold. Chill until set. Unmold salad onto lettuce-lined serving plate. Garnish with parsley, maraschino cherries and mayonnaise.

Ardyth Lehnert, Nevada Star #16

DREAMY LEMON SALAD

Yield:
8 servings
Utensil:
serving dish

Approx Per
Serving:
Cal 292
Prot 3 g
Carbo 61 g
Fiber 2 g
T Fat 6 g
17% Calories
from Fat
Chol 20 mg
Sod 98 mg

1 6-ounce package
   lemon gelatin
2 cups boiling water
1 cup 7-Up
1 cup pineapple juice
1 20-ounce can
   pineapple tidbits,
   drained

2 bananas, sliced
2 cups miniature
   marshmallows
1 cup prepared lemon
   pie filling
1 cup whipped cream

Dissolve gelatin in boiling water in bowl. Add 7-Up and
pineapple juice. Chill until partially set. Fold in pineapple,
bananas and marshmallows. Spoon into 9x13-inch serving
dish. Chill until set. Mix pie filling and whipped cream in
small bowl. Spread over congealed layer. Chill completely.
Cut into squares.

LaVern Albaugh, Mt. Lassen #417

PINEAPPLE GELATIN SALAD

Yield:
8 servings
Utensil:
salad mold

Approx Per
Serving:
Cal 366
Prot 6 g
Carbo 27 g
Fiber 1 g
T Fat 27 g
65% Calories
from Fat
Chol 62 mg
Sod 205 mg

1 3-ounce package
   lemon gelatin
1 cup boiling water
16 ounces cream cheese,
   softened
3/4 cup crushed pecans

1 20-ounce can crushed
   pineapple, drained
1 teaspoon vanilla extract
1 tablespoon sugar
1 7-ounce can 7-Up

Dissolve gelatin in boiling water in large bowl. Add cream
cheese; mix well. Stir in pecans, pineapple, vanilla and
sugar. Add 7-Up; mix well. Spoon into 8-cup salad mold.
Chill until set. Unmold onto serving plate.

Lenora Moore, Palermo #493

STRAWBERRY-PRETZEL SALAD

Yield:
12 servings
Utensil:
baking dish

Approx Per Serving:
Cal 430
Prot 5 g
Carbo 55 g
Fiber 2 g
T Fat 24 g
47% Calories from Fat
Chol 52 mg
Sod 489 mg

3/4 cup melted butter
3 tablespoons brown sugar
2½ cups crushed pretzels
1 6-ounce package strawberry gelatin
2 cups boiling water

1 16-ounce package frozen strawberries, thawed
8 ounces cream cheese, softened
1 cup sugar
8 ounces whipped topping

Combine butter, brown sugar and pretzels in bowl; mix well. Press onto bottom of 9x13-inch baking dish. Bake at 350 degrees for 10 minutes. Dissolve gelatin in boiling water in bowl. Add strawberries; mix well. Chill until partially set. Mix cream cheese and sugar in bowl until smooth. Fold in whipped topping gently. Spread in prepared dish. Spread gelatin mixture over cream cheese layer. Chill until set. Cut into squares.

Doris Stein, Estrella #488

STRAWBERRY CRUNCH SALAD

Yield:
12 servings
Utensil:
baking dish

Approx Per Serving:
Cal 602
Prot 6 g
Carbo 63 g
Fiber 2 g
T Fat 39 g
56% Calories from Fat
Chol 31 mg
Sod 705 mg

2⅔ cups crushed pretzels
1½ cups melted margarine
12 ounces cream cheese, softened
1¼ cups sugar
9 ounces whipped topping

2 cups pineapple juice
1 6-ounce package strawberry gelatin
1 16-ounce package frozen whole strawberries, thawed

Combine pretzels and margarine in bowl; mix well. Press onto bottom of 9x13-inch baking dish. Bake at 400 degrees for 10 minutes. Cool slightly. Mix cream cheese and sugar in bowl until smooth. Spread over warm baked layer. Top with whipped topping, spreading evenly. Let stand until cool. Bring pineapple juice to a boil in saucepan. Pour over gelatin in bowl, stirring until dissolved. Stir in strawberries. Chill until partially set. Spread over whipped topping layer. Chill until set. Cut into squares. May substitute water for pineapple juice if desired.

Clarella Marriott, Mt. Vernon #453

CREAM CHEESE-GELATIN SALAD

Yield:
9 servings
Utensil:
serving dish

Approx Per
Serving:
Cal 111
Prot 2 g
Carbo 15 g
Fiber 1 g
T Fat 6 g
43% Calories
from Fat
Chol 10 mg
Sod 67 mg

1 3-ounce package lime
   gelatin
1 cup boiling water
3 ounces cream cheese,
   softened

1 8-ounce can crushed
   pineapple
Salt to taste
3/4 cup chopped celery
1/4 cup chopped pecans

Dissolve gelatin in boiling water in bowl. Beat cream cheese in mixer bowl until smooth. Add pineapple and salt; mix well. Chill for 30 to 45 minutes or until partially set. Stir in celery and pecans. Spoon into 8x8-inch serving dish. Chill until set. Cut into squares.

Evelyn Campbell, Mt. Vernon #453

GELATIN CHIFFON SALAD

Yield:
12 servings
Utensil:
glass dish

Approx Per
Serving:
Cal 183
Prot 7 g
Carbo 23 g
Fiber 1 g
T Fat 8 g
36% Calories
from Fat
Chol 5 mg
Sod 189 mg

1 3-ounce package lime
   gelatin
1 3-ounce package
   lemon gelatin
2 cups boiling water
1 tablespoon horseradish

2 cups small curd
   cottage cheese
1 16-ounce can crushed
   pineapple
1/2 to 1 cup chopped
   walnuts

Dissolve lime and lemon gelatin in boiling water in bowl. Add horseradish, cottage cheese, pineapple and walnuts in order listed, mixing well after each addition. Spoon into 8x8-inch glass dish. Chill until set. Cut into squares. Serve on lettuce-lined plates.

Georgia Laughlin, Trinity Valley #618

Macaroni-Fruit Salad

Yield:
10 servings
Utensil:
large bowl

Approx Per
Serving:
Cal 475
Prot 9 g
Carbo 85 g
Fiber 5 g
T Fat 12 g
22% Calories
from Fat
Chol 118 mg
Sod 40 mg

1 16-ounce package
   macaroni
1 20-ounce can crushed
   pineapple
1/4 cup lemon juice
2 tablespoons flour
1/2 cup sugar
4 eggs, slightly beaten
6 to 8 red apples
1 cup whipping cream
1/2 cup sugar
1 teaspoon vanilla extract

Cook macaroni using package directions; drain. Drain pineapple, reserving liquid. Combine reserved pineapple liquid, lemon juice, flour, 1/2 cup sugar and eggs in saucepan; mix well. Cook over medium heat until thickened, stirring constantly. Let stand until cool. Peel apples partially, leaving some peel on for color; chop. Combine with macaroni in large bowl; mix well. Fold in cooled sauce. Chill for 4 hours to overnight. Beat whipping cream with 1/2 cup sugar and vanilla in mixer bowl until soft peaks form. Fold into macaroni salad before serving. Spoon into serving dish. Garnish with maraschino cherries.

Edythe Lorang, Ojai Valley #659

Mystery Salad

Yield:
10 servings
Utensil:
large bowl

Approx Per
Serving:
Cal 339
Prot 4 g
Carbo 59 g
Fiber 1 g
T Fat 11 g
28% Calories
from Fat
Chol 14 mg
Sod 81 mg

1 20-ounce can cherry
   pie filling
1 20-ounce can crushed
   pineapple, drained
1 11-ounce can
   mandarin oranges,
   drained
1 cup miniature
   marshmallows
1 14-ounce can
   sweetened condensed
   milk
8 ounces whipped
   topping
1/4 cup walnuts, coarsely
   chopped

Combine pie filling, pineapple, mandarin oranges, marshmallows, condensed milk, whipped topping and walnuts in large bowl; mix well. Spoon into large serving dish. Chill, covered, for several hours. Garnish with additional coarsely chopped walnuts before serving.

Emma Mansfield, Hesperia #682

FRUIT SALAD ⧖

Yield:
10 servings
Utensil:
serving dish

Approx Per Serving:
Cal 257
Prot 7 g
Carbo 29 g
Fiber 1 g
T Fat 13 g
46% Calories from Fat
Chol 6 mg
Sod 211 mg

1 3-ounce package strawberry gelatin
2 cups cottage cheese
1 16-ounce can fruit cocktail, drained

1 8-ounce can crushed pineapple, drained
16 ounces whipped topping

Mix gelatin and cottage cheese in large bowl. Add fruit cocktail and pineapple; mix well. Fold in whipped topping gently. Spoon into large serving dish.

Ila Bravo, Orchard City #333

MOLDED AVOCADO SALAD ⧖

Yield:
6 servings
Utensil:
salad mold

Approx Per Serving:
Cal 299
Prot 3 g
Carbo 19 g
Fiber 7 g
T Fat 25 g
71% Calories from Fat
Chol 33 mg
Sod 485 mg

1 3-ounce package lime gelatin
1 cup boiling water
2 avocados, mashed
1 cup finely chopped celery
1 tablespoon finely chopped onion

1 tablespoon finely chopped green bell pepper
1 teaspoon salt
1 teaspoon lemon juice
1/4 cup mayonnaise
1/2 cup whipping cream

Dissolve gelatin in boiling water in large bowl. Let stand until cool. Mix avocados, celery, onion, green pepper, salt, lemon juice and mayonnaise. Whip whipping cream in mixer bowl until soft peaks form. Fold into avocado mixture gently. Fold into gelatin gently. Spoon into 4-cup salad mold. Chill until set.

Evelyn Ruckman, Morgan Hill #408

BEET-PINEAPPLE SALAD

Yield:
8 servings
Utensil:
serving dish

Approx Per Serving:
Cal 245
Prot 5 g
Carbo 39 g
Fiber 3 g
T Fat 9 g
32% Calories from Fat
Chol 0 mg
Sod 223 mg

1 15-ounce can pickled beets
1 12-ounce can crushed pineapple
1 6-ounce package raspberry gelatin
1 cup chopped celery
1 cup chopped walnuts

Drain beets and pineapple, reserving liquid. Add enough water to reserved liquid to measure 2 cups. Bring liquid to a boil in saucepan. Pour over gelatin in bowl, stirring until dissolved. Chill until partially set. Cut beets into julienne strips. Stir into gelatin with pineapple, celery and walnuts. Spoon into serving dish. Chill until set.

Thelma Jardine, Estrella #488

BROCCOLI SALAD

V.I.P.

Yield:
8 servings
Utensil:
serving dish

Approx Per Serving:
Cal 322
Prot 7 g
Carbo 28 g
Fiber 5 g
T Fat 23 g
59% Calories from Fat
Chol 19 mg
Sod 282 mg

Flowerets of 2 bunches broccoli
1 cup raisins
1/2 cup chopped onion
1/3 cup walnuts
10 to 12 slices crisp-fried bacon, crumbled
2 tablespoons vinegar
2 tablespoons honey
2/3 cup mayonnaise

Combine broccoli, raisins, onion, walnuts and bacon in large bowl; mix well. Mix vinegar, honey and mayonnaise in small bowl. Pour over broccoli salad; toss well. Spoon into serving dish. Chill, covered, overnight. May add cauliflower and bell pepper or may substitute 2 tablespoons sugar for 2 tablespoons honey.

Ruth Verrue, Region 6 GWA Director

SUNNY BROCCOLI SALAD

Yield:
8 servings
Utensil:
serving dish

Approx Per
Serving:
Cal 235
Prot 5 g
Carbo 25 g
Fiber 4 g
T Fat 15 g
52% Calories
from Fat
Chol 8 mg
Sod 136 mg

Flowerets of 2 bunches
  broccoli
1/3 cup raisins
1/3 cup sunflower seed
1/4 red onion, chopped

1/2 cup mayonnaise
1/2 cup sugar
2 tablespoons red wine
  vinegar
2 tablespoons bacon bits

Combine broccoli, raisins, sunflower seed and red onion in bowl; mix well. Mix mayonnaise, sugar and vinegar in small bowl. Pour over broccoli salad just before serving. Add bacon bits; toss well. Spoon into serving dish.

Bernice Albright, Oakdale #435

ORIENTAL CABBAGE SALAD

Yield:
10 servings
Utensil:
serving dish

Approx Per
Serving:
Cal 253
Prot 2 g
Carbo 9 g
Fiber 1 g
T Fat 24 g
83% Calories
from Fat
Chol 0 mg
Sod 159 mg

1 package chicken-
  flavored ramen
  noodles
1 head cabbage, finely
  shredded
8 green onions, chopped

2 teaspoons toasted
  sesame seed
4 teaspoons cider vinegar
4 teaspoons sugar
1 cup oil

Reserve seasoning mix packet from ramen noodles for salad dressing. Crumble ramen noodles into large bowl. Add cabbage, green onions and sesame seed; mix well. Mix vinegar, sugar, oil and reserved seasoning mix in bowl. Pour over salad; toss. Spoon into serving dish. Chill, covered, overnight.

Annetta Griffith, Berry Creek #694

ORIENTAL COLESLAW

Yield:
8 servings
Utensil:
serving dish

Approx Per
Serving:
Cal 213
Prot 3 g
Carbo 11 g
Fiber 2 g
T Fat 18 g
74% Calories
from Fat
Chol 0 mg
Sod 167 mg

1 package ramen noodles
1 head cabbage, finely
  shredded
5 green onions, chopped
1 medium carrot, grated
½ cup sliced almonds

½ cup oil
1 tablespoon seasoned
  rice vinegar
2 teaspoons sugar
Salt and pepper to taste

Boil ramen noodles in water to cover in saucepan until tender; drain. Do not use ramen noodle seasoning mix. Let stand until cool. Combine cooled noodles, cabbage, green onions, carrot and almonds in large bowl; mix well. Mix oil, vinegar, sugar, salt and pepper in small bowl. Pour over noodle mixture; toss well. Spoon into serving dish.

Nutritional information does not include ramen noodle seasoning mix.

Barbara Ann Eye, Wintersburg #583

PEA SALAD

Yield:
8 servings
Utensil:
serving dish

Approx Per
Serving:
Cal 226
Prot 8 g
Carbo 14 g
Fiber 3 g
T Fat 18 g
65% Calories
from Fat
Chol 8 mg
Sod 330 mg

1   16-ounce package
  frozen peas, thawed
1 cup dry roasted
  peanuts
½ cup chopped celery

¼ cup sliced green onions
⅔ cup sour cream
¼ cup creamy Italian
  salad dressing
¼ teaspoon salt

Combine peas, peanuts, celery, green onions, sour cream, salad dressing and salt in bowl; mix well. Spoon into lettuce-lined serving dish. Chill for 2 hours.

Noreen Garloff, Hessel #750

EASY GREEN PEA SALAD

Yield:
4 servings
Utensil:
serving dish

Approx Per Serving:
Cal 263
Prot 7 g
Carbo 47 g
Fiber 7 g
T Fat 8 g
24% Calories from Fat
Chol 0 mg
Sod 87 mg

1 10-ounce package frozen baby peas
1 cup raisins

¹/₂ cup chopped cashews
Mayonnaise to taste

Cook peas using package directions; drain. Let stand until cool. Soften raisins in boiling water to cover in saucepan; drain. Let stand until cool. Combine peas, raisins and cashews in bowl; mix well. Add enough mayonnaise to make of desired consistency. Spoon into serving dish.

Jan Johnson, Pleasant Valley #675

SAUERKRAUT SALAD

Yield:
8 servings
Utensil:
large bowl

Approx Per Serving:
Cal 245
Prot 1 g
Carbo 32 g
Fiber 2 g
T Fat 14 g
49% Calories from Fat
Chol 0 mg
Sod 648 mg

1 27-ounce jar sauerkraut
1 cup chopped celery
1 cup chopped green bell pepper

¹/₂ cup chopped red onion
¹/₂ cup cider vinegar
1 cup sugar
¹/₂ cup oil
¹/₈ teaspoon garlic salt

Rinse sauerkraut; drain. Combine with celery, green pepper and onion in large bowl; mix well. Mix vinegar, sugar, oil and garlic salt in small bowl. Pour over sauerkraut mixture; toss well. May substitute ¹/₈ teaspoon garlic powder for garlic salt.

Lillian Skavland, Sonoma Valley #407

SPRING SPINACH SALAD

Yield:
10 servings
Utensil:
salad bowl

Approx Per
Serving:
Cal 87
Prot 2 g
Carbo 5 g
Fiber 2 g
T Fat 7 g
71% Calories
from Fat
Chol 0 mg
Sod 189 mg

1 clove of garlic, cut into halves
1 pound fresh spinach
1 medium cucumber, scored, sliced
1/4 cup chopped celery
8 radishes, sliced
1/4 cup sliced green onions
1/2 cup French salad dressing
2 tomatoes, cut into quarters

Rub inside of large salad bowl with cut sides of garlic; discard garlic. Tear spinach leaves into bowl, leaving smaller leaves whole. Layer cucumber, celery, radishes and green onions over spinach. Pour salad dressing over top. Arrange tomatoes on salad. May add finely chopped hard-boiled egg yolk if desired.

Gladys Fulton, Jacinto #431

GREEK-STYLE TOMATO SALAD

Yield:
8 servings
Utensil:
glass dish

Approx Per
Serving:
Cal 207
Prot 3 g
Carbo 9 g
Fiber 2 g
T Fat 19 g
78% Calories
from Fat
Chol 13 mg
Sod 313 mg

1/2 cup olive oil
1/3 cup red wine vinegar
2 tablespoons minced parsley
4 teaspoons sugar
1/2 teaspoon basil
1/4 teaspoon salt
1/4 teaspoon cracked pepper
6 medium tomatoes, sliced
1 small onion, sliced
1 3-ounce can pitted black olives, drained, sliced
4 ounces crumbled feta cheese
Lettuce leaves

Mix olive oil, vinegar, parsley, sugar, basil, salt and pepper in small bowl. Arrange tomatoes, onion and black olives in 9x13-inch glass dish. Sprinkle with feta cheese. Pour salad dressing over top. Lift tomatoes and onions, allowing salad dressing to coat both sides. Chill, covered, in refrigerator for 2 hours or longer. Arrange on lettuce-lined platter to serve.

Esther F. Russell, Rainbow Valley #689

STUFFED TOMATO SALAD

Yield:
6 servings
Utensil:
serving plate

Approx Per
Serving:
Cal 47
Prot 4 g
Carbo 7 g
Fiber 2 g
T Fat 1 g
12% Calories
from Fat
Chol 2 mg
Sod 99 mg

6 medium tomatoes, cut
into halves
1/2 cup low-fat cottage
cheese
1/2 cup grated carrot

1/2 cup finely chopped
celery
2 teaspoons chopped
fresh chives
Pepper to taste

Scoop out pulp of tomatoes, reserving 1/4 cup pulp. Combine reserved pulp with cottage cheese, carrot, celery, chives and pepper in bowl; mix well. Fill tomato shells with mixture. Arrange on lettuce-lined serving plate.

Lucella M. Rogers, Orangevale #354

TWENTY-FOUR HOUR SALAD

Yield:
10 servings
Utensil:
glass dish

Approx Per
Serving:
Cal 473
Prot 10 g
Carbo 12 g
Fiber 3 g
T Fat 44 g
82% Calories
from Fat
Chol 123 mg
Sod 776 mg

1 medium head lettuce,
chopped
1 bunch green onions,
finely sliced
1/2 green bell pepper,
finely sliced
1 8-ounce can sliced
water chestnuts
3 stalks celery, thinly
sliced
1 10-ounce package
frozen peas, thawed

2 cups mayonnaise
2 teaspoons sugar
1/2 cup grated Parmesan
cheese
1 teaspoon salt
1/4 teaspoon garlic
powder
3 or 4 hard-boiled eggs,
grated
3/4 pound bacon,
crisp-fried, crumbled
2 tomatoes, sliced

Layer lettuce, green onions, green pepper, water chestnuts, celery and peas in 9x13-inch glass dish. Mix mayonnaise, sugar, Parmesan cheese, salt and garlic powder in bowl. Spread over vegetable layers. Sprinkle with grated egg and crumbled bacon. Chill, covered, for 4 to 24 hours. Arrange tomato slices on top just before serving.

Lela Hughes, Farmersville #637

MACARONI-VEGETABLE SALAD

Yield:
10 servings
Utensil:
salad bowl

Approx Per
Serving:
Cal 252
Prot 2 g
Carbo 12 g
Fiber 1 g
T Fat 22 g
77% Calories
from Fat
Chol 0 mg
Sod 324 mg

2 cups uncooked
  macaroni
2 cups chopped tomatoes
2 cups chopped zucchini
1 small red onion, finely
  chopped
1 cup oil

1/3 cup tarragon vinegar
1/2 teaspoon dry mustard
2 teaspoons dillweed
1 clove of garlic, crushed
1 1/2 teaspoons salt
1/4 teaspoon pepper

Cook macaroni using package directions; drain. Let stand
until cool. Combine with tomatoes and zucchini in large
bowl. Mix red onion, oil, vinegar, dry mustard, dillweed,
garlic, salt and pepper in small bowl. Pour over salad; toss
well. Spoon into salad bowl. Chill, covered, overnight.

Marilyn Reynolds, Elk Creek #441

PASTA SALAD

Yield:
8 servings
Utensil:
salad bowl

Approx Per
Serving:
Cal 412
Prot 15 g
Carbo 47 g
Fiber 4 g
T Fat 19 g
42% Calories
from Fat
Chol 21 mg
Sod 720 mg

16 ounces uncooked rotini
1 teaspoon each garlic
  salt, pepper and parsley
1/4 teaspoon oregano
1/4 teaspoon basil
1/4 cup sunflower oil
1/4 cup vinegar
1 medium carrot,
  shredded
6 small mushrooms, sliced
1 4-ounce can chopped
  black olives

1/2 cup each slivered red,
  green and yellow bell
  pepper
2 ounces mild Cheddar
  cheese, cut julienne-
  style
1 cup chopped dry
  Italian salami
4 slices crisp-fried
  bacon, crumbled
1/2 cup grated Parmesan
  cheese

Cook rotini using package directions; drain. Rinse with
cold water; drain. Mix next 6 ingredients in small bowl.
Pour over rotini in salad bowl; toss. Drizzle with vinegar;
toss lightly. Add carrot, mushrooms, black olives, bell pepper slivers, Cheddar cheese and salami; toss. Let stand for
1 hour. Add bacon and Parmesan cheese just before serving. May chill salad overnight before adding bacon and
Parmesan cheese. May substitute any type pasta for rotini.

Leslie S. Smith, CSG Staff-Bookkeeper, Fair Oaks #724

RICE SALAD

Yield:
8 servings
Utensil:
serving bowl

Approx Per
Serving:
Cal 216
Prot 3 g
Carbo 22 g
Fiber 2 g
T Fat 14 g
55% Calories
from Fat
Chol 8 mg
Sod 589 mg

1 package chicken-
  flavored rice mix
1 9-ounce jar marinated
  artichokes
1/2 green bell pepper,
  chopped

3 small green onions,
  chopped
1/2 cup mayonnaise
1/4 teaspoon curry
  powder

Cook rice according to package directions, omitting butter. Let stand until cool. Combine with artichokes, green
pepper, green onions, mayonnaise and curry powder; mix
well. Spoon into serving bowl. Chill, covered, overnight.

Shirley Stockwell, Berry Creek #694

CABBAGE-CHICKEN SALAD ☺

Yield:
10 servings
Utensil:
salad bowl

Approx Per
Serving:
Cal 230
Prot 9 g
Carbo 11 g
Fiber 2 g
T Fat 18 g
67% Calories
from Fat
Chol 14 mg
Sod 473 mg

1 package chicken-
  flavored ramen noodles
2 cooked chicken breast
  filets, chopped
1/2 head cabbage,
  chopped
4 green onions, chopped
1/2 cup chopped green
  bell pepper
1/2 cup slivered almonds,
  lightly toasted

2 tablespoons toasted
  sesame seed
1 tablespoon soy sauce
2 tablespoons sugar
3 tablespoons rice wine
  vinegar
1/2 cup olive oil
6 cloves of garlic, crushed
1 teaspoon salt
1/2 teaspoon red pepper
  flakes

Reserve seasoning mix packet from ramen noodles.
Crumble ramen noodles into large bowl. Add chicken,
cabbage, green onions, green pepper, almonds and sesame
seed; mix well. Mix soy sauce, sugar, vinegar, olive oil,
garlic, 1/2 packet ramen seasoning mix, salt and red pepper
flakes in small bowl. Pour over salad; toss well. Spoon into
salad bowl. Chill, covered, overnight.

Nutritional information includes 1/2 the ramen noodle
seasoning mix.

Vera Vecchio, Napa #307

FLYING FARMER CHICKEN SALAD

Yield:
12 servings
Utensil:
large bowl

Approx Per Serving:
Cal 500
Prot 21 g
Carbo 29 g
Fiber 2 g
T Fat 35 g
61% Calories from Fat
Chol 68 mg
Sod 401 mg

2 tablespoons oil
2 tablespoons orange juice
2 tablespoons vinegar
1 teaspoon salt
5 cups chopped cooked chicken
1½ cups small green grapes

3 cups cooked rice
1½ cups sliced celery
1 cup pineapple tidbits
1 11-ounce can mandarin oranges, drained
1 cup toasted slivered almonds
1½ cups mayonnaise

Mix oil, orange juice, vinegar and salt in glass bowl; mix well. Add chicken; toss to coat. Marinate in refrigerator to enhance flavor. Combine grapes, rice, celery, pineapple, mandarin oranges, almonds and mayonnaise in large bowl; mix well. Add marinated chicken; toss lightly. Spoon into serving dish. Serve with crackers.

Edna Jones, Dows Prairie #505

OVERNIGHT LAYERED CHICKEN SALAD

Yield:
12 servings
Utensil:
serving dish

Approx Per Serving:
Cal 423
Prot 19 g
Carbo 12 g
Fiber 4 g
T Fat 34 g
71% Calories from Fat
Chol 61 mg
Sod 254 mg

6 cups shredded lettuce
¼ pound bean sprouts
1 8-ounce can sliced water chestnuts, drained
½ cup thinly sliced green onions, including tops
1 medium cucumber, thinly sliced
4 cups cooked chicken breast, cut into strips

2 6-ounce packages frozen pea pods
2 cups mayonnaise
2 teaspoons curry powder
1 tablespoon sugar
½ teaspoon ground ginger
½ cup Spanish peanuts
12 to 18 cherry tomatoes, cut into halves

Spread lettuce over bottom of 4-quart serving dish. Layer bean sprouts, water chestnuts, green onions, cucumber and chicken over top. Thaw pea pods; pat dry. Arrange over chicken layer. Mix mayonnaise, curry powder, sugar and ginger in small bowl. Spread over top of salad. Chill, covered, for several hours to overnight. Top with peanuts and tomato halves before serving.

Evelyn L. Geiser, Lompoc #646

CORNED BEEF SALAD

Yield:
6 servings
Utensil:
serving dish

Approx Per Serving:
Cal 509
Prot 21 g
Carbo 17 g
Fiber 1 g
T Fat 40 g
70% Calories from Fat
Chol 83 mg
Sod 976 mg

1 3-ounce package lemon gelatin
1 cup boiling water
2 tablespoons vinegar
1 15-ounce can corned beef, crumbled

1 small green bell pepper, finely chopped
1 medium onion, finely chopped
1 cup mayonnaise
1/4 cup horseradish

Dissolve gelatin in boiling water in bowl. Chill until partially set. Stir in vinegar, corned beef, green pepper, onion, mayonnaise and horseradish. Spoon into serving dish. Chill until set.

Maxine Dodge, Live Oak #494

HOT HAM SALAD

Yield:
8 servings
Utensil:
baking dish

Approx Per Serving:
Cal 311
Prot 16 g
Carbo 10 g
Fiber 1 g
T Fat 23 g
67% Calories from Fat
Chol 94 mg
Sod 1084 mg

3 cups diced ham
1/2 cup sweet pickle relish
2 teaspoons minced onion
2 teaspoons prepared mustard
3/4 cup mayonnaise

1 cup chopped celery
2 hard-boiled eggs, chopped
1 tablespoon lemon juice
1/4 teaspoon salt
1/4 teaspoon pepper
1 cup crushed potato chips

Combine ham, relish, onion, prepared mustard, mayonnaise, celery, eggs, lemon juice, salt and pepper in bowl; mix well. Spoon into baking dish. Sprinkle with potato chips. Bake, covered, at 425 degrees for 20 minutes.

John A. Valentine, National Grange Treasurer

MACARONI-SHRIMP SALAD

Yield:
8 servings
Utensil:
salad bowl

Approx Per
Serving:
Cal 376
Prot 14 g
Carbo 44 g
Fiber 3 g
T Fat 15 g
37% Calories
from Fat
Chol 162 mg
Sod 450 mg

1 16-ounce package
   macaroni
1 4-ounce can sliced
   pimentos, drained
1 4-ounce can broken
   shrimp
5 hard-boiled eggs,
   chopped
1/2 cup mayonnaise
1/2 teaspoon prepared
   mustard
Salt to taste

Cook macaroni using package directions; drain. Combine with pimentos, shrimp and eggs in bowl; mix well. Mix mayonnaise, mustard and salt. Pour over salad; toss. Spoon into salad bowl. Chill until serving time.

Helen M. Papst, Orangevale #354

SEAFOOD SALAD

Yield:
15 servings
Utensil:
serving dish

Approx Per
Serving:
Cal 432
Prot 9 g
Carbo 11 g
Fiber 1 g
T Fat 40 g
81% Calories
from Fat
Chol 135 mg
Sod 440 mg

1 loaf white sandwich
   bread
2 tablespoons butter,
   softened
1 onion, chopped
4 hard-boiled eggs,
   chopped
1/2 cup chopped celery
6 ounces cooked peeled
   shrimp
6 ounces crab meat
2 to 3 cups mayonnaise
1 hard-cooked egg,
   chopped

Cut crust off bread slices. Spread 1 side with butter. Cut bread into crouton-sized pieces. Combine with onion and 4 eggs in large bowl; mix well. Chill, covered, overnight. Mix celery, shrimp, crab meat and mayonnaise in bowl. Add to bread mixture; toss well. Spoon into large serving dish. Chill for 5 hours or longer.

Hazel Moon, Little Lake #670

Tuna-Apple Salad

Yield:
4 servings
Utensil:
salad plate

Approx Per
Serving:
Cal 211
Prot 16 g
Carbo 22 g
Fiber 3 g
T Fat 7 g
29% Calories
from Fat
Chol 30 mg
Sod 237 mg

4 small new potatoes,
  cooked
1/4 cup plain yogurt
1/4 cup low-fat
  mayonnaise
2 tablespoons lemon
  juice
1/4 teaspoon grated
  lemon rind

1/2 teaspoon dried chervil
1/8 teaspoon pepper
1 apple, chopped
1   6-ounce can tuna,
  flaked
1/2 cup cooked fresh peas
1/4 cup toasted almond
  flakes

Cut potatoes into cubes. Mix yogurt, mayonnaise, lemon juice, grated lemon rind, chervil and pepper in bowl. Stir in apple, tuna, potatoes and peas. Chill completely. Serve on lettuce-lined salad plate; sprinkle with almonds. May substitute 1 teaspoon parsley for chervil.

Joyce Crankshaw, Berry Creek #694

Quick Aioli

Yield:
4 servings
Utensil:
blender

Approx Per
Serving:
Cal 414
Prot 1 g
Carbo 3 g
Fiber <1 g
T Fat 45 g
96% Calories
from Fat
Chol 86 mg
Sod 315 mg

1 to 3 cloves of garlic,
  crushed
1 hard-boiled egg yolk

1 tablespoon lemon juice
1 cup mayonnaise

Combine crushed garlic, egg yolk, lemon juice and 1/4 of the mayonnaise in blender container. Process until smooth. Fold in remaining mayonnaise. Spoon into serving dish. Chill until serving time.

Dicie Goltz, Dows Prairie #505

COLESLAW DRESSING

Yield:
12 servings
Utensil:
bowl

Approx Per
Serving:
Cal 113
Prot 1 g
Carbo 10 g
Fiber 0 g
T Fat 8 g
63% Calories
from Fat
Chol 9 mg
Sod 64 mg

½ cup sugar
½ mayonnaise

½ cup evaporated milk
¼ cup vinegar

Combine sugar, mayonnaise, evaporated milk and vinegar in small bowl; mix well. Serve tossed with shredded cabbage.

Clara Rowe, Nevada Star #16

MY RUSSIAN DRESSING

Yield:
16 servings
Utensil:
saucepan

Approx Per
Serving:
Cal 63
Prot <1 g
Carbo 6 g
Fiber <1 g
T Fat 5 g
63% Calories
from Fat
Chol 0 mg
Sod 98 mg

¼ cup sugar
3 tablespoons water
⅓ cup oil
½ cup catsup
Juice of 1 lemon
1 tablespoon vinegar
½ teaspoon paprika

1½ teaspoons celery
   seed
1 tablespoon
   Worcestershire sauce
2 tablespoons grated
   onion
Salt to taste

Combine sugar and water in small saucepan. Bring to a boil. Remove from heat. Add oil, catsup, lemon juice, vinegar, paprika, celery seed, Worcestershire sauce, onion and salt; mix well. Spoon into serving dish. Chill until serving time.

Muriel Taff, Anderson #418

SIDE DISHES

BREAKFAST CASSEROLE ☺

Yield:
8 servings
Utensil:
baking pan

Approx Per Serving:
Cal 203
Prot 17 g
Carbo 18 g
Fiber 1 g
T Fat 6 g
28% Calories from Fat
Chol 19 mg
Sod 732 mg

1 pound Canadian bacon
1¹/₂ cups egg substitute
2 cups skim milk
1 teaspoon dry mustard

8 slices bread, cubed
1 cup shredded low-calorie American cheese

Fry bacon lightly in skillet; drain. Combine egg substitute, milk and mustard in small bowl; mix well. Layer bread cubes, bacon and cheese in greased baking pan. Pour egg mixture over top. Chill, covered, overnight. Bake at 350 degrees for 45 minutes.

Jean McNary, Riverdale #624

CHRISTMAS BREAKFAST

Yield:
8 servings
Utensil:
baking dish

Approx Per
Serving:
Cal 314
Prot 18 g
Carbo 17 g
Fiber <1 g
T Fat 19 g
55% Calories
from Fat
Chol 205 mg
Sod 584 mg

7 slices white bread,
  crusts, trimmed, cubed
8 ounces Cheddar
  cheese, shredded
6 eggs
3 cups milk
$1/2$ teaspoon salt
$1/4$ teaspoon pepper
1 teaspoon prepared
  mustard
4 slices bacon, cut into
  halves

Combine bread cubes and cheese in bowl. Spread in greased 9x13-inch baking dish. Beat eggs with milk, salt, pepper and mustard in bowl. Pour over bread mixture. Lay bacon slices on top. Chill, covered, overnight. Bake at 350 degrees for 50 to 55 minutes.

Elizabeth Morse, Mt. Hamilton #469

MOTHER'S CHEESE SOUFFLÉ

Yield:
4 servings
Utensil:
soufflé dish

Approx Per
Serving:
Cal 334
Prot 17 g
Carbo 22 g
Fiber 1 g
T Fat 20 g
53% Calories
from Fat
Chol 207 mg
Sod 723 mg

1 cup scalded milk
1 cup bread crumbs
4 ounces Cheddar
  cheese, shredded
1 tablespoon butter
$1/2$ teaspoon salt
3 egg yolks
$1/4$ teaspoon
  Worcestershire sauce
3 egg whites

Combine scalded milk, bread crumbs, cheese, butter and salt in bowl; mix well. Beat egg yolks in small bowl until lemon-colored. Stir into cheese mixture with Worcestershire sauce. Beat egg whites in mixer bowl until stiff peaks form. Fold into cheese mixture. Pour into greased $1 1/2$-quart soufflé dish. Bake at 350 degrees for 20 to 30 minutes or until puffy. Serve immediately.

Diane Risko, Pleasant Valley #675

LETTUCE FIELD
Cuyama Valley, California

CALIFORNIA PEACHES, O'HENRY VARIETY
Esparto, California

BROCCOLI-CHEESE STRATA

Yield:
12 servings
Utensil:
baking dish

*Approx Per
Serving:*
Cal 260
Prot 13 g
Carbo 24 g
Fiber 1 g
T Fat 13 g
*43% Calories
from Fat*
Chol 134 mg
Sod 621 mg

1 16-ounce loaf white bread
1 10-ounce package frozen chopped broccoli, cooked, drained
8 slices sharp American cheese
6 eggs, beaten
3½ cups milk
1 teaspoon minced onion flakes
½ teaspoon salt
¼ teaspoon pepper
¼ teaspoon dry mustard
¼ teaspoon Tabasco sauce

Slice bread into halves lengthwise. Layer half the bread, broccoli, cheese and remaining bread in greased 9x13-inch baking dish. Beat eggs, milk, onion, salt, pepper, mustard and Tabasco sauce in bowl. Pour over layers. Bake at 350 degrees for 45 to 55 minutes or until set. Garnish with paprika and shredded cheese.

Ida Grossi, Lompoc #646

CHEESE STRATA

Yield:
8 servings
Utensil:
casserole

*Approx Per
Serving:*
Cal 308
Prot 15 g
Carbo 9 g
Fiber 1 g
T Fat 24 g
*69% Calories
from Fat*
Chol 141 mg
Sod 459 mg

2 cups crust-trimmed bread cubes
8 ounces sharp Cheddar cheese, cubed
8 ounces bacon, cooked, crumbled
¼ cup melted butter
8 ounces mushrooms, sliced
3 eggs
2 cups milk
1 teaspoon prepared mustard

Layer bread cubes, cheese, bacon and butter ½ at a time in greased 1½-quart casserole. Arrange mushrooms on top. Beat eggs, milk and mustard in bowl. Pour over layers. Place casserole in pan of hot water. Bake at 300 degrees for 1½ hours. May chill overnight before baking.

Aileen Dillow, Apple Valley #593

LASAGNA ROLL-UPS

Yield:
8 servings
Utensil:
baking dish

Approx Per
Serving:
Cal 348
Prot 19 g
Carbo 35 g
Fiber 2 g
T Fat 16 g
40% Calories
from Fat
Chol 65 mg
Sod 479 mg

8 lasagna noodles,
  cooked, drained
1/2 cup chopped onion
2 tablespoons olive oil
1 4-ounce can chopped
  mushrooms
1 14-ounce can Italian-
  style stewed tomatoes
1 6-ounce can tomato
  paste

1/2 cup water
1 cup shredded low-fat
  mozzarella cheese
15 ounces ricotta cheese
1 10-ounce package
  frozen spinach,
  thawed, drained
1 egg, beaten
1/2 cup grated Parmesan
  cheese

Lay noodles flat on waxed paper to cool. Sauté onion in oil in skillet until tender. Add next 4 ingredients. Bring to a boil; reduce heat. Simmer for 5 minutes, stirring frequently. Mix 1/2 cup mozzarella cheese and next 4 ingredients in bowl. Spread 3/4 cup tomato mixture in 9x13-inch baking dish. Spread 1/3 cup spinach mixture on each noodle to within 1 inch of end; roll up. Place in prepared dish. Top with remaining tomato mixture. Bake at 350 degrees for 35 minutes. Sprinkle with 1/2 cup mozzarella cheese. Bake for 5 minutes or until cheese melts.

Marilynn Rasp, Rainbow Valley #689

PEPPERONI PASTA

Yield:
6 servings
Utensil:
skillet

Approx Per
Serving:
Cal 577
Prot 19 g
Carbo 65 g
Fiber 5 g
T Fat 27 g
42% Calories
from Fat
Chol 13 mg
Sod 1067 mg

1 large onion, thinly
  sliced
2 large cloves of garlic,
  minced
8 ounces pepperoni,
  thinly sliced
2 medium green bell
  peppers, sliced

1/4 cup vegetable oil
1 15-ounce can whole
  peeled tomatoes
1 teaspoon oregano
1/2 teaspoon salt
1 16-ounce package
  fettucini

Sauté onion, garlic, pepperoni and green peppers in oil in skillet over medium heat for 5 minutes. Add tomatoes, oregano and salt. Simmer, covered, for 5 minutes longer, stirring frequently. Cook, uncovered, for 1 minute or until sauce is of desired consistency. Cook pasta using package directions; drain. Pour into serving bowl. Pour in sauce, tossing to coat.

Lois Janiak, Lompoc #646

SPRINGTIME PASTA

Yield:
6 servings
Utensil:
skillet

Approx Per
Serving:
Cal 443
Prot 13 g
Carbo 44 g
Fiber 3 g
T Fat 25 g
50% Calories
from Fat
Chol 81 mg
Sod 418 mg

8 ounces fresh
 asparagus, trimmed
8 ounces mushrooms,
 sliced
1/4 cup slivered baked ham
1 medium carrot, thinly
 sliced
1 medium zucchini, cubed
1/4 cup butter
3 green onions with
 tops, sliced
1/2 cup frozen green
 peas, thawed
1 teaspoon dried basil
1/2 teaspoon salt
Nutmeg and white
 pepper to taste
1 cup whipping cream
1 10-ounce package
 angel hair pasta, cooked
1/4 cup grated Parmesan
 cheese

Slice asparagus diagonally into 1-inch pieces, leaving tips whole. Sauté asparagus, mushrooms, ham, carrot and zucchini in butter in large skillet over medium heat for 3 minutes, stirring occasionally. Cook, covered, for 1 minute longer. Add next 7 ingredients; mix well. Cook over high heat until bubbly, stirring constantly. Drain cooked pasta. Add to sauce mixture, tossing to coat. Add Parmesan cheese, tossing to coat. Pour into warmed serving bowl. Garnish with parsley and additional Parmesan cheese.

Kathy Real, Lake Francis #745

CHILI QUICHE

Yield:
12 servings
Utensil:
baking dish

Approx Per
Serving:
Cal 332
Prot 19 g
Carbo 6 g
Fiber <1 g
T Fat 25 g
69% Calories
from Fat
Chol 238 mg
Sod 739 mg

10 eggs
1 pint cottage cheese
1 teaspoon baking
 powder
1 teaspoon salt
10 drops of Tabasco
 sauce
1/2 cup flour
16 ounces Monterey Jack
 cheese, shredded
1 4-ounce can chopped
 green chilies, drained
1/2 cup melted butter

Combine eggs, cottage cheese, baking powder, salt, Tabasco sauce and flour in blender container. Process until smooth. Combine with cheese, chilies and butter in large bowl; mix well. Pour into buttered 9x13-inch baking dish. Bake at 400 degrees for 15 minutes. Reduce oven temperature to 350 degrees. Bake for 25 to 30 minutes longer or until knife inserted near center comes out clean. Let stand for 5 minutes before cutting into serving pieces. Mixture may be prepared 3 to 4 days in advance, refrigerated and baked when needed.

Connie Picotte, Berry Creek #694

THRIFTY VEGETABLE-RICE QUICHE

Yield:
6 servings
Utensil:
glass dish

Approx Per Serving:
Cal 333
Prot 14 g
Carbo 32 g
Fiber 1 g
T Fat 17 g
45% Calories from Fat
Chol 181 mg
Sod 683 mg

3 cups cooked rice
¾ cup shredded
   Cheddar cheese
1 egg, beaten
1 small zucchini, sliced
1 small tomato, chopped
2 tablespoons butter
¾ cup chopped onion

2 tablespoons flour
¾ cup milk
3 eggs, beaten
1¼ teaspoons salt
¼ teaspoon pepper
1 teaspoon marjoram
½ cup shredded
   Cheddar cheese

Combine rice, ¾ cup cheese and egg in small bowl; mix well. Press on bottom and up side of greased 10-inch round glass dish. Layer with zucchini and tomato. Microwave butter in 2-cup glass measure on High for 30 to 60 seconds or until melted. Add onion. Microwave for 1 to 2 minutes or until tender. Stir in flour and ½ cup milk. Microwave for 1 to 2 minutes or until mixture thickens, stirring every minute. Add remaining milk, 3 eggs, salt, pepper and marjoram; mix well. Pour over tomato and zucchini layers. Sprinkle with ½ cup Cheddar cheese. Microwave on Medium for 12 to 14 minutes or until set, turning every 4 minutes. Let stand for 5 to 10 minutes.

Joyce Crankshaw, Berry Creek #694

FRENCH-FRIED DEVILED EGGS

Yield:
8 servings
Utensil:
deep-fryer

Approx Per Serving:
Cal 114
Prot 8 g
Carbo 5 g
Fiber <1 g
T Fat 7 g
53% Calories from Fat
Chol 240 mg
Sod 253 mg

8 hard-boiled eggs
½ teaspoon dry mustard
½ teaspoon salt
Pepper to taste
2 tablespoons vinegar

½ cup fine dry bread
   crumbs
1 egg, beaten
Oil for deep frying

Slice eggs into halves lengthwise. Scoop out yolks. Mash yolks with mustard, salt, pepper and vinegar in small bowl. Fill whites of eggs with mixture. Place egg halves together, securing with wooden picks. Coat with bread crumbs; dip in egg. Coat again with crumbs. Deep-fry in hot oil in deep-fryer until golden brown; drain well. Serve with tomato sauce.

Nutritional information does not include oil for deep frying.

Jean Smith, Quartz Hill #697

RICE CASSEROLE

Yield:
6 servings
Utensil:
baking dish

Approx Per
Serving:
Cal 269
Prot 6 g
Carbo 33 g
Fiber 1 g
T Fat 12 g
41% Calories
from Fat
Chol 12 mg
Sod 1149 mg

2¼ cups water
1 tablespoon butter
¾ teaspoon salt
2 cups uncooked minute
  rice
2 tablespoons chopped
  onion

6 slices bacon, chopped
2 10-ounce cans cream
  of mushroom soup
1 tablespoon garlic
  powder
Salt and pepper to taste

Bring water, butter and salt to a boil in saucepan. Add rice. Cover and remove from heat. Let stand for 5 minutes. Stir in onion, bacon, soup, garlic powder, salt and pepper. Spoon into 1½ quart baking dish. Bake at 350 degrees for 30 minutes.

Elsye Ruport, Mt. Vernon #453

APPLE PIE-IN-A-JAR

Yield:
7 quarts
Utensil:
saucepan

Approx Per
Quart:
Cal 655
Prot <1 g
Carbo 169 g
Fiber 4 g
T Fat 1 g
1% Calories
from Fat
Chol 0 mg
Sod 308 mg

4½ cups sugar
1 teaspoon salt
1 cup cornstarch
10 cups water
2 teaspoons cinnamon

½ teaspoon nutmeg
3 tablespoons lemon
  juice
9 medium apples,
  peeled, sliced

Combine sugar, salt, cornstarch, water, cinnamon and nutmeg in large saucepan; mix well. Cook over medium heat until mixture comes to a boil, stirring frequently. Stir in lemon juice. Place apples in 7 hot sterilized 1-quart jars. Pour in hot syrup. Seal with 2-piece lids. Process in hot water bath for 25 minutes or in pressure cooker at 10 pounds pressure for 10 minutes. May substitute peaches or cherries, omitting spices and adding almond extract with cherries. Great to have on hand to make a quick dessert or apple pie.

Mary and Don Johnson
National Grange Assistant Steward

CARROT MARMALADE

Yield:
46 ounces
Utensil:
saucepan

Approx Per
Ounce:
Cal 63
Prot <1 g
Carbo 14 g
Fiber <1 g
T Fat 1 g
11% Calories
from Fat
Chol 0 mg
Sod 4 mg

1 pound carrots, peeled,
    cut into quarters
3 cups sugar

Juice of 2 lemons
Grated rind of 1 lemon
1/2 cup chopped walnuts

Cook carrots in a small amount of water in saucepan until tender; drain. Mash until smooth. Stir in sugar, lemon juice and lemon rind. Cook over medium heat for 20 minutes, stirring frequently. Stir in walnuts. Pour into hot sterilized jars, leaving 1/2 inch headspace; seal with 2-piece lids. Process in boiling water bath for 10 to 15 minutes.

Ruby L. Tait, Costa Mesa #612

PINEAPPLE-CARROT MARMALADE

Yield:
72 ounces
Utensil:
saucepan

Approx Per
Ounce:
Cal 58
Prot <1 g
Carbo 15 g
Fiber 1 g
T Fat <1 g
1% Calories
from Fat
Chol 0 mg
Sod 9 mg

4 pounds carrots, peeled
3 lemons
4 cups sugar

1 8-ounce can crushed
    pineapple, drained
1 cup orange juice

Process carrots and whole lemons in food chopper until finely chopped. Combine with sugar, pineapple and orange juice in saucepan. Cook over medium heat until syrup is clear, stirring occasionally. Pour into hot sterilized jars, leaving 1/2 inch headspace; seal with 2-piece lids.

Amy A. Stubbs, Lompoc #646

MICROWAVE STRAWBERRY-PEACH JAM

Yield:
16 ounces
Utensil:
glass dish

Approx Per
Ounce:
Cal 56
Prot <1 g
Carbo 14 g
Fiber 1 g
T Fat <1 g
1% Calories
from Fat
Chol 0 mg
Sod 1 mg

1 pint strawberries,
  hulled
1 peach, peeled, chopped

1 cup sugar
1 teaspoon fresh lemon
  juice

Place strawberries in 2-quart glass dish; coarsely mash. Add chopped peach and sugar. Let stand for 10 minutes. Microwave on High for 12 to 14 minutes, stirring every 4 minutes until thickened. Stir in lemon juice; cool. Pour into hot sterilized 1-pint jar. Chill for 3 hours.

Lavene Douglas, Farmerville #637

RHUBARB MARMALADE

Yield:
64 ounces
Utensil:
saucepan

Approx Per
Ounce:
Cal 87
Prot <1 g
Carbo 21 g
Fiber 1 g
T Fat 1 g
6% Calories
from Fat
Chol 0 mg
Sod 2 mg

2 oranges
8 cups chopped rhubarb
5 cups sugar

2 cups raisins
1/2 cup water
1/2 cup chopped walnuts

Chop unpeeled oranges in food processor. Combine with rhubarb, sugar, raisins and water in saucepan. Cook until rhubarb is tender and mixture is thickened, stirring occasionally. Stir in walnuts. Pour into hot sterilized jars, leaving 1/2 inch headspace. Seal with 2-piece lids.

Pearl Harless, Tulelake #468

CHARLES' RED BELL PEPPER SAUCE

Yield:
4 servings
Utensil:
skillet

Approx Per
Serving:
Cal 195
Prot 4 g
Carbo 17 g
Fiber 4 g
T Fat 6 g
27% Calories
from Fat
Chol 8 mg
Sod 959 mg

3 red bell peppers,
  chopped
2 teaspoons olive oil
8 cloves of garlic,
  chopped
Salt and pepper to taste

2 4-ounce cans chopped
  mushrooms, drained
1 tablespoon butter
2 cups white Chablis
2 8-ounce cans tomato
  sauce

Sauté red peppers in olive oil in large skillet over medium low heat for 15 minutes. Add garlic, salt and pepper. Cook for 15 minutes longer. Sauté mushrooms in butter in small skillet over low heat for 15 minutes. Sprinkle with salt and pepper. Add Chablis, tomato sauce, salt, pepper and mushrooms to red pepper mixture. Simmer for 30 minutes over low heat, stirring frequently. This is enough sauce for 1 pound spaghetti.

Thelma Rains, Fort Bragg #672

MOLDED HORSERADISH SOUFFLÉ

Yield:
32 ounces
Utensil:
mold

Approx Per
Serving:
Cal 37
Prot <1 g
Carbo 3 g
Fiber <1 g
T Fat 3 g
64% Calories
from Fat
Chol 10 mg
Sod 82 mg

1 3-ounce package
  lemon gelatin
1 teaspoon salt
1 tablespoon apple
  vinegar

1 cup whipping cream
1 4-ounce bottle of
  prepared horseradish
1/2 cup freshly minced
  parsley

Prepare gelatin using package directions. Stir in salt and vinegar. Chill until partially set. Whip whipping cream in mixer bowl until soft peaks form. Fold into gelatin mixture with horseradish. Spoon into 1-quart mold. Chill until set. Unmold onto serving plate; sprinkle with parsley. Serve with meat or over lettuce.

John C. Swegles, Gazelle #380

PICKLED MUSHROOMS

Yield:
4 servings
Utensil:
saucepan

1 pound fresh
  mushrooms
2 to 4 cups cider vinegar
3 cloves of garlic
1 tablespoon minced
  parsley

2 teaspoons salt
1 cup oil
2 teaspoons crushed
  oregano
1 teaspoon crushed basil

Rinse mushrooms. Place in saucepan; cover with vinegar.
Bring to a boil; remove from heat. Add garlic, parsley, salt,
oil, oregano and basil, stirring to mix. Marinate, covered,
in refrigerator for several hours.

Rosemary Hansen
California State Grange Executive Committee

Approx Per
Serving:
Cal 542
Prot 3 g
Carbo 20 g
Fiber 2 g
T Fat 55 g
84% Calories
from Fat
Chol 0 mg
Sod 1073 mg

FREEZER NO-COOK PICKLES

Yield:
10 servings
Utensil:
bowl

7 cups thinly sliced
  scored cucumbers
1 cup finely chopped
  onion
1/2 cup chopped green or
  red bell pepper

2 cups sugar
1/2 teaspoon celery seed
1 teaspoon canning salt
1 cup vinegar

Combine cucumbers, onion, bell pepper, sugar, celery
seed, canning salt and vinegar in large bowl; mix well.
Pack into freezer containers leaving 1 inch headspace.
Store in freezer until needed. May use juice from pickles
for preparing pickled carrots, cauliflower, onions or three-
bean salad.

Rosetta M. Krause, Mt. Hamilton #469

Approx Per
Serving:
Cal 191
Prot 1 g
Carbo 49 g
Fiber 3 g
T Fat <1 g
1% Calories
from Fat
Chol 0 mg
Sod 219 mg

ZUCCHINI RELISH

Yield:
96 ounces
Utensil:
saucepan

Approx Per Ounce:
Cal 51
Prot 1 g
Carbo 13 g
Fiber 1 g
T Fat <1 g
2% Calories from Fat
Chol 0 mg
Sod 334 mg

10 cups ground peeled zucchini
5 cups ground onion
5 tablespoons salt
5 cups sugar
2½ cups vinegar
1 teaspoon nutmeg
1 tablespoon dry mustard
2 teaspoons turmeric
1 tablespoon cornstarch

Combine zucchini and onion in large bowl. Sprinkle with salt. Add enough water to cover. Let stand overnight; drain. Combine sugar, vinegar, nutmeg, mustard, turmeric and cornstarch in small bowl, stirring to form paste. Stir into zucchini mixture. Spoon into saucepan. Simmer for 30 minutes. Spoon into hot sterilized jars; seal with 2-piece lids. Delicious used in potato salad.

Myra Eberspecher, Anderson #418

HOMEMADE BAKING POWDER

Yield:
16 ounces
Utensil:
bowl

Approx Per Ounce:
Cal 36
Prot <1 g
Carbo 9 g
Fiber <1 g
T Fat <1 g
1% Calories from Fat
Chol 0 mg
Sod 1940 mg

8 ounces cream of tartar
4 ounces cornstarch
4 ounces baking soda

Combine all ingredients in bowl. Sift together three times. Store in covered container until needed. Sift with flour before adding to other ingredients.

June Fredrickson, Freshwater #499

SOUPS & STEWS

ALBONDIGA SOUP

Yield:
16 servings
Utensil:
stockpot

Approx Per Serving:
Cal 157
Prot 10 g
Carbo 15 g
Fiber 2 g
T Fat 6 g
35% Calories from Fat
Chol 29 mg
Sod 305 mg

1 pound lean ground beef
1 pound turkey sausage
1/2 cup uncooked rice
1 onion, finely chopped
1 teaspoon salt
1/2 teaspoon pepper
4 quarts water
3 to 4 stalks celery, cut into 1/2-inch slices
1 16-ounce can tomatoes, chopped
1 16-ounce package frozen mixed vegetables
1/2 cup uncooked rice

Combine ground beef and turkey sausage in bowl. Stir in 1/2 cup uncooked rice, half the onion, salt and pepper. Shape into 1 1/2-inch balls. Bring water to a boil in large stockpot. Add meatballs, celery and tomatoes. Simmer for 45 minutes or until meatballs are cooked through. Add mixed vegetables and 1/2 cup rice. Cook for 45 minutes longer or until vegetables and rice are tender. May serve with garlic bread or breadsticks.

Eloise Knight Sharp, Apple Valley #593

BROCCOLI CHOWDER

Yield:
8 servings
Utensil:
saucepan

Approx Per
Serving:
Cal 357
Prot 18 g
Carbo 8 g
Fiber 1 g
T Fat 29 g
72% Calories
from Fat
Chol 93 mg
Sod 678 mg

2 10-ounce cans chicken broth
1 bunch broccoli, trimmed, cut up
1 cup milk
2 cups half and half
2 cups shredded Swiss cheese
1/2 cup butter
1 cup chopped cooked ham

Combine chicken broth and broccoli in large saucepan. Bring to a boil. Simmer, covered, for 10 to 15 minutes or until broccoli is tender. Remove broccoli with slotted spoon; cool. Add milk, half and half, Swiss cheese, butter and ham to broth. Chop broccoli. Add to broth. Simmer, covered, for 10 minutes. Serve with hot sourdough bread.

Jan Hartz, CSG Staff-Production Manager
L.A. Metro #826

CHICKEN-VEGGIE SOUP

Yield:
8 servings
Utensil:
stockpot

Approx Per
Serving:
Cal 235
Prot 27 g
Carbo 17 g
Fiber 2 g
T Fat 7 g
26% Calories
from Fat
Chol 76 mg
Sod 731 mg

1 3-pound chicken, skinned, cut up
3 chicken bouillon cubes
3 large carrots, sliced
2 large potatoes, cubed
2 stalks celery, sliced
1 medium zucchini, cubed
1 large onion, sliced
2 cloves of garlic, minced
1 8-ounce can whole kernel corn
1 teaspoon poultry seasoning
1 teaspoon parsley flakes
1/2 teaspoon thyme
1/2 teaspoon sage
1 bay leaf
1/2 teaspoon salt
1/2 teaspoon pepper

Rinse chicken. Place in stockpot with enough water to cover. Cook over medium heat until tender. Remove chicken; cool. Shred chicken, discarding bones. Return to stockpot. Add bouillon cubes, carrots, potatoes, celery, zucchini, onion, garlic and corn. Season with poultry seasoning, parsley, thyme, sage, bay leaf, salt and pepper. Add 2 cups additional water. Bring to a boil; reduce heat. Simmer for 45 minutes or until vegetables are tender. Remove bay leaf before serving.

Pauline Stinnett, North Shore #822

LENTIL SOUP

⌛

Yield:
8 servings
Utensil:
slow cooker

Approx Per Serving:
Cal 249
Prot 20 g
Carbo 35 g
Fiber 7 g
T Fat 4 g
13% Calories from Fat
Chol 11 mg
Sod 217 mg

1   16-ounce package lentils
¾ cup dried mixed carrots, peas and oats
3 to 4 cloves of garlic, minced
6 to 8 cups water
2 ham hocks

Rinse lentils and drain. Place in slow cooker with dried vegetables, garlic and 4 cups water. Add ham hocks, stirring to mix. Add enough remaining water to cover. Cook, covered, on High for 4 to 6 hours or until ham begins to fall off the bone. Remove ham hocks, discarding fat and bone. Stir ham into mixture. Cook, covered, on Medium for an additional 2 hours.

Ruby L. Tait, Costa Mesa #612

LINDA'S TWENTY-MINUTE MINESTRONE

⌛

Yield:
6 servings
Utensil:
saucepan

Approx Per Serving:
Cal 128
Prot 7 g
Carbo 25 g
Fiber 7 g
T Fat 1 g
5% Calories from Fat
Chol 4 mg
Sod 1066 mg

2   14-ounce cans beef broth
1   15-ounce can kidney beans, drained
1 cup frozen mixed vegetables
½ small onion, chopped
½ cup uncooked noodles
1 teaspoon basil
1 teaspoon coarsely ground pepper
1   8-ounce can Italian-style zucchini
1   14-ounce can Italian stewed tomatoes

Combine beef broth, kidney beans, mixed vegetables, onion, noodles, basil and pepper in 3-quart saucepan. Bring to a boil; reduce heat. Simmer, covered, for 10 minutes. Add zucchini and tomatoes. Simmer, covered, for 7 to 10 minutes longer. Serve with warm bread.

Margaret Daley, Wyandotte #495

Minestrone Soup

Yield:
8 servings
Utensil:
saucepan

Approx Per
Serving:
Cal 100
Prot 5 g
Carbo 14 g
Fiber 2 g
T Fat 3 g
27% Calories
from Fat
Chol 3 mg
Sod 685 mg

3 slices bacon, chopped
1 cup chopped onion
1/2 cup chopped celery
2 cloves of garlic, minced
1 teaspoon basil
1 14-ounce can beef broth
1 10-ounce can bean
   and bacon soup
1 1/2 soup cans water
1 16-ounce can tomatoes
1/2 cup uncooked small
   macaroni
1/2 teaspoon salt
1 cup shredded cabbage
1 cup cubed zucchini

Sauté bacon, onion, celery, garlic and basil in saucepan until tender. Add broth, soup, water, undrained tomatoes, macaroni and salt. Simmer for 20 minutes, stirring occasionally. Add cabbage and zucchini. Simmer for 30 minutes longer or until zucchini is tender. Ladle into serving bowls. Garnish with Parmesan cheese.

Linda Rasmusson, Palermo #493

Potato Soup

Yield:
6 servings
Utensil:
saucepan

Approx Per
Serving:
Cal 238
Prot 6 g
Carbo 28 g
Fiber 2 g
T Fat 12 g
44% Calories
from Fat
Chol 37 mg
Sod 647 mg

4 cups cubed potatoes
2 medium onions, sliced
3/4 cup water
1 teaspoon salt
1/2 teaspoon garlic salt
1/2 teaspoon oregano
1/4 teaspoon pepper
3 cups milk
1/4 cup butter

Combine potatoes, onions, water, salt, garlic salt, oregano and pepper in saucepan; cover. Bring to a boil; reduce heat. Simmer for 20 minutes or until potatoes are tender. Mash potatoes slightly. Stir in milk and butter. Simmer until heated through. Ladle into serving bowls.

Joy Beatie, State Women's Activities Director

SUPER TACO SOUP

Yield:
8 servings
Utensil:
saucepan

Approx Per
Serving:
Cal 184
Prot 11 g
Carbo 26 g
Fiber 6 g
T Fat 5 g
24% Calories
from Fat
Chol 19 mg
Sod 862 mg

8 ounces ground beef
1/2 cup chopped onion
1 1/2 tablespoons flour
2 cups water
1   17-ounce can whole
    kernel corn, drained
1   16-ounce can kidney
    beans
1   16-ounce can tomatoes

2 tablespoons taco
    seasoning
1 tablespoon mild taco
    sauce
1 teaspoon seasoned salt
1/4 teaspoon garlic
    powder
Salt to taste

Brown ground beef and onion in skillet, stirring frequently; drain. Add flour, stirring until dissolved. Add water. Pour into large saucepan. Add corn, beans, tomatoes, taco seasoning, taco sauce, seasoned salt, garlic powder and salt. Bring to a boil; reduce heat. Simmer for 20 minutes, stirring occasionally. Ladle into serving bowls. Garnish with shredded Cheddar cheese, sliced green onions, crushed tortilla chips and sour cream.

Mary Thornton, Hornbrook #391

TOMATO SOUP

Yield:
6 servings
Utensil:
saucepan

Approx Per
Serving:
Cal 203
Prot 8 g
Carbo 37 g
Fiber 2 g
T Fat 3 g
13% Calories
from Fat
Chol 7 mg
Sod 329 mg

1   8-ounce package shell
    macaroni
1   10-ounce can tomato
    soup

1 cup plus 2 tablespoons
    milk

Cook macaroni using package directions; drain. Combine with soup and milk in saucepan. Simmer for 5 to 10 minutes or until heated through. Serve immediately.

Sara Sarazen, Oakdale #435

BURGUNDY-BEEF STEW

Yield:
6 servings
Utensil:
saucepan

*Approx Per
Serving:*
Cal 310
Prot 25 g
Carbo 32 g
Fiber 4 g
T Fat 8 g
*23% Calories
from Fat*
Chol 64 mg
Sod 718 mg

1 10-ounce can tomato
  soup
1 10-ounce can beef
  broth
1/2 cup red Burgundy
1 tablespoon flour
1/2 teaspoon salt
Pepper to taste

1/2 teaspoon basil
1 1/2 pounds beef stew
  meat
4 medium potatoes,
  peeled, cut into halves
4 medium carrots, cut
  into quarters
1 large onion, sliced

Combine tomato soup, beef broth and wine in large saucepan. Stir in flour, salt, pepper and basil. Add stew meat, potatoes, carrots and onion; mix well. Simmer, covered, for 1 1/2 hours, stirring occasionally. May be frozen for later use.

Thelma Hylton, Anderson #418

FOUR-HOUR OVEN STEW

Yield:
6 servings
Utensil:
Dutch oven

*Approx Per
Serving:*
Cal 389
Prot 33 g
Carbo 39 g
Fiber 6 g
T Fat 10 g
*23% Calories
from Fat*
Chol 85 mg
Sod 679 mg

1 onion
3 potatoes, peeled
6 carrots, peeled
2 pounds 2-inch beef
  cubes
1/2 green bell pepper, cut
  into chunks
2 cups sliced fresh
  mushrooms

1/4 cup quick-cooking
  tapioca
1/4 cup dry bread crumbs
1 teaspoon salt
1/4 teaspoon pepper
1 28-ounce can tomatoes
3/4 cup dry red wine

Cut onion and potatoes into fourths and carrots into halves. Combine with beef cubes, green pepper and mushrooms in 5-quart Dutch oven. Sprinkle with tapioca, bread crumbs, salt and pepper. Add undrained tomatoes and wine; mix well. Bake, tightly covered, at 300 degrees for 4 hours. Do not uncover while cooking. Serve with green salad and hot rolls. May omit potatoes and serve over rice.

Rosemarie E. Garner, Durham #460

CHAMPIONSHIP TEXAS CHILI

Yield:
12 servings
Utensil:
stockpot

Approx Per
Serving:
Cal 239
Prot 30 g
Carbo 7 g
Fiber 3 g
T Fat 10 g
37% Calories
from Fat
Chol 85 mg
Sod 953 mg

4 pounds beef chuck, cut
  into 1/2-inch cubes
1 1/3 cups beef broth
1   12-ounce can tomato
  sauce
2 1/2 medium onions,
  chopped
2 1/2 tablespoons cumin
1 tablespoon paprika

1 tablespoon salt
3 tablespoons garlic
  powder
1/2 cup chili powder
1 cup chicken broth
1 teaspoon oregano
1 teaspoon cayenne
  pepper
1 teaspoon white pepper

Brown beef cubes in skillet; drain. Combine with beef broth, tomato sauce and onions in stockpot. Cook until onions are tender. Add cumin, paprika, salt, garlic powder, chili powder, chicken broth, oregano, cayenne pepper and white pepper; mix well. Simmer over medium heat for 3 hours, stirring occasionally. May also add 4 cloves of garlic and 1 1/2 cups chopped celery. I have won many chili cook-offs with this recipe.

Vera Woodard-Snyder, Ostrom #751

CREOLE CHILI

Yield:
8 servings
Utensil:
skillet

Approx Per
Serving:
Cal 284
Prot 19 g
Carbo 27 g
Fiber 11 g
T Fat 12 g
38% Calories
from Fat
Chol 37 mg
Sod 1038 mg

1/4 cup chopped onion
2 tablespoons oil
1 pound ground chuck
2   16-ounce cans kidney
  beans, drained
2   16-ounce cans
  tomatoes
1   6-ounce can tomato
  paste
1 1/2 teaspoons salt

2 to 3 teaspoons chili
  powder
1/2 teaspoon oregano
1/2 teaspoon pepper
1 bay leaf
1 1/2 cups water
1 cup chopped celery
1 cup chopped green
  bell pepper
Tabasco sauce to taste

Sauté onion in oil in large skillet until tender. Add ground chuck. Cook until browned and crumbly, stirring often. Add kidney beans, tomatoes, tomato paste, salt, chili powder, oregano, pepper, bay leaf, water, half the celery and half the green pepper. Simmer for 1 hour, stirring occasionally. Stir in Tabasco sauce and remaining celery and green pepper. Simmer for 10 minutes longer. Remove bay leaf before serving.

Marjorie Long, Montgomery #442

HUNTER'S STEW

Yield:
8 servings
Utensil:
Dutch oven

Approx Per
Serving:
Cal 502
Prot 26 g
Carbo 50 g
Fiber 7 g
T Fat 25 g
42% Calories
from Fat
Chol 46 mg
Sod 2818 mg

1 pound ham, chopped
1 pound bacon, chopped
1 large onion, chopped
3 16-ounce cans
  prepared spaghetti
  with sauce
1 17-ounce can cream-
  style corn
1 32-ounce can
  tomatoes, sliced
2 8-ounce cans tomato
  hot sauce
1 6-ounce can sliced
  mushrooms
1 6-ounce can pitted
  black olives
Salt and pepper to taste

Sauté ham, bacon and onion in Dutch oven until bacon is crisp and onion is tender; drain. Stir in spaghetti, corn, tomatoes, hot sauce, mushrooms, olives, salt and pepper. Bake at 350 degrees for 3 hours, stirring occasionally.

Ruth N. Toreson, Centerville #797

ONE-STOP DINNER

Yield:
12 servings
Utensil:
saucepan

Approx Per
Serving:
Cal 329
Prot 21 g
Carbo 44 g
Fiber 12 g
T Fat 9 g
24% Calories
from Fat
Chol 37 mg
Sod 507 mg

1½ pounds ground beef
¼ cup chopped onion
1 gallon water
4 beef bouillon cubes
1 tablespoon taco
  seasoning
1 tablespoon oregano
¼ teaspoon salt
½ teaspoon pepper
1½ cups chopped celery
5 potatoes, peeled,
  chopped
7 large carrots, chopped
2 large bunches broccoli,
  chopped
3 cups whole kernel corn
4 cups chopped tomatoes
4 cups kidney beans
1 cup cut green beans

Brown ground beef in large saucepan, stirring until crumbly; drain. Add onion, water, bouillon cubes, taco seasoning, oregano, salt and pepper; mix well. Bring to a boil over medium-low heat. Add celery, potatoes, carrots, broccoli, corn, tomatoes and beans; mix well. Add additional water if necessary to cover completely. Cook for 30 to 40 minutes or until vegetables are tender. Garnish servings with shredded cheese. Serve with French bread or corn bread.

Terry Stuart, Feather River #440

VEGETABLES

BAKED BEANS

Yield:
16 servings
Utensil:
baking dish

**Approx Per
Serving:**
*Cal 209
Prot 8 g
Carbo 38 g
Fiber 6 g
T Fat 4 g
16% Calories
from Fat
Chol 11 mg
Sod 515 mg*

4   16-ounce cans pork
   and beans
8 ounces bacon, cut into
   1-inch pieces
1 medium onion,
   chopped
³/₄ cup packed brown
   sugar
¹/₄ cup catsup
4 cloves of garlic, chopped
4 teaspoons prepared
   mustard

Combine pork and beans, bacon and onion in bowl. Add brown sugar, catsup, garlic and mustard; mix well. Spoon into 9x13-inch baking dish. Bake at 325 degrees for 2 hours, stirring once.

Sam Raygor, Rincon Valley #710

IAMMA'S BAKED BEANS

Yield:
12 servings
Utensil:
baking dish

Approx Per
Serving:
Cal 312
Prot 11 g
Carbo 56 g
Fiber 10 g
T Fat 6 g
17% Calories
from Fat
Chol 17 mg
Sod 807 mg

6 slices bacon, chopped
1 onion, chopped
1   28-ounce can pork
    and beans
1   16-ounce can kidney
    beans, drained
1   16-ounce can lima
    beans, drained

1 cup packed brown
    sugar
1 cup catsup
2 teaspoons
    Worcestershire sauce
4 ounces Cheddar
    cheese, cubed

Fry bacon in skillet until crisp; remove with slotted spoon, reserving drippings. Add onion to drippings in skillet. Sauté until tender. Combine with pork and beans, kidney beans, lima beans, brown sugar, catsup and Worcestershire sauce in bowl; mix well. Stir in cheese and bacon. Spoon into baking dish. Bake at 325 degrees until bubbly.

Harriet J. Bettinger, Brownsville #708

GRANDMA'S BOSTON BAKED BEANS

Yield:
8 servings
Utensil:
beanpot

Approx Per
Serving:
Cal 375
Prot 14 g
Carbo 71 g
Fiber 1 g
T Fat 5 g
11% Calories
from Fat
Chol 7 mg
Sod 448 mg

2 cups dried navy beans
1 teaspoon salt
8 ounces salt pork
1 cup (scant) brown
    sugar

1/2 cup dark molasses
1 teaspoon prepared
    mustard

Combine beans with water to cover by 3 inches and 1 teaspoon salt in saucepan. Soak overnight. Simmer in same water just until skins on a spoonful of beans will curl when blown upon; drain. Combine with salt pork, brown sugar, molasses and mustard in beanpot; mix well. Bake at 250 degrees for 6 to 8 hours, adding water when beans become dry. May substitute 2 ham hocks for salt pork or dry mustard for prepared mustard.

Marian Harris, Meadow Vista #721

CHILI BEANS

Yield:
12 servings
Utensil:
saucepan

Approx Per
Serving:
Cal 343
Prot 24 g
Carbo 32 g
Fiber 14 g
T Fat 14 g
36% Calories
from Fat
Chol 49 mg
Sod 113 mg

1 large green bell
 pepper, chopped
2 large red bell peppers,
 chopped
2 tablespoons oil
1 large onion, chopped
2 stalks celery, chopped
1 clove of garlic, minced
2 pounds ground beef

1 tablespoon chili
 powder
1 teaspoon cilantro
1/2 teaspoon cumin
1/2 teaspoon seasoned
 salt
Salt to taste
1/2 teaspoon pepper
8 cups cooked pinto beans

Sauté bell peppers in oil in large saucepan for 5 minutes. Add onion, celery and garlic. Sauté for 5 minutes or until tender. Brown ground beef in skillet, stirring until crumbly; drain. Add to saucepan with chili powder; mix well. Cook for 10 minutes. Stir in cilantro, cumin, seasoned salt, salt and pepper. Add beans; mix well. Simmer, covered, for 1 hour. Simmer, uncovered, for 30 minutes longer.

Bob Grogan, Estrella #488

GLEN'S SLOW-COOKER BEANS

Yield:
12 servings
Utensil:
slow cooker

Approx Per
Serving:
Cal 188
Prot 13 g
Carbo 27 g
Fiber 8 g
T Fat 4 g
18% Calories
from Fat
Chol 13 mg
Sod 791 mg

12 ounces dried beans
4 cups chicken stock
1   16-ounce can tomato
 sauce
2 cloves of garlic, crushed
2 teaspoons cider vinegar
2 tablespoons
 Worcestershire sauce
1 teaspoon Tabasco sauce
1/2 teaspoon cumin
1/2 teaspoon celery seed
1 tablespoon oregano

3 tablespoons chili powder
2 bay leaves
1/4 teaspoon cayenne
 pepper
8 ounces ground beef
1 large onion, chopped
1 green bell pepper,
 chopped
1   16-ounce can
 tomatoes, chopped
2 tablespoons brown sugar
1 teaspoon salt

Measure beans. Combine with water equal to 3 times the measurement of beans in bowl. Soak for 1 hour. Combine with next 12 ingredients in saucepan. Boil mixture for 1 hour. Brown ground beef with onion and green pepper in skillet, stirring frequently; drain. Combine bean mixture and ground beef mixture in slow cooker. Add tomatoes, brown sugar and salt. Cook on High for 12 hours. Discard bay leaves. Serve with French bread or corn bread.

Lucille Poteet, Los Banos #79

MICHIGAN BEAN BAKE

Yield:
12 servings
Utensil:
baking dish

1½ pounds lean pork
1   48-ounce jar Great
    Northern beans
1   14-ounce bottle of
    catsup
½ large onion, chopped

3 tablespoons prepared
    mustard
1½ cups packed brown
    sugar
½ teaspoon salt

Approx Per
Serving:
Cal 394
Prot 15 g
Carbo 66 g
Fiber 1 g
T Fat 9 g
20% Calories
from Fat
Chol 14 mg
Sod 1277 mg

Cut pork into 1-inch cubes. Combine with beans, catsup, onion, mustard, brown sugar and salt in bowl; mix gently. Spoon into 9x13-inch baking dish. Bake at 300 degrees for 5 to 6 hours or until of desired consistency, covering during last hour of cooking time. May cook on Low in slow cooker overnight.

Charlotte Harrell, Montgomery #442

ZESTY RED BEANS

Yield:
3 servings
Utensil:
saucepan

1   16-ounce can red
    beans, drained
2 tablespoons margarine

1 green onion, chopped
1 teaspoon dillweed
¼ teaspoon salt

Combine beans, margarine, green onion, dillweed and salt in 2-quart saucepan; mix well. Simmer until heated through. This makes a good relish.

Evelyne Hall Adams, Vista #609

Approx Per
Serving:
Cal 192
Prot 8 g
Carbo 23 g
Fiber 11 g
T Fat 8 g
37% Calories
from Fat
Chol 0 mg
Sod 792 mg

TIN CAN CASSEROLE

Yield:
6 servings
Utensil:
baking dish

Approx Per
Serving:
Cal 201
Prot 6 g
Carbo 27 g
Fiber 4 g
T Fat 9 g
39% Calories
from Fat
Chol 7 mg
Sod 1310 mg

1 29- ounce can French-style green beans, drained
1 8-ounce can sliced water chestnuts, drained
1 4-ounce can sliced mushrooms, drained
1 10-ounce can cream of celery soup
1 10-ounce can cream of mushroom soup
1 3-ounce can chow mein noodles

Combine green beans, water chestnuts, mushrooms and soups in bowl; mix well. Mix in noodles gently. Spoon into 2-quart baking dish. Bake at 350 degrees for 30 minutes.

Sylvia DeMello, Wyandotte #495

BROCCOLI CASSEROLE

Yield:
8 servings
Utensil:
baking dish

Approx Per
Serving:
Cal 421
Prot 10 g
Carbo 17 g
Fiber 2 g
T Fat 37 g
76% Calories
from Fat
Chol 101 mg
Sod 1230 mg

2 10-ounce packages frozen chopped broccoli
2 eggs, beaten
1 cup mayonnaise
1 10-ounce can cream of celery soup
1 5-ounce can evaporated milk
1 tablespoon minced onion
1 cup shredded sharp Cheddar cheese
Garlic powder to taste
1 teaspoon MSG
1 cup butter cracker crumbs
2 tablespoons butter

Cook broccoli using package directions; drain. Add eggs, mayonnaise, soup, evaporated milk, onion, cheese, garlic powder and MSG; mix well. Spoon into 2-quart baking dish. Sprinkle with cracker crumbs; dot with butter. Bake at 350 degrees for 30 to 45 minutes or until heated through.

Lisa Giustini, Sacramento #12

Microwave Broccoli Casserole

Yield:
4 servings
Utensil:
glass dish

Approx Per Serving:
Cal 320
Prot 6 g
Carbo 5 g
Fiber 3 g
T Fat 33 g
93% Calories from Fat
Chol 93 mg
Sod 557 mg

6 ounces cream cheese
6 tablespoons butter
1 10-package frozen chopped broccoli
1/2 teaspoon salt

Combine cream cheese and butter in small bowl. Microwave on Low for 3 minutes or until melted; mix gently. Place broccoli in 1-quart glass dish. Microwave, covered, on High for 5 minutes; drain. Add cream cheese mixture and salt; mix gently. Microwave, covered, on High for 3 minutes. Let stand for 2 minutes before serving.

Roma Gardiner, Palermo #493

Broccoli and Cauliflower Ring

Yield:
8 servings
Utensil:
bundt pan

Approx Per Serving:
Cal 78
Prot 2 g
Carbo 5 g
Fiber 3 g
T Fat 6 g
63% Calories from Fat
Chol 16 mg
Sod 135 mg

1 small tomato
4 cups fresh broccoli flowerets
4 cups fresh cauliflowerets
1/4 cup water
1/4 cup butter
1 tablespoon lemon juice
1/4 teaspoon salt
1/8 teaspoon pepper

Cut tomato into 6 wedges. Arrange skin side down in 9-cup microwave-safe bundt pan. Combine broccoli and cauliflower in 3-quart glass dish; sprinkle with water. Microwave, covered, on High for 9 to 13 minutes or until tender-crisp, stirring halfway through cooking time; drain well. Arrange in prepared bundt pan, pressing to pack firmly. Microwave butter on High in 1-cup glass measure for 45 to 60 seconds or until melted. Stir in lemon juice, salt and pepper. Pour over vegetables. Microwave on High for 3 minutes, turning dish 1/2 turn every 30 seconds. Invert onto serving plate.

Mary R. Buffington, National Grange Lecturer

Broccoli and Corn Casserole

1 10-ounce package frozen cut broccoli, thawed, drained
1 16-ounce can cream-style corn
1 egg, beaten
1 envelope onion soup mix
1/2 teaspoon pepper
1/4 cup cracker crumbs
2 tablespoons melted butter

Combine broccoli, corn, egg, soup mix and pepper in bowl; mix well. Spoon into buttered 1-quart baking dish. Top with mixture of cracker crumbs and melted butter. Bake, covered, at 350 degrees for 40 minutes or until heated through.

Lois Galli, Orchard City #333

Broccoli and Rice Casserole

1 cup uncooked quick-cooking rice
2 10-ounce packages frozen chopped broccoli, cooked, drained
1/2 small onion, chopped
1/2 cup milk
2 tablespoons melted butter
1 10-ounce can cream of chicken soup
1 8-ounce jar Cheez Whiz
1 teaspoon salt

Combine rice, broccoli, onion, milk, butter, soup, Cheez Whiz and salt in bowl; mix well. Spoon into 9x13-inch baking dish. Bake at 350 degrees until casserole is heated through and rice is tender.

Margaret Davison, Marshall #451

BROCCOLI SOUFFLÉ

Yield:
6 servings
Utensil:
baking dish

Approx Per Serving:
Cal 523
Prot 12 g
Carbo 20 g
Fiber 5 g
T Fat 47 g
76% Calories from Fat
Chol 88 mg
Sod 868 mg

2 16-ounce packages frozen chopped broccoli
1 10-ounce can cream of mushroom soup
1 cup mayonnaise
1 small onion, minced
1 cup shredded Cheddar cheese
1 egg, beaten
16 butter crackers, crushed
2 tablespoons butter

Cook broccoli using package directions; drain. Add soup, mayonnaise, onion, cheese and egg; mix well. Spoon into 2-quart baking dish. Sprinkle with cracker crumbs; dot with butter. Bake at 350 degrees for 45 minutes.

Betty Ferriera, Hollister #578

MANDARIN CAULIFLOWER AND BROCCOLI

Yield:
4 servings
Utensil:
wok

Approx Per Serving:
Cal 110
Prot 3 g
Carbo 11 g
Fiber 3 g
T Fat 7 g
55% Calories from Fat
Chol 0 mg
Sod 283 mg

2 tablespoons oil
1/2 teaspoon salt
10 small mushrooms, sliced
1 small onion, minced
1 cup water
1 1/2 cups coarsely chopped cauliflower
1 1/2 cups coarsely chopped broccoli
1/2 cup water
2 teaspoons sugar
2 teaspoons cornstarch
1 tablespoon water

Heat oil with salt in wok or skillet. Add mushrooms and onion. Stir-fry for 2 minutes or until tender. Add 1 cup water. Bring to a boil. Add cauliflower. Steam, covered, for 5 minutes. Add broccoli. Steam, covered, for 10 minutes, stirring occasionally. Add 1/2 cup water and sugar. Bring to a simmer. Stir in mixture of cornstarch and 1 tablespoon water. Cook until thickened, stirring constantly.

Lois R. McCutcheon, Palermo #493

Green Chili Casserole

2 7-ounce cans green
   chilies, seeded
2 cups shredded
   Cheddar cheese
1 cup baking mix
3 eggs, beaten
3 cups milk
1 teaspoon salt

Arrange chilies in buttered 9x13-inch baking dish; sprinkle with cheese. Combine baking mix, eggs, milk and salt in bowl; mix well. Spoon over cheese. Bake at 350 degrees for 45 minutes.

Mary N. Davis, Tulare #198

Corn Casserole

2 eggs, beaten
1 16-ounce can whole
   kernel corn
1 16-ounce can cream-
   style corn
1 medium onion, chopped
1 7-ounce package corn
   muffin mix
1/4 cup melted butter
1 cup shredded Cheddar
   cheese

Combine eggs, whole kernel corn, cream-style corn, onion, corn muffin mix and butter in bowl; mix well. Spoon into buttered 9x13-inch baking dish. Sprinkle with cheese. Bake at 400 degrees for 30 minutes.

Marie Streyle, Lompoc #646

SOUR CREAM-CORN CASSEROLE

Yield:
8 servings
Utensil:
baking dish

Approx Per Serving:
Cal 326
Prot 6 g
Carbo 32 g
Fiber 2 g
T Fat 21 g
55% Calories from Fat
Chol 66 mg
Sod 601 mg

1 16-ounce can whole kernel corn, drained
1 16-ounce can cream-style corn
2 eggs, slightly beaten
1 8-ounce package corn bread mix
1/2 cup melted margarine
1 cup sour cream

Combine whole kernel corn, cream-style corn, eggs, corn bread mix and margarine in bowl; mix well. Stir in sour cream. Spoon into greased 2-quart baking dish. Bake at 350 degrees for 1 hour.

June Thomson, Sonoma Valley #407

SCALLOPED EGGPLANT

V.I.P.

Yield:
4 servings
Utensil:
baking dish

Approx Per Serving:
Cal 416
Prot 17 g
Carbo 32 g
Fiber 9 g
T Fat 26 g
54% Calories from Fat
Chol 172 mg
Sod 601 mg

1 1/2 to 2 pounds eggplant, peeled, chopped
2 tablespoons chopped parsley
1 small onion, finely chopped
1 tablespoon butter
1/2 cup milk
2 eggs, beaten
1/2 cup bread crumbs
3 tablespoons melted butter
1/4 teaspoon paprika
1/4 teaspoon salt
1 cup shredded Cheddar cheese

Simmer eggplant in water in saucepan until tender; drain. Sprinkle with parsley. Sauté onion in 1 tablespoon butter in skillet. Add sautéed onion, milk and eggs to eggplant; mix gently. Toss bread crumbs with 3 tablespoons melted butter in bowl. Alternate layers of eggplant mixture, seasonings and bread crumbs in 9x9-inch baking dish until all ingredients are used. Top with cheese. Bake at 375 degrees for 30 minutes.

William R. Booth, Master, California State Grange

EGGPLANT CASSEROLE

Yield:
6 servings
Utensil:
baking dish

Approx Per
Serving:
Cal 120
Prot 3 g
Carbo 10 g
Fiber 2 g
T Fat 8 g
60% Calories
from Fat
Chol 56 mg
Sod 396 mg

1 medium eggplant,
  peeled
1 egg
1/2 cup milk
2/3 teaspoon salt
12 to 14 crackers,
  crumbled
3 tablespoons butter

Cut eggplant into 1 to 2-inch cubes. Cook in water to cover in saucepan for 2 minutes; drain. Beat egg with milk and salt in small bowl. Add to cooked eggplant; mix well. Sprinkle cracker crumbs in baking dish. Add eggplant mixture; mix lightly. Dot with butter. Bake at 325 degrees for 30 to 40 minutes or until set. May add chopped ham or bacon if desired.

Mildred H. Seale, Mt. Lassen #417

EGGPLANT AND RICOTTA CHEESE CASSEROLE

Yield:
6 servings
Utensil:
baking dish

Approx Per
Serving:
Cal 176
Prot 6 g
Carbo 13 g
Fiber 6 g
T Fat 12 g
58% Calories
from Fat
Chol 19 mg
Sod 491 mg

1 2-pound eggplant,
  peeled, chopped
1 teaspoon salt
1 1/2 cups canned
  tomatoes
3 tablespoons olive oil
1 cup water
Salt and pepper to taste
8 ounces ricotta cheese

Soak eggplant in water with 1 teaspoon salt in bowl for 5 minutes; drain well. Bring tomatoes, olive oil and water to a boil in saucepan. Add salt and pepper to taste. Stir in eggplant. Simmer for 30 minutes. Spoon into baking dish. Dollop ricotta cheese by teaspoonfuls over top. Bake at 350 degrees for 15 minutes. May add 1 pound browned ground beef or substitute sliced mozzarella cheese for ricotta cheese if desired.

Ellen F. Spoon, Mt. Lassen #417

EGGPLANT SURPRISE

Yield:
8 servings
Utensil:
baking dish

Approx Per
Serving:
Cal 417
Prot 20 g
Carbo 25 g
Fiber 2 g
T Fat 27 g
57% Calories
from Fat
Chol 118 mg
Sod 957 mg

1 eggplant, peeled, sliced
2 eggs, beaten
1 cup flour
Oil for frying
2 10-ounce cans cream
   of mushroom soup
1 cup milk
Italian seasoning to
   taste

2 cups shredded
   Cheddar cheese
2 cups shredded white
   Cheddar cheese
1 onion, chopped
1 green bell pepper,
   chopped
4 cloves of garlic,
   chopped

Dip eggplant in eggs; coat with flour. Fry in oil in skillet until brown on both sides; drain. Mix soup with milk and Italian seasoning in bowl. Layer soup mixture, eggplant, cheeses, onion, green pepper and garlic 1/2 at a time in baking dish. Bake at 350 degrees for 40 minutes. May add sausage, ground beef or olives if desired.

Nutritional information does not include oil for frying.

Joy MacGregor, Fort Bragg #672

EGGPLANT STUFFING

Yield:
8 servings
Utensil:
slow cooker

Approx Per
Serving:
Cal 118
Prot 5 g
Carbo 9 g
Fiber 2 g
T Fat 7 g
53% Calories
from Fat
Chol 69 mg
Sod 318 mg

1 large eggplant, peeled,
   chopped
1 small onion, chopped
1 3/4 cups seasoned
   croutons, crushed
2 teaspoons baking
   powder
2 eggs

2 tablespoons melted
   butter
2 tablespoons
   evaporated milk
Salt and pepper to taste
1/2 cup shredded
   American cheese

Cook eggplant in water to cover in saucepan for 8 minutes or until tender; drain. Add onion, crouton crumbs, baking powder, eggs, butter, evaporated milk, salt and pepper; mix well. Spoon into slow cooker. Sprinkle with cheese. Cook on Low for 6 hours or on High for 1 1/2 hours.

Sharon M. Maylone, Sierra Nevada #454

Broccoli and Cheese-Stuffed Baked Potatoes

Yield:
6 servings
Utensil:
baking sheet

Approx Per
Serving:
Cal 400
Prot 11 g
Carbo 55 g
Fiber 6 g
T Fat 16 g
36% Calories
from Fat
Chol 44 mg
Sod 373 mg

6 medium potatoes
1/2 cup sour cream
3 tablespoons butter
2 green onions, thinly
  sliced
1 1/2 cups cooked
  chopped broccoli
1/2 teaspoon salt
1/4 teaspoon pepper
1 cup shredded Cheddar
  cheese
Paprika to taste

Bake potatoes in 425-degree oven for 45 to 60 minutes or until tender. Cut lengthwise slice from each potato. Scoop pulp into bowl, reserving shells. Mash pulp until smooth. Add sour cream, butter, green onions, broccoli, salt, pepper and 3/4 cup cheese to potato pulp; mix well. Spoon into reserved shells; place on baking sheet. Top with remaining 1/4 cup cheese; sprinkle with paprika. Bake at 425 degrees for 20 to 25 minutes or until heated through.

Diane Bettinger, Wyandotte #495

Hashed Brown Potatoes

Yield:
8 servings
Utensil:
baking dish

Approx Per
Serving:
Cal 789
Prot 20 g
Carbo 45 g
Fiber 3 g
T Fat 61 g
70% Calories
from Fat
Chol 81 mg
Sod 932 mg

1 32-ounce package
   frozen hashed brown
   potatoes, partially
   thawed
1 10-ounce can cream
   of chicken soup
3/4 cup melted margarine
2 cups sour cream
1 small onion, chopped
14 ounces Cheddar
   cheese, shredded
1 cup crushed cornflakes

Combine potatoes, soup, margarine, sour cream, onion and cheese in bowl; mix well. Spoon into 9x13-inch baking dish. Top with cornflake crumbs. Bake at 350 degrees for 1 hour.

Readon M. Silva, Lompoc #646

OVEN-FRIED POTATOES

Yield:
6 servings
Utensil:
baking dish

Approx Per
Serving:
Cal 388
Prot 5 g
Carbo 51 g
Fiber 5 g
T Fat 19 g
43% Calories
from Fat
Chol 1 mg
Sod 225 mg

6 large baking potatoes
1/2 cup oil
2 tablespoons grated
   Parmesan cheese
1/2 teaspoon paprika

1/2 teaspoon garlic
   powder
1/2 teaspoon salt
1/4 teaspoon pepper

Scrub potatoes and cut into 4 to 8 wedges. Arrange skin side down in 9x13-inch baking dish. Combine oil, cheese, paprika, garlic powder, salt and pepper in small bowl; mix well. Brush over potatoes. Bake at 375 degrees for 45 minutes or until potatoes are tender and golden brown, brushing occasionally with butter mixture.

Dorthy Burns, Concow #735

SPINACH CASSEROLE

Yield:
8 servings
Utensil:
baking dish

Approx Per
Serving:
Cal 281
Prot 7 g
Carbo 17 g
Fiber 4 g
T Fat 22 g
67% Calories
from Fat
Chol 31 mg
Sod 380 mg

3 10-ounce packages
   frozen chopped
   spinach, thawed
8 ounces cream cheese,
   softened

1 8-ounce can water
   chestnuts, drained
1/2 cup margarine
3/4 cup Italian bread
   crumbs

Drain spinach well. Combine with cream cheese, water chestnuts and margarine in bowl; mix well. Spread evenly in 8x12-inch baking dish. Sprinkle with bread crumbs. Bake at 350 degrees for 30 minutes.

Katherine Hinkle, Wintersburg #583

HAWAIIAN SQUASH

Yield:
6 servings
Utensil:
saucepan

1   9-ounce can crushed
pineapple
3 cups chopped
Hubbard squash
1/2 cup margarine

2 tablespoons brown
sugar
1 teaspoon salt
1/4 teaspoon pepper

Drain pineapple, reserving juice. Cook squash in a small amount of water in saucepan until tender; drain. Mash with butter until smooth. Add pineapple, brown sugar, salt and pepper; beat until light and fluffy, adding a small amount of reserved pineapple juice if needed for desired consistency. Serve immediately.

Pearl Helmuth, Sanger #478

*Approx Per
Serving:*
Cal 199
Prot 1 g
Carbo 16 g
Fiber 1 g
T Fat 15 g
*67% Calories
from Fat*
Chol 0 mg
Sod 538 mg

DOROTHY'S HOT SQUASH CASSEROLE

Yield:
8 servings
Utensil:
baking dish

3 cups chopped yellow
squash
1 large green bell
pepper, chopped
1 large onion, chopped
1/4 cup oil
2 jalapeño peppers,
chopped

2   10-ounce cans cream
of mushroom soup
2 cups shredded
Cheddar cheese
2 cups cracker crumbs
6 tablespoons melted
butter

Sauté squash, green pepper and onion in oil in skillet until tender but not brown. Add jalapeño peppers. Spoon into buttered 5x9-inch baking dish. Spread with soup; sprinkle with cheese. Top with mixture of cracker crumbs and melted butter. Bake at 350 degrees for 45 minutes.

Ferne C. Jones, Hessel #750

*Approx Per
Serving:*
Cal 431
Prot 10 g
Carbo 26 g
Fiber 2 g
T Fat 32 g
*67% Calories
from Fat*
Chol 61 mg
Sod 1095 mg

SQUASH PATTIES

Yield:
4 servings
Utensil:
skillet

2 cups grated yellow
  squash
2 tablespoons finely
  chopped onion
2 teaspoons sugar

1/2 teaspoon salt
1/8 teaspoon pepper
6 tablespoons flour
2 eggs, beaten
2 tablespoons butter

Approx Per
Serving:
Cal 169
Prot 6 g
Carbo 17 g
Fiber 2 g
T Fat 9 g
46% Calories
from Fat
Chol 122 mg
Sod 353 mg

Combine squash, onion, sugar, salt and pepper in medium bowl; mix well. Let stand, covered, for 30 minutes; drain well. Add flour and eggs; mix well. Heat butter in large skillet over medium heat. Drop squash mixture by tablespoonfuls into butter. Cook until golden brown on both sides, turning once. May substitute zucchini squash for yellow squash.

Christine Chambers, Feather River #440

PORTUGUESE ZUCCHINI PANCAKE

Yield:
8 servings
Utensil:
electric skillet

2 pounds zucchini,
  coarsely chopped
1 large onion, chopped
1 green bell pepper,
  chopped
1 clove of garlic, minced
3 sprigs of parsley,
  chopped
1 stalk celery, chopped
5 tablespoons olive oil

1 8-ounce can tomato
  sauce
1 teaspoon basil
1 teaspoon oregano
Salt and pepper to taste
5 eggs
1/2 cup milk
1 cup shredded sharp
  Cheddar cheese

Approx Per
Serving:
Cal 226
Prot 10 g
Carbo 9 g
Fiber 2 g
T Fat 17 g
68% Calories
from Fat
Chol 150 mg
Sod 317 mg

Combine zucchini, onion, green pepper, garlic, parsley and celery with olive oil in electric skillet. Cook, covered, on Low until zucchini is tender-crisp. Add tomato sauce, basil, oregano, salt and pepper; mix well. Simmer until mixture is of desired consistency; mixture should not be soupy. Beat eggs and milk with fork in bowl. Pour over eggplant mixture. Cook, covered, on Low until eggs begin to set. Sprinkle with cheese. Cook until cheese melts.

Melba Penhall, Hornbrook #391

ZUCCHINI QUICHE

Yield:
6 servings
Utensil:
baking dish

Approx Per
Serving:
Cal 140
Prot 6 g
Carbo 9 g
Fiber 1 g
T Fat 9 g
59% Calories
from Fat
Chol 81 mg
Sod 269 mg

2 slices bread
1½ cups grated zucchini
¾ cup grated carrots
2 ounces Cheddar
  cheese, shredded
2 eggs
1 ounce onion, chopped
¼ teaspoon salt
⅛ teaspoon pepper
2 tablespoons melted
  margarine

Process bread in blender until crumbled. Combine half the crumbs with zucchini, carrots, cheese, eggs, onion, salt and pepper in bowl; mix well. Spoon into lightly greased 6x9-inch baking dish. Top with mixture of remaining bread crumbs and margarine. Bake at 325 degrees for 1 hour. Cut into squares. Serve hot or cold.

Adeline Blanke, Woodbridge #482

ZUCCHINI-CHILI CASSEROLE

Yield:
8 servings
Utensil:
baking dish

Approx Per
Serving:
Cal 391
Prot 21 g
Carbo 17 g
Fiber 2 g
T Fat 27 g
62% Calories
from Fat
Chol 177 mg
Sod 1101 mg

2 pounds zucchini,
  chopped
1 pound Monterey Jack
  cheese, cubed
4 eggs
½ cup milk
2 tablespoons flour
2 tablespoons baking
  powder
1 4-ounce can chopped
  green chilies
1 teaspoon salt
1 cup bread crumbs
¼ cup melted butter

Combine zucchini and cheese in bowl; mix well. Spoon into buttered 2-quart baking dish. Beat eggs in bowl. Add milk, flour, baking powder, green chilies and salt; mix well. Pour over zucchini mixture. Top with mixture of bread crumbs and melted butter. Bake at 350 degrees for 40 to 45 minutes or until set.

Jean Grogan, Estrella #488

ZUCCHINI-CORN CASSEROLE

Yield:
8 servings
Utensil:
baking dish

Approx Per Serving:
Cal 214
Prot 8 g
Carbo 19 g
Fiber 3 g
T Fat 13 g
51% Calories from Fat
Chol 85 mg
Sod 647 mg

1½ pounds small zucchini, chopped
1 large onion, chopped
¼ cup butter
1 16-ounce can cream-style corn
2 eggs, beaten
1½ cups soft bread cubes
Thyme to taste
1 teaspoon salt
⅛ teaspoon pepper
¾ cup shredded sharp Cheddar cheese
¼ cup cracker crumbs
¼ cup shredded sharp Cheddar cheese
Paprika to taste

Cook zucchini in a small amount of water in saucepan until tender-crisp; drain. Cool to room temperature. Sauté onion in butter in skillet. Add zucchini, corn, eggs, bread cubes, thyme, salt, pepper and ¾ cup cheese; mix well. Spoon into buttered 8x12-inch baking dish. Top with cracker crumbs, ¼ cup cheese and paprika. Bake at 350 degrees for 45 to 50 minutes or until knife inserted in center comes out clean.

Marguerite Kessy, Dos Palos #541

ZUCCHINI TORTE

Yield:
8 servings
Utensil:
baking dish

Approx Per Serving:
Cal 319
Prot 9 g
Carbo 21 g
Fiber 2 g
T Fat 22 g
62% Calories from Fat
Chol 137 mg
Sod 438 mg

5 eggs
4 cups grated zucchini
1½ cups baking mix
½ cup grated Parmesan cheese
1 small onion, grated
½ cup oil
Basil, parsley, salt and pepper to taste

Beat eggs in bowl. Combine zucchini, baking mix, cheese, onion, oil, basil, parsley, salt and pepper in bowl; mix well. Fold into eggs. Spoon into 9x13-inch baking dish. Bake at 350 degrees for 40 to 45 minutes or just until set; do not overbake. Add seasonings to suit individual taste.

Sarah Swanson, Region 4 GWA Director

GREEN AND GOLD CASSEROLE

Yield:
8 servings
Utensil:
baking dish

Approx Per Serving:
Cal 208
Prot 12 g
Carbo 20 g
Fiber 2 g
T Fat 10 g
42% Calories from Fat
Chol 76 mg
Sod 625 mg

1 pound zucchini, sliced
1 16-ounce can whole
   kernel corn, drained
2 tablespoons chopped
   green chilies
1½ cups cottage cheese
2 tablespoons sour cream
2 tablespoons flour

2 eggs
Tabasco sauce to taste
¾ teaspoon salt
½ cup shredded
   Cheddar cheese
½ cup bread crumbs
2 tablespoons melted
   butter

Cook zucchini in a small amount of water in saucepan until tender; drain. Add corn; mix well. Combine green chilies, cottage cheese, sour cream, flour, eggs, Tabasco sauce and salt in blender container; process until smooth. Fold into zucchini mixture. Spoon into 1-quart baking dish. Top with cheese and mixture of bread crumbs and butter. Bake at 350 degrees for 45 minutes.

Marie T. Haley, Mt. Lassen #417

GERMAN GREEN BEANS AND CABBAGE

Yield:
6 servings
Utensil:
saucepan

Approx Per Serving:
Cal 77
Prot 2 g
Carbo 15 g
Fiber 2 g
T Fat 2 g
18% Calories from Fat
Chol 3 mg
Sod 513 mg

3 slices bacon, chopped
½ cup vinegar
¼ cup sugar
3 tablespoons chopped
   onion

3 cups shredded cabbage
¾ teaspoon salt
¼ teaspoon pepper
1 16-ounce can green
   beans, drained

Fry bacon in saucepan until crisp; remove with slotted spoon. Add vinegar, sugar, onion, cabbage, salt and pepper to drippings in skillet. Simmer, covered, for 5 minutes. Add beans. Cook for 5 minutes. Spoon into serving dish. Top with crisp bacon.

E. Lucille Brinser, Centerville #797

SUPER VEGETABLES

Yield:
6 servings
Utensil:
saucepan

Approx Per Serving:
Cal 103
Prot 5 g
Carbo 9 g
Fiber 3 g
T Fat 6 g
49% Calories from Fat
Chol 10 mg
Sod 211 mg

8 ounces bacon, chopped
1 pound tiny carrots

¹/₂ medium head cabbage, chopped
1 cup water

Fry bacon partially in medium saucepan. Add carrots, cabbage and water. Cook just until vegetables are tender.

Emma Dudal, Dows Prairie #505

VEGETABLE MEDLEY

Yield:
6 servings
Utensil:
saucepan

Approx Per Serving:
Cal 29
Prot 1 g
Carbo 6 g
Fiber 2 g
T Fat <1 g
8% Calories from Fat
Chol 0 mg
Sod 19 mg

2 cups chopped zucchini
2 cups chopped tomatoes
²/₃ cup chopped onion
²/₃ cup chopped celery

²/₃ cup chopped green bell pepper
Garlic, salt and pepper to taste

Combine zucchini, tomatoes, onion, celery, green pepper, garlic, salt and pepper in saucepan. Simmer until vegetables are tender. May serve immediately, can or cool and freeze. May use other kinds of squash or a mixture. This is a good way to use an abundant garden harvest, keeping proportions of vegetables the same.

Edith West, Fort Bragg #672

Substitution Chart

	Instead of	Use
Baking	1 teaspoon baking powder	¼ teaspoon baking soda plus ½ teaspoon cream of tartar
	1 tablespoon cornstarch (for thickening)	2 tablespoons flour or 1 tablespoon tapioca
	1 cup sifted all-purpose flour	1 cup plus 2 tablespoons sifted cake flour
	1 cup sifted cake flour	1 cup minus 2 tablespoons sifted all-purpose flour
	1 cup dry bread crumbs	¾ cup cracker crumbs
Dairy	1 cup buttermilk	1 cup sour milk or 1 cup yogurt
	1 cup heavy cream	¾ cup skim milk plus ⅓ cup butter
	1 cup light cream	⅞ cup skim milk plus 3 tablespoons butter
	1 cup sour cream	⅞ cup sour milk plus 3 tablespoons butter
	1 cup sour milk	1 cup milk plus 1 tablespoon vinegar or lemon juice or 1 cup buttermilk
Seasoning	1 teaspoon allspice	½ teaspoon cinnamon plus ⅛ teaspoon cloves
	1 cup catsup	1 cup tomato sauce plus ½ cup sugar plus 2 tablespoons vinegar
	1 clove of garlic	⅛ teaspoon garlic powder or ⅛ teaspoon instant minced garlic or ¾ teaspoon garlic salt or 5 drops of liquid garlic
	1 teaspoon Italian spice	¼ teaspoon each oregano, basil, thyme, rosemary plus dash of cayenne pepper
	1 teaspoon lemon juice	½ teaspoon vinegar
	1 tablespoon mustard	1 teaspoon dry mustard
	1 medium onion	1 tablespoon dried minced onion or 1 teaspoon onion powder
Sweet	1 1-ounce square chocolate	¼ cup baking cocoa plus 1 teaspoon shortening
	1⅔ ounces semisweet chocolate	1 ounce unsweetened chocolate plus 4 teaspoons granulated sugar
	1 cup honey	1 to 1¼ cups sugar plus ¼ cup liquid or 1 cup corn syrup or molasses
	1 cup granulated sugar	1 cup packed brown sugar or 1 cup corn syrup, molasses or honey minus ¼ cup liquid

Equivalent Chart

	When the recipe calls for	Use
Baking	½ cup butter 2 cups butter 4 cups all-purpose flour 4½ to 5 cups sifted cake flour 1 square chocolate 1 cup semisweet chocolate chips 4 cups marshmallows 2¼ cups packed brown sugar 4 cups confectioners' sugar 2 cups granulated sugar	4 ounces 1 pound 1 pound 1 pound 1 ounce 6 ounces 1 pound 1 pound 1 pound 1 pound
Cereal – Bread	1 cup fine dry bread crumbs 1 cup soft bread crumbs 1 cup small bread cubes 1 cup fine cracker crumbs 1 cup fine graham cracker crumbs 1 cup vanilla wafer crumbs 1 cup crushed cornflakes 4 cups cooked macaroni 3½ cups cooked rice	4 to 5 slices 2 slices 2 slices 28 saltines 15 crackers 22 wafers 3 cups uncrushed 8 ounces uncooked 1 cup uncooked
Dairy	1 cup shredded cheese 1 cup cottage cheese 1 cup sour cream 1 cup whipped cream ⅔ cup evaporated milk 1⅔ cups evaporated milk	4 ounces 8 ounces 8 ounces ½ cup heavy cream 1 small can 1 13-ounce can

Fruit	4 cups sliced or chopped apples
	1 cup mashed bananas
	2 cups pitted cherries
	2½ cups shredded coconut
	4 cups cranberries
	1 cup pitted dates
	1 cup candied fruit
	3 to 4 tablespoons lemon juice plus
	  1 tablespoon grated lemon rind
	⅓ cup orange juice plus 2 teaspoons
	  grated orange rind
	4 cups sliced peaches
	2 cups pitted prunes
	3 cups raisins
		4 medium
		3 medium
		4 cups unpitted
		8 ounces
		1 pound
		1 8-ounce package
		1 8-ounce package
		1 lemon
		
		1 orange
		
		8 medium
		1 12-ounce package
		1 15-ounce package

When the recipe calls for	Use
Meats 4 cups chopped cooked chicken 3 cups chopped cooked meat 2 cups cooked ground meat	1 5-pound chicken 1 pound, cooked 1 pound, cooked
Nuts 1 cup chopped nuts	4 ounces shelled 1 pound unshelled
Vegetables 2 cups cooked green beans 2½ cups lima beans or red beans 4 cups shredded cabbage 1 cup grated carrot 8 ounces fresh mushrooms 1 cup chopped onion 4 cups sliced or chopped potatoes 2 cups canned tomatoes	½ pound fresh or 1 16-ounce can 1 cup dried, cooked 1 pound 1 large 1 4-ounce can 1 large 4 medium 1 16-ounce can

Measurement Equivalents

1 tablespoon = 3 teaspoons
2 tablespoons = 1 ounce
4 tablespoons = ¼ cup
5⅓ tablespoons = ⅓ cup
8 tablespoons = ½ cup
12 tablespoons = ¾ cup
16 tablespoons = 1 cup
1 cup = 8 ounces or ½ pint
4 cups = 1 quart
4 quarts = 1 gallon

1 6½ to 8-ounce can = 1 cup
1 10½ to 12-ounce can = 1¼ cups
1 14 to 16-ounce can = 1¾ cups
1 16 to 17-ounce can = 2 cups
1 18 to 20-ounce can = 2½ cups
1 29-ounce can = 3½ cups
1 46 to 51-ounce can = 5¾ cups
1 6½ to 7½-pound can or
   Number 10 = 12 to 13 cups

Metric Equivalents

Liquid

1 teaspoon   = 5 milliliters
1 tablespoon   = 15 milliliters
1 fluid ounce   = 30 milliliters
1 cup   = 250 milliliters
1 pint   = 500 milliliters

Dry

1 quart   = 1 liter
1 ounce   = 30 grams
1 pound   = 450 grams
2.2 pounds   = 1 kilogram

NOTE: The metric measures are approximate benchmarks for purposes of home food preparation.

Nutritional Guidelines

The editors have attempted to present these family recipes in a form that allows approximate nutritional values to be computed. Persons with dietary or health problems or whose diets require close monitoring should not rely solely on the nutritional information provided. They should consult their physicians or a registered dietitian for specific information.

Abbreviations for Nutritional Analysis

Cal — Calories
Prot — Protein
Carbo — Carbohydrates

Dietary Fiber — Fiber
T Fat — Total Fat
Chol — Cholesterol

Sod — Sodium
gr — gram
mg — milligrams

Nutritional information for these recipes is computed from information derived from many sources, including materials supplied by the United States Department of Agriculture, computer databanks and journals in which the information is assumed to be in the public domain. However, many specialty items, new products and processed foods may not be available from these sources or may vary from the average values used in these analyses. More information on new and/or specific products may be obtained by reading the nutrient labels. Unless otherwise specified, the nutritional analysis of these recipes is based on all measurements being level.

- **Artificial sweeteners** vary in use and strength so should be used "to taste," using the recipe ingredients as a guideline. Sweeteners using aspartame (NutraSweet and Equal) should not be used as a sweetener in recipes involving prolonged heating which reduces the sweet taste. For further information, refer to package information.
- **Alcoholic ingredients** have been analyzed for the basic ingredients, although cooking causes the evaporation of alcohol thus decreasing caloric content.
- **Buttermilk, sour cream** and **yogurt** are types available commercially.
- **Cake mixes** which are prepared using package directions include 3 eggs and ½ cup oil.
- **Chicken**, cooked for boning and chopping, has been roasted; this method yields the lowest caloric values.
- **Cottage cheese** is cream-style with 4.2% creaming mixture. Dry-curd cottage cheese has no creaming mixture.
- **Eggs** are all large. To avoid raw eggs that may carry salmonella as in eggnog or 6-week muffin batter, use an equivalent amount of commercial egg substitute.
- **Flour** is unsifted all-purpose flour.
- **Garnishes**, serving suggestions and other optional additions and variations are not included in the analysis.
- **Margarine** and **butter** are regular, not whipped or presoftened.
- **Milk** is whole milk, 3.5% butterfat. Lowfat milk is 1% butterfat. Evaporated milk is whole milk with 60% of the water removed.
- **Oil** is any type of vegetable cooking oil. Shortening is hydrogenated vegetable shortening.
- **Salt** and other ingredients to taste as noted in the ingredients have not been included in the nutritional analysis.
- If a choice of ingredients has been given, the nutritional analysis information reflects the first option. If a choice of amounts has been given, the nutritional analysis reflects the greater amount.

Index

ACCOMPANIMENTS
Carrot Marmalade, 182
Freezer No-Cook Pickles, 185
Microwave Strawberry-Peach Jam, 183
Molded Horseradish Soufflé, 184
Pickled Mushrooms, 185
Pineapple-Carrot Marmalade, 182
Rhubarb Marmalade, 183
Zucchini Relish, 186

APPETIZERS
Artichoke Dip, 7
Artichoke Squares, 10
Butter Dips, 10
Curried Cheese Yummies, 11
Ham and Cheese Ball, 12
Ham and Cheese Puffs, 12
Hot Cheese Dip, 8
Hummus, 9
Mexican Layered Dip, 9
Party Pizza Cups, 13
Spinach Balls, 13
Spinach Pinwheels, 14
Spinach Roll-Ups, 14
Stuffed Cheese Rolls, 11
The Haystack, 8
Zucchini Finger Food, 15

BEEF. *See also* Ground Beef; Stews
Barbecued Short Ribs, 113
Easy Beef Stroganoff, 115
Hawaiian Short Ribs, 114
One-Two-Three Baked Hash, 129
Prime Rib Roast, 112
Spanish Round Steak, 113
Sweet-and-Sour Beef, 115
Teriyaki Steak, 114

BEVERAGES
Fruit Punch, 15

BREADS
Apricot and Prune Coffee Cake, 21
Black Pepper Bread, 31
Blueberry Corn Bread, 26
Bran Muffins, 17
California Chili Bread, 32
Cheesy Garlic Biscuits, 16
Coffee Cake, 21
Crispy Cookie Coffee Cakes, 22
Crusty Irish Soda Bread, 33
Feather-Light Pancakes, 25
German Beer Coffee Cake, 22
Grandma's Gingerbread, 28
Grandmother Tooter's Doughnuts, 24
Haddon Hall Gingerbread, 27
Holiday French Toast, 25

Homemade Baking Powder, 186
Lemon Bread, 28
Lemon Sauce for Gingerbread, 27
Mother's Brown Bread, 26
No-Knead Whole Wheat Bread, 33
Orange Glaze, 19
Pineapple-Zucchini Bread, 31
Poppy Seed Bread, 29
Portuguese Easter Bread, 32
Prune Ambrosia Pinwheels, 19
Rhubarb-Strawberry Coffee Cake, 23
Sourdough Rolls, 20
Sourdough Starter, 20
Strawberry-Nut Bread, 29
Streusel-Filled Coffee Cake, 23
Sugar-Free Applesauce-Raisin Muffins, 17
Super Pecan-Caramel Rolls, 18
Wesson Oil Coffee Cake, 24
Zucchini Bread, 30
Zucchini-Nut Bread, 30

CAKES
Apple Cake, 34
Applesauce Cakes, 36
Applesauce Fruitcakes, 45
Aunt Christine's Orange Cake, 49
Black Bottom Cupcakes, 59
Butterscotch Chiffon Cake, 37
Butterscotch-Nut Torte, 37
Chocolate Cake, 39
Chocolate-Cherry Cake, 39
Chocolate-Mallo Cake, 41
Chocolate-Zucchini Cake, 58
Classic German Chocolate Cake, 40
Crunch-Topped Oatmeal Cake, 47
Dark Fruitcakes, 44
Dutch Boiled Spice Cake, 55
Earthquake Cake, 41
Easy Raw Apple Cake, 35
Eggless and Sugarless Apple-Raisin
Cake, 36
Eggless-Milkless-Butterless Cake, 43
Fast Fruit and Cake, 44
Fresh Apple Cake, 35
Fresh Pear Cake, 51
Grandma's Easy Cupcakes, 59
Lazy Daisy Cake, 45
Lucerne Lost Cake, 46
Mayonnaise Cake, 46
Mississippi Mud Cake, 42
Mom's Sponge Cake, 56
Moonshine Cake, 47
Old-Fashioned Devil's Food Cake, 42
1-2-3-4 Cake, 48
Orange Kiss-Me Cake, 48
Orange-Pineapple Cake, 49
Orange Slice Cake, 50

Peaches and Cream Cake, 50
Pineapple Cake, 52
Pineapple-Carrot Cake, 38
Poppy Seed Cake, 53
Pumpkin Cake, 54
Quick Prune Cake, 53
Savarin, 54
Spice Cake, 55
Spicy Persimmon Cake, 51
Surprise Cake, 57
Swiss Carrot Cakes, 38
Triple Chocolate Cake, 43
Upside-Down Strawberry Shortcake, 56
Wine Cake, 57
Yellow Cake with Pudding Frosting, 52
Zucchini-Pumpkin Cake, 58

CANDY
Almond Roca, 60
Cathedral Windows, 61
Cinnamon Nuts, 61
Crispy Treats, 62
Graham Cracker Fudge, 63
Kevin's Favorite Fudge, 64
No-Cook Divinity, 62
Peanut Brittle, 63
Peanut Butter Fudge, 64

CHICKEN. *See also* Salads, Chicken
Baked Chicken Sandwiches, 144
Basque Chicken and Rice, 135
Black Wings, 142
Chicken and Spaghetti, 146
Chicken Bordelaise, 144
Chicken-Bread Pudding, 145
Chicken-Broccoli Oriental, 143
Chicken Casserole, 145
Chicken Piccata, 141
Chicken Solo, 142
Hawaiian Kabobs, 138
Homestyle Chicken and Dumplings, 143
Honey Chicken, 136
Italian Chicken in Foil, 136
Lemon-Butter-Garlic Chicken, 139
Lemon Chicken with Thyme, 139
Macaroni and Chicken, 146
Mexican Chicken Casserole, 140
Orange Chicken, 137
Orange-Honey Chicken, 137
Overnight Chicken, 147
Parmesan Chicken, 140
Peach Barbecued Chicken, 138
Salt-Free Crispy Chicken, 141
Skillet Chicken 'n Biscuit Pie, 147
Sonora Chicken, 148

COOKIES
Angel Food Cookies, 65
Applesauce Cookies, 65
Best Sugar Cookies, 84

Carrot-Walnut Cookies, 67
Chocolate Chip Cookies, 67
Chocolate Waffle Cookies, 69
Christmas Treats, 82
Coconut Macaroons, 73
Cornmeal Cookies, 66
Crisp Cookies, 74
Date Dab Cookies, 74
Deluxe Chocolate Chip Cookies, 68
Double Chocolate-Oatmeal Cookies, 72
Easy German Christmas Cookies, 75
Fruity Oatmeal Cookies, 78
Fudge-Oatmeal Cookies, 72
German Chocolate-Cream Brownies, 69
Grandmother's Scottish Shortbread, 83
Gumdrop Cookies, 76
Kiwifruit Bars, 75
Lemon Fingers, 76
Magic Cookie Bars, 70
Melt-Aways, 77
Mincemeat Bars, 77
Molasses Cookies, 78
Mrs. Fields Chocolate Chip Cookies, 68
Oatmeal Cookies, 79
Old-Fashioned Buttermilk Cookies, 66
One Darn Good Cookie, 71
Peanut Butter Cookies, 79
Persimmon Bars, 80
Persimmon Cookies, 80
Potato Chip-Butterscotch Cookies, 81
Potato Chip Cookies, 81
Raisin Cremes, 82
Rice Crisp Squares, 83
Soft Sugar Cookies, 84
Sour Cream-Coconut-Walnut Squares, 87
Sugar-Free Fruit Bars, 85
Surprise Meringues, 70
Swedish Heirloom Cookies, 85
Sweet Dreams, 73
Teatime Tassies, 86
The One, 86
$250.00 Cookie, 71
Walnut Squares, 87

DESSERTS. See also Cakes; Candy; Cookies;
          Pies; Puddings
Apple Dish, 89
Banana-Cookie Freeze, 89
Blackberry Cobbler, 90
Boston Cream Pie, 90
Boysenberry Crunch, 91
Candied Dried Figs, 92
Cherry Dessert, 91
Crown Jewel Dessert, 92
Farmers' Dessert, 95
Floating Islands, 96
Food for the Gods, 96
Gladys' Torte, 97
Heavenly Rice, 97
Lemon Curd, 93

Old English Apple Dessert, 88
Peach Surprise, 93
Plum Cobbler, 94
Prune Soufflé, 94
Pudding Cake, 98
Ritz Cracker-Coconut Dessert, 98
Strawberry Devonshire Tart, 95

EGG DISHES
Breakfast Casserole, 175
Broccoli-Cheese Strata, 177
Cheese Strata, 177
Chili Quiche, 179
Christmas Breakfast, 176
Mother's Cheese Soufflé, 176

GROUND BEEF
Baked Enchiladas, 122
Barbecued Meatballs, 119
Beefy Cajun Polenta, 117
Beefy French Rolls, 117
California Meat Loaf, 120
Cheddar-Beef Pie, 116
Easy Noodle Stroganoff, 128
Enchilada Casserole, 123
Favorite Tamale Pie, 125
Glazed Meat Loaf, 120
Ground Beef Casserole, 116
Ground Beef-Potato Dish, 118
Ground Beef-Tater Tot Casserole, 118
Meat Loaf, 121
Mexican Casserole, 123
Mexican Pie, 124
Noodle Stroganoff, 128
Porcupines, 126
Seven-Layer Casserole, 126
Shenanigan Pie, 121
Slow-Cooker Dinner, 119
Spaghetti Pie, 127
Stuffed Spanish Rolls, 127
Swedish Cabbage Rolls, 122
Taco Casserole, 124
Tagliarini, 129
Tortilla Casserole, 125

MEATS. *See also* Beef; Sausage
Breaded Roast Lamb, 130
Creamy Veal and Mushrooms, 134
Creole Wieners, 134
Glazed Spareribs, 131
Grandfather's Swedish Pork Chops, 130

PIES
Apple Pie-in-a-Jar, 181
Buttermilk Pie, 102
Cottage Cheese Pie, 103
Cream Pie As-You-Like-It, 104
Easy Pumpkin Pie, 107
Egg Custard Pie, 104
Extra-Tender Pastry, 111

Fresh Peach Pie, 106
Fresh Strawberry Pie, 108
Grandma Fairbanks' Boysenberry Pie, 102
Green Tomato Pie, 109
Lemon Cream Pie, 105
Lemon Pie, 105
Mother's Chocolate Pie, 103
Peanut Butter Pie, 106
Rhubarb Custard Pie, 108
Sour Cream-Raisin Pie, 107
Strawberry Pie, 109
Wild Blackberry Pie, 101
Zucchini (Mock Apple) Pie, 111
Zucchini Crumb Pies, 110
Zucchini Custard Pies, 110

POULTRY. *See also* Chicken
Stuffed Cornish Game Hens, 148
Swedish Turkey Meatballs, 149
Terrific Turkey Casserole, 149
Turkey Meat Loaf, 150

PUDDINGS
Bread Pudding, 99
Brownie Pudding, 100
Grandma's Lemon Pudding, 101
Grape Nut-Custard Pudding, 100
Swedish Apple-Bread Pudding, 99

SALADS, CHICKEN
Cabbage-Chicken Salad, 169
Flying Farmer Chicken Salad, 170
Overnight Layered Chicken Salad, 170

SALADS, DRESSINGS
Coleslaw Dressing, 174
My Russian Dressing, 174
Quick Aioli, 173

SALADS, FRUIT
Buttermilk-Apricot Gelatin Salad, 155
Cranberry Salad, 156
Cream Cheese-Gelatin Salad, 159
Dreamy Lemon Salad, 157
Fruit Salad, 161
Gelatin Chiffon Salad, 159
Holiday Cranberry Salad, 156
Macaroni-Fruit Salad, 160
Molded Avocado Salad, 161
Mystery Salad, 160
Pineapple Gelatin Salad, 157
Strawberry Crunch Salad, 158
Strawberry-Pretzel Salad, 158

SALADS, MAIN DISH. *See also* Salads, Chicken
Corned Beef Salad, 171
Hot Ham Salad, 171
Macaroni-Shrimp Salad, 172
Seafood Salad, 172
Tuna-Apple Salad, 173

SALADS, VEGETABLE
Beet-Pineapple Salad, 162
Broccoli Salad, 162
Easy Green Pea Salad, 165
Greek-Style Tomato Salad, 166
Macaroni-Vegetable Salad, 168
Oriental Cabbage Salad, 163
Oriental Coleslaw, 164
Pasta Salad, 168
Pea Salad, 164
Rice Salad, 169
Sauerkraut Salad, 165
Spring Spinach Salad, 166
Stuffed Tomato Salad, 167
Sunny Broccoli Salad, 163
Twenty-Four Hour Salad, 167

SAUSAGE
Kielbasa with Sauerkraut and New
        Potatoes, 133
Lasagna, 133
Savory Italian Sausage-Rice Bake, 131
Spaghetti Pizza, 132
Spaghetti Sauce with Sausage, 132

SEAFOOD
Baked Salmon, 153
Clam Spaghetti, 150
Easy Paella, 153
Easy Potluck Noodle 'n Tuna Florentine, 154
Paella, 152
Prawns Fettucini Alfredo, 151
Shrimp Provençale, 151
Tuna on-a-Shoestring, 154

SIDE DISHES. *See also* Accompaniments
Charles' Red Bell Pepper Sauce, 184
French-Fried Deviled Eggs, 180
Lasagna Roll-Ups, 178
Pepperoni Pasta, 178
Rice Casserole, 181
Springtime Pasta, 179
Thrifty Vegetable-Rice Quiche, 180

SOUPS
Albondiga Soup, 187
Broccoli Chowder, 188
Chicken-Veggie Soup, 188
Lentil Soup, 189
Linda's Twenty-Minute Minestrone, 189
Minestrone Soup, 190
Potato Soup, 190
Super Taco Soup, 191
Tomato Soup, 191

STEWS
Burgundy-Beef Stew, 192

Championship Texas Chili, 193
Creole Chili, 193
Four-Hour Oven Stew, 192
Hunter's Stew, 194
One-Stop Dinner, 194

VEGETABLES. *See also* Salads, Vegetable
Broccoli and Cheese-Stuffed Baked
        Potatoes, 207
Corn Casserole, 203
German Green Beans and Cabbage, 213
Green Chili Casserole, 203
Hashed Brown Potatoes, 207
Oven-Fried Potatoes, 208
Sour Cream-Corn Casserole, 204
Spinach Casserole, 208
Super Vegetables, 214
Tin Can Casserole, 199
Vegetable Medley, 214

VEGETABLES, BEANS
Baked Beans, 195
Chili Beans, 197
Glen's Slow-Cooker Beans, 197
Grandma's Boston Baked Beans, 196
Iamma's Baked Beans, 196
Michigan Bean Bake, 198
Zesty Red Beans, 198

VEGETABLES, BROCCOLI
Broccoli and Cauliflower Ring, 200
Broccoli and Corn Casserole, 201
Broccoli and Rice Casserole, 201
Broccoli Casserole, 199
Broccoli Soufflé, 202
Mandarin Cauliflower and Broccoli, 202
Microwave Broccoli Casserole, 200

VEGETABLES, EGGPLANT
Eggplant and Ricotta Cheese Casserole, 205
Eggplant Casserole, 205
Eggplant Stuffing, 206
Eggplant Surprise, 206
Scalloped Eggplant, 204

VEGETABLES, SQUASH
Dorothy's Hot Squash Casserole, 209
Hawaiian Squash, 209
Squash Patties, 210

VEGETABLES, ZUCCHINI
Green and Gold Casserole, 213
Portuguese Zucchini Pancake, 210
Zucchini-Chili Casserole, 211
Zucchini-Corn Casserole, 212
Zucchini Quiche, 211
Zucchini Torte, 212

Cookbook Order Form

You may order additional cookbooks for the price of $12.00 each which includes tax, postage and handling. Mail this form to:

California State Grange
Attn: Cookbook Order
2101 Stockton Blvd.
Sacramento, CA 95817

Total number of books ordered _____ x $12.00 = $ _____

Total Enclosed = $ _____

Please make check or money order payable to:
California State Grange

SHIP ORDER TO:
(Please Print)

Name _____

Address _____

City _____ State _____ Zip _____

Telephone No. _____
(In case there is a question about your order)

Bon Appétit